P9-DDE-917

12th Edition

Leases & Rental Agreements

**Marcia Stewart, Ralph Warner, J.D.,
& Attorney Janet Portman**

TWELFTH EDITION	AUGUST 2017
Book Design	TERRI HEARSH
Proofreading	IRENE BARNARD
Index	SONGBIRD INDEXING SERVICES
Printing	BANG PRINTING

ISSN: 1555-5291 (print)

ISSN: 2328-059X (online)

ISBN: 978-1-4133-2450-1 (pbk)

ISBN: 978-1-4133-2451-8 (epub ebook)

This book covers only United States law, unless it specifically states otherwise.

Please note

We believe accurate, plain-English legal information should help you solve many of your own legal problems. But this text is not a substitute for personalized advice from a knowledgeable lawyer. If you want the help of a trained professional—and we'll always point out situations in which we think that's a good idea—consult an attorney licensed to practice in your state.

Acknowledgments

Special thanks to Mary Randolph, editor and friend extraordinaire, who contributed many valuable ideas to this book.

Many other Nolo colleagues and friends helped with this book. Special thanks to: Stephen Stine and Jessica Gillespie for their excellent legal research, and to the Production team (Jaleh, Susan, and Rebecca), who always make the book production process go so smoothly.

About the Authors

Marcia Stewart is the coauthor of *Every Landlord's Legal Guide*, *First-Time Landlord*, *Every Tenant's Legal Guide*, *Renters' Rights*, *Nolo's Essential Guide to Buying Your First Home*, and *The Legal Answer Book for Families*. Marcia received a Master's degree in Public Policy from the University of California at Berkeley.

Ralph Warner is Nolo's cofounder. He has dedicated his professional life to making plain-English legal information accessible and affordable to all Americans. He is the author of a number of self-help law titles, including *Everybody's Guide to Small Claims Court*, and many landlord/tenant and real estate publications. He holds a law degree from Boalt Hall School of Law at the University of California at Berkeley.

Janet Portman, an attorney and Nolo's Executive Editor, received undergraduate and graduate degrees from Stanford and a law degree from Santa Clara University. She is an expert on landlord-tenant law and the coauthor of *Every Tenant's Legal Guide*, *Renters' Rights*, *The California Landlord's Law Book: Rights & Responsibilities*, *California Tenants' Rights*, *Every Landlord's Legal Guide*, *First-Time Landlord*, *Negotiate the Best Lease for Your Business*, and the author of *Every Landlord's Guide to Finding Great Tenants*.

Table of Contents

Appendixes

Your Lease and Rental Documents Companion

The rental agreement or lease that you and your tenant sign forms the contractual basis of your relationship. Taken together with the laws of your state—and, in a few areas, local and federal laws—it sets out almost all the legal and practical rules you and your tenant must follow—such as how many people can occupy your property and for how long, the amount of the rent and deposit, and you (and your tenant's) repair and maintenance responsibilities.

We'll take you step by step through preparing a lease or rental agreement, plus key forms that supplement them, including a rental application designed to help you choose the best tenants (and weed out the bad ones) and a landlord-tenant checklist to document the condition of the rental unit at the beginning and end of the tenancy (and avoid disputes over security deposits).

Fortunately, you don't need a lawyer to draft these important rental documents—just this book. Here's how we can help you.

State-specific legal information. We'll show you how to easily create an effective and legal rental agreement or lease that you can tailor to fit your situation using the 50-state law charts in Appendix A. Want to know about security deposit rules in your state? The "State Security Deposit Rules" chart has what you need, including the deposit limit, whether you need to keep the deposit in a separate account or pay interest on it, when you must return the deposit, and whether you're exempt from the rules based on the number of rental properties you own.

Where to find forms in this book. You'll find copies of the lease and rental agreement, rental application, and other forms in this book available for download on the Nolo website on a special companion page for this book (described below).

Both the print copy and e-book versions include blank versions of the forms (found in Appendix C), which you can either tear out or print, as well as filled-in samples in the text.

> ⓘ **CAUTION**
>
> **Who shouldn't use our lease or rental agreement?** Don't use the forms in this book if you're renting out property that is subsidized by the government; mobile homes; hotels; or commercial property. Landlords who accept Section 8 vouchers will need to use the HUD addendum, which will add to the terms and conditions of the lease you draft using this product (the HUD terms will prevail in case of any inconsistencies). If you are renting out your condominium or townhouse, use this book in conjunction with your homeowners' association CC&Rs (covenants, conditions, and restrictions).

Get Updates, Forms, and More at This Book's Companion Page on Nolo.com

You can download the lease, rental agreement, and all of the other forms in this book at

www.nolo.com/back-of-book/LEAR.html

When there are important changes to the information in this book, we'll post updates on this same dedicated page (what we call the book's companion page). (See Appendix B, "How to Use the Downloadable Forms on the Nolo Website," for a complete list of forms available on Nolo.com.)

Other Helpful Nolo Titles and Online Information and Resources for Landlords

A lease or rental agreement is only one part of a landlord-tenant legal relationship. Nolo publishes several other books for landlords (most with legal forms and state-by-state information) that complement this book, including:

- *Every Landlord's Legal Guide*, by Marcia Stewart, Ralph Warner, and Janet Portman. A comprehensive explanation of landlord-tenant laws and the practical steps rental property owners can take to comply with them (while at the same time running an efficient and profitable business). It covers most key laws affecting landlords in all 50 states, including your repair and maintenance responsibilities and your liability for crime and environmental health hazards such as lead, mold, and bedbugs; rules and procedures for collecting and returning security deposits; antidiscrimination laws; privacy rules; employment laws affecting managers; tenants' rights to break a lease and leave early; how to resolve problems with tenants or begin the eviction process; issues such as meth labs; and more.

- *First-Time Landlord: Your Guide to Renting Out a Single-Family Home*, by Janet Portman, Ilona Bray, and Marcia Stewart. A starter guide for people who are renting out a house for the first time (or are considering doing so) and want a basic overview of the legal, practical, and financial issues involved, including estimating costs and profits, co-owning rental property with family, and managing rental income to maximize tax deductions.

- *Every Landlord's Guide to Finding Great Tenants*, by Janet Portman. A detailed guide to attracting, screening, and choosing the best tenants possible.

- *Every Landlord's Guide to Managing Property*, by Michael Boyer. Provides practical and legal compliance advice for small-time landlords who manage property and tenants on the side (while holding down a day job).Includes do-it-yourself advice on handling day-to-day issues, such as nitty-gritty maintenance and conflicts with tenants regarding late rent, pets, and unauthorized occupants. Explains how to manage and grow a successful rental property business with minimal hassle and cost.

- *Every Landlord's Tax Deduction Guide*, by Stephen Fishman. A comprehensive explanation of deductions and other tax write-offs available to landlords, such as depreciation and insurance. Includes instructions for filling out Schedule E.

- For California landlords: *The California Landlord's Law Book: Rights & Responsibilities*, by David Brown, Janet Portman, and Nils Rosenquest, and *The California Landlord's Law Book: Evictions*, by David Brown and Nils Rosenquest. These books contain all the information California landlords need to run their business and handle an eviction in court by themselves.

You can order these landlord titles from Nolo's website (www.nolo.com) or by phone (800-728-3555). You can also find Nolo books at bookstores and libraries.

The Nolo website has many online state-specific leases and other landlord forms for sale, plus lots of free information of interest to landlords, including legal updates, and 50-state charts of state laws, such as tenants' rights to withhold rent, eviction rules, restrictions on smoking in residential units, and small claims court limits. (Check out the "Landlords and Tenants" section at www.nolo.com.) The Legal Research section on the Nolo website will also help you find federal and state laws that affect your property (look for the Legal Research link at the bottom of www.nolo.com).

You can also find an experienced landlord's attorney at Nolo's Lawyer Directory (see www.nolo.com/lawyers).

11 Tips for Being a Successful Landlord

1. **Don't rent to anyone before checking their credit history, references, and background.** Haphazard screening too often results in problems—a tenant who pays the rent late or not at all, trashes your place, moves in undesirable friends, or worse.

2. **Avoid illegal discrimination.** Comply with all federal and state laws prohibiting discrimination on the basis of race or color, national origin, gender, age, familial status, disability, and other protected categories.

3. **Get all the important terms of the tenancy in writing.** Beginning with the rental application and lease or rental agreement, be sure to document important aspects of your relationship with your tenants—including when and how you handle tenant complaints and repair problems, the amount of notice you must give to enter a tenant's apartment, and the like.

4. **Establish a clear, fair system of setting, collecting, holding, and returning security deposits.** Inspect and document the condition of the rental unit before the tenant moves in to avoid disputes over security deposits when the tenant moves out.

5. **Stay on top of repair and maintenance needs and make repairs when requested.** If the property is not kept in good repair, you'll alienate good tenants. And they may have the right to withhold rent, sue for any injuries caused by defective conditions, or move out without notice.

6. **Don't let your tenants and property be easy marks for a criminal.** You could well be liable for the tenant's losses. Landlords are sued more than any other group of business owners in the country.

7. **Respect your tenants' privacy.** Notify tenants whenever you plan to enter their rental unit, and provide at least 24 hours' notice or the minimum amount required by state law.

8. **Disclose environmental hazards such as lead.** Landlords are increasingly being held liable for tenant health problems resulting from exposure to environmental poisons in the rental premises.

9. **Choose and supervise your manager carefully.** If a manager commits a crime or is incompetent, you may be held financially responsible. Do a thorough background check and clearly spell out the manager's duties to help prevent problems down the road.

10. **Purchase enough liability and other property insurance.** A well-designed insurance program can protect your rental property from losses caused by everything from fire and storms to burglary, vandalism, and personal injury and discrimination lawsuits.

11. **Try to resolve disputes with tenants without lawyers and lawsuits.** If you have a conflict with a tenant over rent, repairs, your access to the rental unit, noise, or some other issue that doesn't immediately warrant an eviction, meet with the tenant to see if the problem can be resolved informally. If that doesn't work, consider mediation by a neutral third party, often available at little or no cost from a publicly funded program. If your dispute involves money and all attempts to reach agreement fail, try small claims court, where you can represent yourself. Use it to collect unpaid rent or to seek money for property damage after a tenant moves out and the deposit is exhausted.

Get a Little Help From Your Friends

Many landlords have discovered the value of belonging to a local or state association of rental property owners. These organizations range from small, volunteer-run groups to substantial city, county, or statewide organizations. Many offer a wide variety of services to members, including:

- legal information and updates through newsletters and seminars
- tenant-screening and credit check services
- training and practical advice on compliance with legal responsibilities
- a place to meet other rental property owners and exchange information and ideas, and
- referrals to professionals, including attorneys, accountants, maintenance firms, and property management companies.

If you can't find an association of rental property owners in your phone book or online, ask other landlords for references. You can also contact the National Apartment Association (www.naahq.org), a national organization whose members include many individual state associations.

Preparing a Lease or Rental Agreement

This chapter provides step-by-step instructions on how to prepare a lease or rental agreement form. It discusses important issues that relate to your choices—as to both the type of document and the specific provisions—including any state, federal, and local laws that may apply.

SEE AN EXPERT

The lease and rental agreement forms are legally sound as designed. If you change important terms or make major changes, however, you may affect a form's legal validity. In this case, you may wish to have your work reviewed by an experienced landlords' lawyer.

Which Is Better, a Lease or a Rental Agreement?

One of the key decisions you need to make is whether to use a lease or a rental agreement. Often, but by no means always, your choice will depend on how long you want a tenant to stay. But, since other factors can also come into play, read what follows carefully before evaluating your own situation and making a decision.

Month-to-Month Rental Agreement

A written rental agreement provides for a tenancy for a short period of time. The law refers to these agreements as periodic or month-to-month tenancies, although it is often legally possible to base them on other time periods, as would be the case if the rent must be paid every two weeks. A month-to-month tenancy automatically renews each month—or other agreed-upon period—unless the landlord or tenant gives the other the proper amount of written notice (typically 30 days) and terminates the agreement.

Month-to-month rental agreements give landlords more flexibility than leases. You may increase the rent or change other terms of the tenancy on relatively short notice (subject to any restrictions of local rent control ordinances—see "Rent Control," below). And with proper notice, you may also end the tenancy at any time (again, subject to any rent control restrictions). (Chapter 4 discusses notice requirements to change or end a rental agreement.) Not surprisingly, many landlords prefer to rent month to month, particularly in urban areas with tight rental markets where new tenants are usually easily found and rents are trending upwards.

On the flip side, a month-to-month tenancy almost guarantees more tenant turnover. Tenants who may legally move out with only 30 days' notice may be more inclined to do so than tenants who make a longer commitment. Some landlords base their rental business strategy on painstakingly seeking high-quality, long-term renters. If you're one of those, or if you live in an area where it's difficult to fill vacancies, you will probably want tenants to commit for a longer period, such as a year. As discussed below, a fixed-term lease, especially when combined with tenant-friendly management policies, may encourage tenants to stay longer. However, it is no guarantee against turnover.

Fixed-Term Lease

A lease is a contract that obligates both you and the tenant for a set period of time—usually six months or a year, but sometimes longer. With a fixed-term lease, you can't raise the rent or change other terms of the tenancy until the lease runs out, unless the lease itself allows future changes or the tenant agrees in writing to the changes.

In addition, you usually can't ask a tenant to move out or prevail in an eviction lawsuit before the lease term expires unless the tenant fails to pay the rent or violates another significant term of the lease or the law, such as repeatedly making too much noise, damaging the rental unit, or selling drugs on your property. This restriction can sometimes be problematic if you end up with a tenant you would like to be rid of but don't have sufficient cause to evict.

To take but one example, if you wish to sell the property halfway into the lease, the existence of long-term tenants—especially if they are paying less than the market rate—may be a negative factor. The new owner usually purchases all the obligations of the previous owner, including the obligation to honor existing leases. Of course, the opposite can also be true: If you have good, long-term tenants paying a fair rent, the property may be very attractive to potential new owners.

At the end of the lease term, you have several options. You can:

- decline to renew the lease, except in the few areas where local rent control requirements prohibit that
- sign a new lease for a set period, or
- do nothing—which means, under the law of most states, your lease will usually turn into a month-to-month tenancy if you continue to accept monthly rent from the tenant.

(Chapter 4 discusses in more detail how fixed-term leases end.)

Although leases restrict your flexibility, there's often a big plus to having long-term tenants. Some tenants make a serious personal commitment when they enter into a long-term lease, in part because they think they'll be liable for several months' rent if they leave early. And people who plan to be with you over the long term are often more likely to respect your property and the rights of other tenants, making the management of your rental units far easier and more pleasant.

CAUTION

A lease guarantees less income security than you think. As experienced landlords know well, it's usually not hard for a determined tenant to break a lease and avoid paying all of the money theoretically owed for the unused portion of the lease term. A few states allow tenants to break a lease without penalty in specific circumstances, such as the need to move to a nursing home. (In addition, tenants who enter military service are entitled to break a lease, as explained in "Special Rules for Active Military Tenants" in Chapter 4.) And many states require landlords to "mitigate" (minimize) the loss they suffer as a result of a broken lease—meaning that if a tenant moves out early, you must try to find another suitable tenant at the same or a greater rent. If you rerent the unit immediately (or if a judge believes it could have been rerented with a reasonable effort), the lease-breaking tenant is off the hook—except for the obligation to pay for the few days or weeks the unit was vacant, plus (sometimes) any costs you incurred in rerenting it. (Chapter 4 discusses a landlord's responsibility to mitigate damages if the tenant leaves early.)

As mentioned, you'll probably prefer to use leases in areas where there is a high vacancy rate or it is difficult to find tenants for one season of the year. For example, if you are renting near a college that is in session for only nine months a year, or in a vacation area that is deserted for months, you are far better off with a year's lease. This is especially true if you have the market clout to charge a large deposit, so that a tenant who wants to leave early has an incentive to find someone to take over the tenancy.

TIP

Always put your agreement in writing. Oral leases or rental agreements are perfectly legal for month-to-month tenancies and for leases of a year or less in most states. While oral agreements are easy and informal, it is never wise to use one. As time passes, people's memories (even yours) have a funny habit of becoming unreliable. You can almost count on tenants claiming that you made, but didn't keep, certain oral promises—for example, to repaint their kitchen or to not increase the rent. Tenants may also forget their own key agreements, such as no subletting. And other issues—for example, how deposits may be used—probably aren't covered at all. Oral leases are especially dangerous, because they require that both parties accurately remember one important term—the length of the lease—over a considerable time. If something goes wrong with an oral rental agreement or lease, you and your tenants are all too likely to end up in court, arguing over who said what to whom, when, and in what context.

Tips for Landlords Taking Over Rental Property

If you've recently bought (or inherited) property, you will likely be inheriting tenants with existing rental agreements or leases. Be sure the last owner gives you copies of all tenant and property files, including leases and rental agreements, details on deposits (location and amounts), house rules, maintenance and repair records, and all other paperwork and records relevant to the property. If you want to change any of the terms of the lease or rental agreement, follow our advice in the first part of Chapter 4.

Instructions for Completing the Lease or Rental Agreement Form

This section explains each clause in the lease and rental agreement forms that are provided in this book, and how to fill in any blanks (in many cases, there will be nothing to fill in). When relevant, you will be asked to check the state law charts in Appendix A to see whether your state has a specific rule that you'll need to enter, such as the amount

of notice you give tenants before entering the rental property. Except for Clause 4, Term of the Tenancy, the lease and rental agreement forms are identical, covering the basic terms of the tenancy, such as the amount of rent and due date.

Check Your Local Laws

In some cities or counties, local ordinances or laws (particularly rent control laws) may apply to your rental business. In addition, these laws may affect the lease itself by requiring certain language or information to be in the document. We cannot list local requirements for every locality in the United States, but we can suggest that, to be extra careful, you take a moment to find out whether local laws affect your residential lease.

Fortunately, many cities and counties have placed their local laws online. To find out whether your local government has done so, go to www. statelocalgov.net and look for your state and city. A useful source of city codes is www.municode. com. Or, simply call your local government offices, ask whether residential rentals are covered by local ordinances and, if so, where you can obtain a copy. If local law varies from your state law—by imposing an interest requirement for security deposits, for example—be sure to follow the local rule. You may need to modify this lease accordingly.

You may be tempted to simply use the form in the back of this book (if you're using a print copy), or download the lease or rental agreement from the Nolo website, and skip over detailed instructions. This would be a mistake. If there is one area of landlord-tenant law where details count, this is it. Make sure you really do have the information necessary to create a lease or a rental agreement that accurately reflects your business strategy and complies with all the laws of your state.

How to Edit (or Add) a Lease or Rental Agreement Clause

You may want to change our lease and rental agreement forms in some situations, and the instructions suggest possible modifications for doing so, including how to prepare an attachment (see "How to Prepare an Attachment Page," below, for advice).

It's easy to make changes to the lease or rental agreement form by using the electronic versions available for download on the Nolo website—for example, if you want to:

- edit or add something to a clause
- delete a clause (for example, Clause 18 on tenant rules and regulations, if you don't have a separate set of these), or
- add a new clause.

If your additions or modifications are very slight, and can be done in the margins of the lease or rental agreement, you may choose instead to enter them on the hard copy. If you do this, be sure that you and all tenants initial and date the insertions.

Be sure to renumber the clauses if you add or delete a clause. And if you make extensive changes on your own, you may wish to have your work reviewed by an experienced landlords' lawyer.

TIP

Don't be tempted to cram too many details into your lease or rental agreement. Instead, send new tenants a move-in letter that dovetails with your lease or rental agreement and highlights important terms of the tenancy—for example, how and where to report maintenance problems, procedures for returning security deposits, or special rules for use of a pool or laundry room. (See Chapter 3 for advice on preparing a move-in letter.)

 FORM

Rental agreement and lease forms. You'll find copies of the Month-to-Month Residential Rental Agreement and the Fixed-Term Residential Lease (in English and in Spanish) in Appendix C of this book. You can also download these forms on the Nolo website; the link is included in Appendix B of this book. A filled-in sample rental agreement is shown at the end of this chapter.

Clause 1. Identification of Landlord and Tenant

This Agreement is entered into between

_____ (Tenant)

and _____

(Landlord). Each Tenant is jointly and severally liable for the payment of rent and performance of all other terms of this Agreement.

Every lease or rental agreement must identify the tenant and the landlord or property owner— usually called the "parties" to the agreement. The term "Agreement" (a synonym for contract) refers to either the lease or the rental agreement.

Any competent adult—at least 18 years of age—may be a party to a lease or rental agreement. (A teenager under age 18 may also be a party to a lease if he or she has achieved legal adult status through court order, military service, or marriage.)

The last sentence of Clause 1 states that if you have more than one tenant, they (the cotenants) are all "jointly and severally" liable (legally responsible) for paying rent and abiding by all the terms of the agreement. This essential bit of legalese simply means that each tenant is legally responsible for the whole rent and complying with the lease. This part of the clause gives you important rights; it means you can legally seek the entire rent from any one of the tenants should the others skip out or be unable to pay. A "jointly and severally liable" clause also gives you the right to evict all of the tenants even if just one has broken the terms of the lease—for example, by seriously damaging the property.

How to Fill In Clause 1

In the first blank, fill in the names of all tenants—adults who will live in the premises, including both members of a married couple. It's crucial that everyone who lives in your rental unit signs the lease or the rental agreement. This underscores your expectation that each individual is responsible for the rent, the use of the property, and all terms of the agreement. Also, make sure the tenant's name matches his or her legal documents, such as a driver's license. You may set a reasonable limit on the number of people per rental unit. (See "How Many Tenants to Allow," below.)

In the second blank, list the names of all landlords or property owners who will be signing the lease or rental agreement. If you are using a business name, enter your name, followed by your business name.

> **EXAMPLE:** Joe Smith, doing business as Apple Lane Apartments.

If more than one landlord or owner is signing the lease (such as husband and wife property owners), you may want to put both names on the lease if both of you plan to actively participate in managing the property.

> **RELATED TOPIC**
> **More on choosing tenants.** Chapter 2 provides detailed advice on choosing tenants.

Clause 2. Identification of Premises

> Subject to the terms and conditions in this Agreement, Landlord rents to Tenant, and Tenant rents from Landlord, for residential purposes only, the premises located at _____
> _____(the premises), together with the following furnishings and appliances: _____
> _____ . Rental of the premises also includes
> _____ .

Clause 2 identifies the street address of the property being rented (the premises) and provides details on furnishings and extras, such as a parking space. The words "for residential purposes only" are to prevent a tenant from using the property for conducting a business that might affect your insurance or violate zoning laws, or that might burden other tenants or neighbors.

How to Fill In Clause 2

In the first blank, fill in the street address of the unit or house you are renting. If there is an apartment or building number, specify that as well as the city and state.

In the second blank, add details on furnishings and appliances. If the rental unit has only a few basic furnishings, list them in the text of Clause 2.

> **EXAMPLE:** Double bed, night table, blue sofa, and round kitchen table and two matching chairs.

If the rental is fully furnished—for example, complete living room, dining room, and bedroom sets, plus a fully equipped kitchen (dinnerware, pots and pans, flatware, etc.), it makes sense to attach a separate room-by-room list to the lease or rental agreement. In this case, simply write in something like this: "The rental unit is fully

Home Businesses on Rental Property

Over 20 million Americans run a business from their house or apartment. If a tenant wants you to modify Clause 2 to allow the operation of a business, you have some checking to do—even if you are inclined to say yes. For starters, you'll need to check local zoning laws for restrictions on home-based businesses, including the type of businesses allowed (if any), the amount of car and truck traffic the business can generate, outside signs, on-street parking, the number of employees, and the percentage of floor space devoted to the business. And if your rental is in a planned unit or a condominium development, check the CC&Rs of the homeowners' association.

You'll also want to consult your insurance company as to whether you'll need a different policy to cover the potential liability of tenants' employees or guests. In many situations, a home office for occasional use will not be a problem. But if the tenant wants to operate a business that involves people and deliveries coming and going, such as a therapy practice, jewelry importer, or small business consulting firm, you should seriously consider whether to expand or add coverage. You may also want to require that the tenant maintain certain types of liability insurance, so that you won't wind up paying if someone gets hurt on the rental property—for example, a business customer who trips and falls on the front steps.

Finally, be aware that if you allow a residence to be used as a commercial site, your property may need to meet the accessibility requirements of the federal Americans with Disabilities Act (ADA). For more information on the ADA, see www.ada.gov or contact the U.S. Department of Justice, Disability Rights Section, Civil Rights Division, in Washington, DC, at 800-514-0301.

> **CAUTION**
>
> **You may not be able to restrict a child care home business.** A tenant who wants to do child care in the rental may be entitled to do so, despite your general prohibition against businesses. In California and New York, for example, legislators and courts have declared a strong public policy in favor of home-based child care, in single-family homes or in multifamily settings, and have limited a landlord's ability to say no. (Cal. Health & Safety Code § 1597.40; *Haberbaum v. Gotbaum*, 698 NYS 2d 406 (N.Y. City Civ. Ct. 1999).) If you're concerned about a tenant running a child care business in the apartment, check with your state's office of consumer protection (find yours at www.usa. gov) for information on laws that cover in-home child care in residential properties.

If you ultimately decide to allow a tenant to run a business from your rental property, you may want to provide details in Clause 22 (Additional Provisions) of your lease or rental agreement.

furnished. See Attachment 1, Addition to Clause 2, Identification of Premises, for a complete list of furnishings." Or you can provide information on furnishings on the Landlord-Tenant Checklist included in Chapter 3.

In some circumstances, you may want to elaborate on exactly what the premises include (do so in the third blank of Clause 2). For example, if the rental unit includes a parking space, storage in the garage or basement, or other use of the property, such as a gardening shed in the backyard or the use of a barn in rural areas, specifically include it in your description of the premises.

> **EXAMPLES:**
>
> Parking space #5 in underground garage
>
> Open parking in lot on west side of building
>
> Storage unit #5 in basement
>
> Storage space available on west side of garage

If your parking rules are quite detailed—for example, covering guest parking—you may want to include them in Clause 18 (Tenant Rules and Regulations) of your lease or rental agreement.

How to Prepare an Attachment Page

An attachment is simply a separate sheet with specific details relevant to a clause, such as a list of furnishings (Clause 2) or detailed rules and regulations (Clause 18). Every time you make an attachment, number and name it by referring to the relevant clause—for example, "Attachment 1, Addition to Clause 2, Identification of Premises," "Attachment 2, Addition to Clause 18, Tenant Rules and Regulations." Then, in the lease itself, refer to the attachment by name, like this: "See 'Attachment 2, Addition to Clause 18, Tenant Rules and Regulations.'" Everyone signing the lease or rental agreement should sign and date each page of an attachment, and you should staple the attachment to the lease or rental agreement.

Possible Modifications to Clause 2

If a particular part of the rental property that a tenant might reasonably assume to be included is not being rented, such as a garage or storage shed you wish to use yourself or rent to someone else, explicitly exclude it from your description of the premises. Simply add the following sentence, with details on what part of the property is excluded from the rental: "Rental of the premises excludes the following areas: _____ ."

Clause 3. Limits on Use and Occupancy

> The premises are to be used only as a private residence for Tenant(s) listed in Clause 1 of this Agreement, and their minor children. Occupancy by guests for more than _____ is prohibited without Landlord's written consent and will be considered a breach of this Agreement.

Clause 3 specifies that the rental unit is the residence of the tenants and their minor children only. It lets the tenants know that they may not move anyone else in as a permanent resident without your consent. The value of this clause is that a tenant who tries to move in a relative or friend for a longer period has clearly violated a defined standard, which gives you grounds for eviction. (New York landlords, however, are subject to the "Roommate Law." See "How Many Tenants to Allow," below, for details.)

Clause 3 also allows you to set a time limit for guest stays. Even if you do not plan to strictly enforce restrictions on guests, this provision will be very handy if a tenant tries to move in a friend or relative for a month or two, calling that person a guest. It will give you the leverage you need to ask the guest to leave, request that the guest apply to become a tenant with an appropriate increase in rent, or, if necessary, evict the tenant for violating this lease provision.

How Many Tenants to Allow

Two kinds of laws affect the number of people who may live in a rental unit.

State and local health and safety codes typically set *maximum* limits on the number of tenants, based on the size of the unit and the number of bedrooms and bathrooms.

Even more important, the federal government has taken the lead in establishing *minimum* limits on the number of tenants, through passage of the Fair Housing Act (42 U.S. C. §§ 3601–3619, 3631) and by means of regulations from the Department of Housing and Urban Development (HUD). HUD generally considers a limit of two persons per bedroom a reasonable occupancy standard. Because the number of bedrooms is not the only factor—the size of the bedrooms and configuration of the rental unit are also considered—the federal test has become known as the "two per bedroom plus" standard. States and localities can set their own occupancy standards as long as they are more generous than the federal government's—that is, by allowing more people per rental unit.

The Fair Housing Act is designed primarily to disallow illegal discrimination against families with children, but it also allows you to establish your own "reasonable" restrictions on the number of people per rental unit—as long as your policy is truly tied to health and safety needs. In addition, you can adopt standards that are driven by a legitimate business reason or necessity, such as the capacities of the plumbing or electrical systems. Your personal preferences (such as a desire to reduce wear and tear by limiting the number of occupants or to ensure a quiet, uncrowded environment for upscale tenants),

however, do not constitute a legitimate business reason. If your occupancy policy limits the number of tenants for any reason other than health, safety, and legitimate business needs, you risk charges that you are discriminating against families.

Figuring out whether your occupancy policy is legal is not always a simple matter. Furthermore, laws on occupancy limits often change. For more information, call HUD's Housing Discrimination Hotline at 800-669-9777, or check the HUD website at www.hud.gov. Check your local and state housing authority for other occupancy standards that may affect your rental property. The HUD website includes contact information for these agencies.

TIP

New York landlords should check out the state's "Roommate Law." New York landlords must comply with the "Unlawful Restrictions on Occupancy" law, commonly known as the Roommate Law. (N.Y. RPL § 235-f.) The Roommate Law prohibits New York landlords from limiting occupancy of a rental unit to just the tenant named on the lease or rental agreement. It permits tenants to share their rental units with their immediate family members, and, in many cases, with unrelated, nontenant occupants, too, so long as a tenant (or tenant's spouse) occupies the unit as a primary residence. The number of total occupants is still restricted, however, by local laws governing overcrowding.

How to Fill In Clause 3

Fill in the number of days you allow guests to stay over a given time period without your consent. We suggest you allow up to two consecutive weeks in any six-month period, but, of course, you may want to modify this based on your own preferences.

 CAUTION

Don't discriminate against families with children. You can legally establish reasonable space-to-people ratios, but you cannot use overcrowding as an excuse for refusing to rent to tenants with children, especially if you would rent to the same number of adults. (See "How Many Tenants to Allow," above.) Discrimination against families with children is illegal, except in housing reserved for senior citizens only. Just as important as adopting a reasonable people-to-square-foot standard in the first place is the maintenance of a consistent occupancy policy. If you allow three adults to live in a two-bedroom apartment, you had better let a couple with a child live in the same type of unit, or you are leaving yourself open to charges that you are illegally discriminating.

Clause 4. Term of the Tenancy

This clause sets out the key difference between a lease and a rental agreement: how long a rent-paying tenant is entitled to stay. The early part of this chapter discusses the pros and cons of leases and rental agreements.

Lease Provision

> The term of the rental will begin on _____, and end on _____ . If Tenant vacates before the term ends, Tenant will be liable for the balance of the rent for the remainder of the term.

This lease provision sets a definite date for the beginning and the expiration of the lease and obligates both the landlord and the tenant for a specific term.

Most leases run for one year. This makes sense, because it allows you to raise the rent at reasonably frequent intervals if market conditions allow. Leases may be shorter (six months) or longer (24 months). This, of course, is up to you and the tenants. A long period—two, three, or even five years—can be appropriate, for example, if you're renting out your own house because you're taking a two-year sabbatical or if you have agreed to allow a tenant to make major repairs or remodel your property at his expense.

How to Fill In Clause 4 (Lease)

In the first blank, fill in the starting date of the lease. The starting date is the date the tenant has the right to move in, such as the first of the month. This date does not have to be the date that you and the tenant sign the lease. The lease signing date is simply the date that you're both bound to the terms of the lease. If the tenant moves in before the regular rental period—such as the middle of the month and you want rent due on the first of every month—you will need to prorate the rent for the first partial month as explained in Clause 5 (Payment of Rent).

In the second blank, fill in the expiration date—in most leases, this will be a year from the starting date. Leases may be shorter (six months) or longer (two years), depending on your situation.

Rental Agreement Provision

> The rental will begin on _____, and continue on a month-to-month basis. Landlord may terminate the tenancy or modify the terms of this Agreement by giving the Tenant _____ days' written notice. Tenant may terminate the tenancy by giving the Landlord _____ days' written notice.

This rental agreement provides for a month-to-month tenancy and specifies how much written notice you must give a tenant to change or end a tenancy, and how much notice the tenant must provide you before moving out. (Chapter 4 discusses changing or ending a month-to-month rental agreement.)

How to Fill In Clause 4 (Rental Agreement)

In the first blank, fill in the date the tenancy will begin. The date the tenancy will begin is the date the tenant has the right to move in, such as the first of the month. This date does not have to be the date that you and the tenant sign the rental agreement. The agreement signing date is simply the date that you're both bound to the terms of the rental agreement. If the tenant moves in before the regular rental period—such as the middle of the month, and you want rent due on the first of every month—you will need to prorate the rent for the first partial month as explained in Clause 5 (Payment of Rent).

In the next two blanks, fill in the amount of written notice you'll need to give tenants to end or change a tenancy and the amount of notice tenants must provide to end a tenancy. In most cases, to comply with the law of your state, this will be 30 days for both landlord and tenant in a month-to-month tenancy. (See the "State Rules on Notice Required to Change or Terminate a Month-to-Month Tenancy" chart in Appendix A for a list of each state's notice requirements.)

Possible Modifications to Clause 4 (Rental Agreement)

This rental agreement is month to month, although you can change it to a different interval as long as you don't go below the minimum notice period required by your state's law. If you do, be aware that notice requirements to change or end a tenancy may also need to differ from those required for standard month-to-month rental agreements, because state law often requires that all key notice periods be the same.

RENT CONTROL

Rent control may limit your right to terminate or change the terms of a tenancy. Even a month-to-month tenancy can be limited by a rent control ordinance. Check local rules for details.

Clause 5. Payment of Rent

Regular monthly rent.

Tenant will pay to Landlord a monthly rent of $_____ , payable in advance on the first day of each month, except when that day falls on a weekend or legal holiday, in which case rent is due on the next business day. Rent will be paid in the following manner, unless Landlord designates otherwise:

Delivery of payment.

Rent will be paid:
- ☐ by mail, to _____
- ☐ in person, at _____

Form of payment.

Landlord will accept payment in these forms:
- ☐ personal check made payable to _____
- ☐ cashier's check made payable to _____
- ☐ credit card
- ☐ money order
- ☐ automatic credit card debit
- ☐ cash
- ☐ other electronic funds transfer

Prorated first month's rent.

For the period from Tenant's move-in date, _____ , through the end of the month, Tenant will pay to Landlord the prorated monthly rent of $ _____ . This amount will be paid on or before the date the Tenant moves in.

This clause provides details on the amount of rent and when, where, and how it's paid. It requires the tenant to pay rent monthly on the first day of the month, unless the first day falls on a weekend or a legal holiday, in which case rent is due on the next business day. (Extending the rent due date for holidays is legally required in some states and is a general rule in most.) Clause 5 also covers prorating rent if a tenant moves in before the regular rental period.

How to Fill In Clause 5

Regular monthly rent. In the first blank, state the amount of monthly rent. Unless your premises are subject to a local rent control ordinance, you can legally charge as much rent as you want (or, more practically speaking, as much as the market will bear).

Delivery of payment. Next, specify to whom and where the rent is to be paid. If you accept payment by mail (most common), list the specific person (such as yourself) to whom rent checks will be mailed. Be sure the tenant knows the exact address, including the building or office name and suite number for mailing rent checks. If the tenant will pay rent in person, specify the address, such as your office or the manager's unit at the rental property. Be sure to specify the hours when rent can be paid in person, such as 9 a.m. to 5 p.m. weekdays and 9 a.m. to noon on Saturdays.

CAUTION

California landlords should take special care to inform tenants of where and how rent is paid. State law (Cal. Civ. Code §§ 1962 and 1962.5) requires landlords to notify tenants (either in a separate writing or in a written rental agreement or lease) of the name and street address of the owner or manager responsible for collection of rent, how rent is to be paid, and who is available for services of notices. A landlord in California may not evict for nonpayment of any rent that came due during any period that the landlord was not in compliance with this requirement.

Form of payment. Note all the forms of payment you'll accept, such as personal check and money order, and to whom payment must be made. You can require that tenants pay rent only by check, or give them several options, such as personal check, money order, cashier's check, credit card, automatic credit card debit, or other electronic funds transfer, such as PayPal.

TIP

Looking for ways to ensure that rent payments are timely and reliable? Credit card and automatic debit are two common methods, especially for landlords with large numbers of rental units. If you accept credit cards, you must pay a fee—a percentage of the amount charged—for the privilege, but the cost may be worth it if accepting credit cards results in more on-time rent payments and less hassle for you and your tenants. In terms of automatic debit, you can get tenants' permission to have rent payments debited automatically each month from the tenants' bank accounts and transferred into your account. This may be a good option for tenants who are in the military. Some tenants will be resistant to this idea, however, and it's not worth insisting on.

CAUTION

Don't accept cash unless you have no choice. You face an increased risk of robbery if word gets out that you are taking in large amounts of cash once or twice a month. And if you accept cash knowing that the tenant earned it from an illegal act such as drug dealing, the government could seize the money from you under federal and state forfeiture laws. For both these reasons, we recommend that you insist that rent be paid by check, money order, or credit card. If you do accept cash, be sure to provide a written, dated receipt stating the tenant's name and the amount of rent paid. Such a receipt is required by law in a few states, and it's a good idea everywhere. Also, check your state law for any other restrictions regarding cash payments. For example, California landlords cannot demand that rent be paid only in cash, unless a tenant has previously bounced a check and the landlord has given the tenant notice to that effect;

in that event, the landlord's demand for cash only may last no longer than three months. (Cal. Civ. Code § 1947.3.)

Prorated first month's rent. If the tenant moves in before the regular rental period—say in the middle of the month, and you want rent due on the first of every month—you can specify the prorated amount due for the first partial month. To figure out prorated rent, divide the monthly rent by 30 days and multiply by the number of days in the first (partial) rental period. That will avoid confusion about what you expect to be paid. Enter the move-in date, such as "June 21, 20xx," and the amount of prorated monthly rent.

> **EXAMPLE:** Meg rents an apartment for $2,100 per month, with rent due on the first of the month. She moves in on June 21, so she should pay ten days' prorated rent of $700 when she moves in. ($2,100 ÷ 30 = $70 x 10 days = $700.) Beginning with July 1, Meg's full $2,100 rent check is due on the first of the month.

If the tenant is moving in on the first of the month, or the same day rent is due, write "N/A" or "Not Applicable" in the section on prorated rent, or delete this section of the clause.

Possible Modifications to Clause 5

Here are a few common ways to modify Clause 5.

Rent due date. You can establish a rent due date different from the first of the month, such as the day of the month on which the tenant moves in. For example, if the tenant moved in on July 10, rent would be due on that date, a system which of course saves the trouble of prorating the first month's rent.

Frequency of rent payments. You are not legally required to have your tenant pay rent on a monthly basis. You can modify the clause and require that the rent be paid twice a month, each week, or by whatever schedule suits you.

RELATED TOPIC

See the following chapters for rent-related discussions:

- collecting deposits and potential problems with calling a deposit the "last month's rent": Clause 8, this chapter
- the value of highlighting your rent rules in a move-in letter to new tenants, and collecting the first month's rent: Chapter 3
- tenant's obligations to pay rent when breaking a lease: Chapter 4, and
- legal citations for state rent rules: Appendix A.

Rent Control

Communities in only five states—California, the District of Columbia, Maryland, New Jersey, and New York—have laws that limit the amount of rent landlords may charge and how and when rent may be increased. Typically, only a few cities or counties in each of these states have enacted local rent control ordinances (also called rent stabilization, maximum rent regulation, or a similar term), but often these are some of the state's largest cities—for example, San Francisco, Los Angeles, New York City, and Newark all have some form of rent control.

Rent control laws commonly regulate much more than rent. For example, owners of rent-controlled properties must often follow specific "just cause" eviction procedures. And local rent control ordinances may require that your lease or rental agreement include certain information—for example, the address of the local rent control board.

If you own rental property in a city that has rent control, you should always have a current copy of the ordinance and any regulations interpreting it. Check with your local rent control board or city manager's or mayor's office for more information on rent control, and modify our forms accordingly.

Clause 6. Late Charges

> If Tenant fails to pay the rent in full before the end of the _____ day after it's due, Tenant will pay Landlord a late charge as follows:
>
> _____ .
>
> Landlord does not waive the right to insist on payment of the rent in full on the date it is due.

It is your legal right in most states to charge a late fee if rent is not paid on time. This clause spells out details of your policy on late fees. Charging a late fee does not mean that you give up your right to insist that rent be paid on the due date. To bring this point home, Clause 6 states that you do not waive the right to insist on full payment of the rent on the date it is due. A late fee is simply one way to motivate tenants to pay rent on time.

A few states have statutes that put precise limits on the amount of late fees or when they can be collected. (See the Late Fees column in the "State Rent Rules" chart in Appendix A before completing this clause.)

 RENT CONTROL

Some rent control ordinances also regulate late fees. If you own rental units in a municipality with rent control, check the ordinances carefully.

But even if your state doesn't have specific rules restricting late fees, you are still bound by general legal principles (often expressed in court decisions) that prohibit unreasonably high fees. Unless your state imposes more specific statutory rules on late fees, you should be on safe ground if you adhere to these principles:

- The total late charge should not exceed 4%–5% of the rent. That's $40 to $50 on a $1,000-per-month rental.
- If the late fee increases each day the rent is late, it should be moderate and have an

upper limit. A late charge that increases without a maximum could be considered interest charged at an illegal ("usurious") rate. Although state usury laws don't directly apply to late charges, judges often use these laws as one guideline in judging whether a particular provision is reasonable. Most states set the maximum interest rate that may be charged for a debt at about 10% to 12%. A late charge that would generally be acceptable for a $1,000 per month rent would be a charge of $10 if rent is not paid by the end of the second business day after it is due, plus $5 for each additional day, up to a maximum of 5% of the monthly rental amount.

 CAUTION

Don't try to disguise excessive late charges by giving a "discount" for early payment. One landlord we know concluded that he couldn't get away with charging a $100 late charge on an $850 rent payment, so, instead, he designed a rental agreement calling for a rent of $950 with a $100 discount if the rent was not more than three days late. Ingenious as this ploy sounds, it is unlikely to stand up in court in many states, unless the discount for timely payment is modest. Giving a relatively large discount is, in effect, the same as charging an excessive late fee, and a judge is likely to see it as such.

How to Fill In Clause 6

In the first blank, specify how many days (if any) you will allow as a grace period before you charge a late fee. You don't have to give a grace period, but many landlords don't charge a late fee until the rent is two or three days late. If you don't allow any grace period, simply cross out the first blank and the word "after," so that the first line reads "If Tenant fails to pay the rent in full before the end of the day it's due...."

Next, fill in details on your late rent fee, such as the daily charge and any maximum fee.

Possible Modifications to Clause 6

If you decide not to charge a late fee (something we consider highly unwise), you may simply delete this clause, or write the words "N/A" or "Not Applicable" on it.

Clause 7. Returned Check and Other Bank Charges

If any check offered by Tenant to Landlord in payment of rent or any other amount due under this Agreement is returned for lack of sufficient funds, a "stop payment," or any other reason, Tenant will pay Landlord a returned check charge of $ _____ .

As with late charges, any bounced-check charges you require must be reasonable. Some states regulate the amount you can charge; in the absence of such regulation, you should charge no more than the amount your bank charges you for a returned check, probably $25 to $35 per returned item, plus a few dollars for your trouble. Some states regulate the maximum amount you can charge. Check with your state consumer protection agency for any restrictions on bounced-check charges. A list of state consumer protection agencies is available at www.usa.gov.

TIP

Don't tolerate repeated bad checks. If a tenant habitually pays rent late or gives you bad checks, give written notice demanding that the tenant pay the rent or move within a few days. How long the tenant is allowed to stay depends on state law; in most places, it's about three to 15 days. In most instances, the tenant who receives this kind of "pay rent or quit" notice pays up and reforms his ways, and that's the end of it. But, if the tenant doesn't pay the rent (or move), you can file an eviction lawsuit. An alternative is to serve the tenant with a 30-day notice to change Clause 5 of the lease or rental agreement to require payment with a money order or a verified credit card transaction.

How to Fill In Clause 7

In the blank, fill in the amount of the returned check charge. If you won't accept checks, fill in "N/A" or "Not Applicable," or simply delete this clause.

Clause 8. Security Deposit

On signing this Agreement, Tenant will pay to Landlord the sum of $ _____ as a security deposit. Tenant may not, without Landlord's prior written consent, apply this security deposit to the last month's rent or to any other sum due under this Agreement. Within _____ after Tenant has vacated the premises, returned keys, and provided Landlord with a forwarding address, Landlord will return the deposit in full or give Tenant an itemized written statement of the reasons for, and the dollar amount of, any of the security deposit retained by Landlord, along with a check for any deposit balance.

Most landlords quite sensibly ask for a security deposit before entrusting hundreds of thousands of dollars' worth of real estate to a tenant. But it's easy to get into legal trouble over deposits, because they are strictly regulated by state law and, sometimes, also by city ordinance. The law of most states dictates how large a deposit you can require, how you can use it, when you must return it, and more. Several states require you to put deposits in a separate account and pay interest on them.

The use and return of security deposits is a frequent source of disputes between landlords and tenants. To avoid confusion and legal hassles, this clause is clear on the subject, including:

- the dollar amount of the deposit
- the fact that the deposit may not be used for the last month's rent without your prior approval, and
- when the deposit will be returned, along with an itemized statement of deductions.

This section discusses the basic information you need to complete Clause 8. Check the "State Security Deposit Rules" chart in Appendix A for specific details that apply to your situation.

If, after reviewing these tables, you have any questions of what's allowed in your state, you should get a current copy of your state's security deposit statute or an up-to-date summary from a landlords' association. In addition, be sure to check local ordinances in all areas where you own property. Cities, particularly those with rent control, may have additional rules on security deposits, such as a limit on the amount you can charge or a requirement that you pay interest on deposits.

Basic State Rules on Security Deposits

All states allow you to collect a security deposit when a tenant moves in and hold it until the tenant leaves. The general purpose of a security deposit is to give the landlord a source of funds if a tenant fails to pay the rent when it is due or doesn't pay for damage to the rental unit. Rent you collect in advance for the first month is not considered part of the security deposit.

State laws typically control the amount you can charge and how and when you must return security deposits:

- Many states limit the amount you can collect as a deposit to a maximum of one or two months' rent. Sometimes, the limit in a particular state is higher for furnished units.
- Several states and cities (particularly those with rent control) require landlords to pay tenants interest on security deposits, and establish detailed requirements as to the interest rate that must be paid and when payments must be made. Some states require you to put deposits in a separate account, sometimes called a "trust" account, rather than mixing the funds with your personal or business accounts. In most

states, however, you don't have to pay tenants interest on deposits or put them in a separate bank account. In other words, you can simply put the money in your pocket or bank account and use it, as long as you have it available when the tenant moves out.

- When a tenant moves out, you will have a set amount of time (usually from 14 to 30 days, depending on the state) to either return the tenant's entire deposit or provide an itemized statement of deductions and refund any deposit balance, including any interest that is required.
- You can generally withhold all or part of the deposit to pay for:
  - unpaid rent
  - repairing damage to the premises (except for "ordinary wear and tear") caused by the tenant, a family member, or a guest
  - cleaning necessary to restore the rental unit to its condition at the beginning of the tenancy (over and above "ordinary wear and tear"), and
  - restoring or replacing rental unit property taken by the tenant. States typically also allow you to use a deposit to cover the tenant's other obligations under the lease or rental agreement, which may include payment of utility charges.
- The laws of many states set heavy penalties for violation of security deposit statutes.

See Chapter 4 for a discussion of inspecting the rental unit and returning deposits when a tenant leaves.

How Much Deposit Should You Charge?

Normally, the best advice is to charge as much as the market will bear, within any legal limits. The more the tenant has at stake, the better the chance your property will be respected. And, the larger the deposit, the more financial protection you will have if a tenant leaves owing you rent.

Don't Charge Nonrefundable Fees

State laws are often muddled on the subject of whether charging nonrefundable deposits and fees is legal. Some specifically allow landlords to collect a fee that is not refundable—such as for pets, cleaning, or redecorating—as long as this is clearly stated in the lease or rental agreement. In addition, most states allow landlords to charge prospective tenants a nonrefundable fee for the cost of a credit report and related screening fees (discussed in Chapter 3).

But many states—and this is clearly the trend—have enacted security deposit statutes that specifically prohibit nonrefundable fees such as a fixed fee for cleaning drapes or carpets or for painting; all such fees are legally considered security deposits, no matter what they are labeled in the lease or rental agreement, and must be refundable. It is also illegal in many states to make the return of deposits contingent upon a tenant staying for a minimum period of time.

Generally, it's best to avoid the legal uncertainties and not try to collect any nonrefundable fees from tenants. In addition, most landlords have found that making all deposits refundable avoids many time-consuming arguments and even lawsuits with tenants. We believe it's much simpler just to consider the expenses these fees cover as part of your overhead and figure them into the rent, raising it, if necessary.

If you have a specific concern about a particular tenant—for example, you're afraid a tenant's pet will damage the carpets or furniture— just ask for a higher security deposit (but do check your state's maximum). That way, you're covered if the pet causes damage, and if it doesn't, the tenant won't have to shell out unnecessarily.

If, despite our advice, you want to charge a nonrefundable fee, check your state's law to find what (if any) kinds of nonrefundable fees are allowed. Then, make sure your lease or rental agreement is clear on the subject.

The market, however, often keeps the practical limit on deposits lower than the maximum allowed by law. Your common sense and your business sense need to work together in setting security deposits. Here are a number of considerations to keep in mind:

- **Charge the full limit in high-risk situations:** where there's a lot of tenant turnover, if the tenant has a pet and you're concerned about damage, or if the tenant's credit is shaky and you're worried about unpaid rent.
- **Consider the psychological advantage of a higher rent rather than a high deposit.** Many tenants would rather pay a slightly higher rent than an enormous deposit. Also, many acceptable, solvent tenants have a hard time coming up with several months' rent, especially if they are still in a rental unit and are awaiting the return of a previous security deposit.
- **Charge a bigger deposit for single-family homes.** Unlike multiunit residences, where close-by neighbors or a manager can spot, report, and quickly stop any destruction of the premises, the single-family home is somewhat of an island. The condition of the interior and even the exterior may be hard to assess, unless you live close by or can frequently check the condition of a single-family rental. And, of course, the cost of repairing damage to a house is likely to be higher than for an apartment.
- **Gain a marketing advantage by allowing a deposit to be paid in installments.** If rentals are plentiful in your area, with comparable units renting at about the same price, you might gain a competitive edge by allowing tenants to pay the deposit in several installments, rather than one lump sum.

TIP

Require renters' insurance as an alternative to a high security deposit. If you're worried about damage but don't think you can raise the deposit any higher, require renters' insurance. You can give your property an extra measure of protection by insisting that the tenant purchase renters' insurance, which may cover damage done by the tenant or guests. (See "Renters' Insurance" under Clause 12.)

Last Month's Rent

It's a common—but often unwise—practice to collect a sum of money called "last month's rent" from a tenant who's moving in. Landlords tend to treat this money as just another security deposit, and use it to cover not only the last month's rent, but also other expenses such as repairs or cleaning.

Problems can arise because some states restrict the use of money labeled as the "last month's rent" to its stated purpose: the rent for the tenant's last month of occupancy. If you use any of it to repair damage by the former tenant, you're violating the law. Also, using the "last month's rent" for cleaning and repairs may lead to a dispute with a tenant who feels that the last month's rent is taken care of and resents having to pay all or part of it. You would be better off if the tenant paid the last month's rent when it came due, leaving the entire security deposit available to cover any necessary cleaning and repairs.

Avoiding the term "last month's rent" also keeps things simpler if you raise the rent, but not the deposit, before the tenant's last month of occupancy. The problem arises when rent for the tenant's last month becomes due. Has the tenant already paid in full, or does he owe more because the monthly rent is now higher? Legally, there is often no clear answer. In practice, it's a hassle you are best to avoid by not labeling any part of the security deposit "last month's rent."

Clause 8 of the form agreements makes it clear that the tenant may not apply the security deposit to the last month's rent without your prior written consent.

How to Fill In Clause 8

Once you decide how much security deposit you can charge (see "State Security Deposit Rules" in Appendix A), fill in the amount in the first blank. Unless there's a lower limit, we suggest about two months as your rent deposit, assuming your potential tenants can afford that much. (See "How Much Deposit Should You Charge?" above.) In no case is it wise to charge less than one month's rent.

Next, fill in the time period when you will return the deposit, also using the chart "State Security Deposit Rules" in Appendix A. If there is no statutory deadline for returning the deposit, we recommend 14 to 21 days as a reasonable time to return a tenant's deposit. Establishing a fairly short period (even if the law of your state allows more time) will discourage anxious tenants from repeatedly bugging you or your manager for their deposit refund. (See the discussion of returning security deposits in Chapter 4.)

Possible Modifications to Clause 8

The laws of several states require you to give tenants written information on various aspects of the security deposit, including where the security deposit is being held, interest payments, and the terms of and conditions under which the security deposit may be withheld. The "State Security Deposit Rules" chart in Appendix A gives you information on disclosures you may need to add to Clause 8.

Even if it's not required, you may want to provide additional details on security deposits in your lease or rental agreement. Here are optional clauses you may add to the end of Clause 8.

OPTIONAL CLAUSES

The security deposit will be held at: _____
(name and address of financial institution) .
Landlord will pay Tenant interest on all security deposits at the prevailing bank rate.

Landlord may withhold only that portion of Tenant's security deposit necessary to: (1) remedy any default by Tenant in the payment of rent; (2) repair damage to the premises, except for ordinary wear and tear caused by Tenant; (3) clean the premises, if necessary; and (4) compensate Landlord for any other losses as allowed by state law.

Disclose Shared Utility Arrangements

If there are not separate gas and electric meters for each unit, or a tenant's meter serves any areas outside his or her unit (such as a water heater used in common with other tenants or even a lightbulb not under the tenant's control in a common area), you should disclose this in your lease or rental agreement. Simply add details to Clause 9. This type of disclosure is required by law in some states, and is only fair in any case. The best solution is to put in a separate meter for the areas served outside the tenant's unit. If you don't do that, you should:

- pay for the utilities for the tenant's meter yourself by placing that utility in your name
- reduce the tenant's rent to compensate for payment of utility usage outside of his or her unit (this will probably cost you more in the long run than if you either added a new meter or simply paid for the utilities yourself), or
- sign a separate written agreement with the tenant, under which the tenant specifically agrees to pay for others' utilities, too.

Clause 9. Utilities

Tenant will pay all utility charges, except for the following, which will be paid by Landlord:
_____
_____ .

This clause helps prevent misunderstandings as to who's responsible for paying utilities. Normally, landlords pay for garbage (and sometimes water, if there is a yard) to help make sure that the premises are well maintained. Tenants usually pay for other services, such as gas, electricity, cable TV, and Internet access.

How to Fill In Clause 9

In the blank, fill in the utilities you—not the tenants—will be responsible for paying. If you will not be paying for any utilities, simply delete the last part of the clause ("except … Landlord: _____ ").

Clause 10. Prohibition of Assignment and Subletting

Tenants will not sublet any part of the premises or assign this Agreement without the prior written consent of Landlord.

☐ a. Tenants shall not sublet or rent any part of the Premises for short-term stays of any duration, including but not limited to vacation rentals.

☐ b. Short-stay rentals are prohibited except as authorized by law. Any short-stay rental is expressly conditioned upon the tenants' following all regulations, laws, and other requirements as a condition to offering a short-stay rental. Failure to follow all laws, ordinances, regulations, and other requirements, including any registration requirement, will be deemed a material, noncurable breach of this Agreement and will furnish cause for termination.

Clause 10 is an antisubletting clause, the breach of which is grounds for eviction. It prevents a tenant from subleasing during a vacation or renting out a room to someone unless you specifically agree.

Clause 10 is also designed to prevent assignments, a legal term that means your tenant transfers her tenancy to someone else. Practically, you need this clause to prevent your tenant from leaving in the middle of the month or lease term and moving in a replacement—maybe someone you wouldn't choose to rent to—without your consent.

Should You Allow a Sublet or Assignment?

As a general rule, your best bet when a tenant asks to sublease or assign is to simply insist that the tenancy terminate and a new one begin—with the proposed "subtenant" or "assignee" as the new tenant who signs a new lease or rental agreement. This gives you the most direct legal relationship with the substitute. There are a few situations, however, in which you may want to agree to a subtenancy or assignment.

You might, for example, want to accommodate —and keep—an exceptional, long-term tenant who has every intention of returning and whose judgment and integrity you have always trusted. If the proposed stand-in meets your normal tenant criteria, you may decide that it is worth the risk of a subtenancy or assignment in order to keep the original tenant.

Another good reason is a desire to have a sure source of funds in the background. This might come up if your original tenant is financially sound and trustworthy, but a proposed stand-in is less secure but acceptable in every other respect. By agreeing to a sublet or assignment, you have someone in the background (the original tenant) still responsible for the rent. The risk you incur by agreeing to set up a subtenancy or assignment and the hassle that comes with dealing with more than one person may be worth what you gain in keeping a sure and reliable source of funds on the hook.

Subletting and Short-Term Stays (Airbnb)

Online businesses such as Airbnb have acted as clearinghouses for short-term, or short-stay rentals (less than 30 days), for use by vacationers or visiting businesspersons. Tenants using these platforms sublet their rentals and pocket the rent, turning your property into a hotel. Landlords are universally opposed to this practice, though even they have joined the bandwagon, taking regular rental property out of circulation in order to operate it solely as a short-term rental.

If you want to restrict tenants from running a short-term rental business, be sure your lease is clear on this. First, however, check local law: Bowing to political pressure, many municipalities are changing their laws concerning short-stay tenancies, by requiring registration and limiting the number of short-stay days per year. It is possible that your locality has granted tenants the right to rent on Airbnb or other services under specific conditions and requirements.

After you have determined whether any local ordinances regulate short-term rentals, choose the appropriate alternative language for Clause 10. Alternate (a) flatly prohibits such rentals, while alternate (b) advises tenants that they must follow the short-term stay law or risk termination of their tenancies.

By including Clause 10 in your lease or rental agreement, you have the option not to accept the person your tenant proposes to take over the lease. Under the law of most states, however, you should realize that if a tenant who wishes to leave early provides you with another suitable tenant, you can't both unreasonably refuse to rent to this person and hold the tenant financially liable for breaking the lease. Typically, state law requires that you must try to rerent the property reasonably quickly and subtract any rent you receive from the amount the original tenant owed you for the remainder of the agreed-upon rental period. Lawyers call this the mitigation-of-damages rule, a bit of legalese it's valuable to know.

How to Fill In Clause 10

You don't need to add anything to this clause in most situations. There may be local laws, however, that do apply.

RESOURCE
For a related discussion of subleases, assignments, and the landlord's duty to mitigate damages, see Chapter 4.

Clause 11. Tenant's Maintenance Responsibilities

> Tenant will: (1) keep the premises clean, sanitary, and in good condition and, upon termination of the tenancy, return the premises to Landlord in a condition identical to that which existed when Tenant took occupancy, except for ordinary wear and tear; (2) immediately notify Landlord of any defects or dangerous conditions in and about the premises of which Tenant becomes aware; and (3) reimburse Landlord, on demand by Landlord, for the cost of any repairs to the premises damaged by Tenant or Tenant's guests or business invitees through misuse or neglect.
>
> Tenant has examined the premises, including appliances, fixtures, carpets, drapes, and paint, and has found them to be in good, safe, and clean condition and repair, except as noted in the Landlord-Tenant Checklist.

Clause 11 makes the tenant responsible for keeping the rental premises clean and sanitary, and makes it clear that if the tenant damages the premises— for example, by breaking a window—it's the tenant's responsibility to pay for the damage.

It is the law in some states (and a wise practice in all) to notify tenants in writing of procedures for making complaint and repair requests. Clause 11 requires the tenant to alert you to defective or dangerous conditions.

Clause 11 also states that the tenant has examined the rental premises, including appliances, carpets, and paint, and found them to be safe and clean, except as noted in a separate form (the Landlord-Tenant Checklist, described in Chapter 4). Before the tenant moves in, you and the tenant should inspect the rental unit and fill out the Landlord-Tenant Checklist, describing what is in the unit and noting any problems. Doing so will help you avoid security deposit disputes when the tenant moves out.

Ten Elements of a Good Maintenance and Repair System

As a general rule, landlords are legally required to offer livable premises when a tenant originally rents an apartment or rental unit and to maintain the premises throughout the rental term. If rental property is not kept in good repair, the tenant may have the right to repair the problem and deduct the cost from the rent, withhold rent, sue for any injuries caused by defective conditions, or move out without notice. Your best defense against rent withholding hassles and other disputes with tenants is to establish and communicate a clear, easy-to-follow procedure for tenants to ask for repairs, and for you to document all complaints, respond quickly when complaints are made, and schedule annual safety inspections. And, if you employ a manager or management company, make sure they fully accept and implement your guidelines.

Follow these steps to avoid maintenance and repair problems with tenants:

- **Regularly look for dangerous conditions on the property and fix them promptly.** Reduce risk exposure as much as possible—for example, by providing sufficient lighting in hallways, parking garages, and other common areas, strong locks on doors and windows, and safe stairs and handrails.
- **Scrupulously comply with all public health and safety codes.** Your local building or housing authority and health or fire department can provide any information you need. Also, check state housing laws governing landlords' repair and maintenance responsibilities. (Appendix A includes citations for the major state laws affecting landlords. Check your statutes under headings such as Landlord Obligations to Maintain Premises.)
- **Clearly set out the tenant's responsibilities for repair and maintenance in your lease or rental agreement.** (See Clauses 11, 12, and 13 of the agreements in this chapter.)
- **Use the written Landlord-Tenant Checklist form in Chapter 3 to check over the premises and fix any problems before new tenants move in.**

- **Encourage tenants to immediately report plumbing, heating, weatherproofing, or other defects and safety or security problems—** whether in the tenant's unit or in common areas such as hallways and parking garages.
- **Handle repairs (especially urgent ones, such as a broken door lock or lack of heat in winter) as soon as possible.** Notify the tenant by phone and follow up in writing if repairs will take more than 48 hours, excluding weekends. Keep the tenant informed—for example, if you have problems scheduling a plumber, let your tenant know with a phone call or a note. For nonurgent repairs, be sure to give the tenant proper notice as required by state law. (See Clause 15 for details on notice required to enter rental premises.)
- **Keep a written log of all tenant complaints, including those made orally.** Record your immediate and any follow-up responses (and subsequent tenant communications) and details as to how and when the problem was fixed, including reasons for any delay.
- **Twice a year, give your tenants a checklist on which to report any potential safety hazards or problems that might have been overlooked—** for example, low water pressure in the shower, peeling paint, or noisy neighbors. This is also a good time to remind tenants of their repair and maintenance responsibilities. Respond promptly and in writing to all repair requests, keeping copies in your file.
- **Once a year, inspect all rental units for safety and maintenance problems, using the Landlord-Tenant Checklist as a guide.** Make sure smoke detectors, heating and plumbing systems, and major appliances are, in fact, safe and in good working order. (Keep copies of the filled-in checklist in your file.)
- **Get a good liability insurance policy to cover injuries or losses suffered by others as the result of defective conditions on the property and lawyers' bills for defending personal injury suits.**

Renters' Insurance

It is becoming increasingly popular, especially in high-end rentals, to require tenants to obtain renters' insurance. This insurance covers losses of the tenant's belongings as a result of fire or theft. Often called a "Tenant's Package Policy," renters' insurance also covers the tenant if his or her negligence causes injury to other people or property damage (to the tenant's property or to yours). Besides protecting the tenant from personal liability, renters' insurance benefits you, too: If damage caused by the tenant could be covered by either the tenant's insurance policy or yours—for example, the tenant accidentally starts a fire by leaving the stove on—a claim made on the tenant's policy will affect the tenant's premiums, not yours.

If you decide to require insurance, insert a clause like the following example at the end of your lease or rental agreement, under Clause 22, Additional Provisions. This will help assure that the tenant purchases and maintains a renters' insurance policy throughout his tenancy.

Renters' Insurance

Within ten days of the signing of this Agreement, Tenant will obtain renters' insurance and provide proof of purchase to Landlord. Tenant further agrees to maintain the policy throughout the duration of the tenancy, and to furnish proof of insurance on a ☐ yearly ☐ semiannual basis.

CAUTION

Check with your insurance agent or lawyer before requiring tenants to carry renters' insurance. Landlords subject to rent control may not be able to require renters' insurance, and some states restrict a landlord's rights to require renters' insurance.

How to Fill In Clause 11

You do not need to add anything to this clause.

RESOURCE

Comprehensive landlord law resource. Several times in this book, we recommend *Every Landlord's Legal Guide,* by Marcia Stewart, Ralph Warner, and Janet Portman (Nolo). It is especially useful for its detailed discussion of landlords' and tenants' rights and responsibilities for repair and maintenance under state and local laws and judicial decisions. It provides practical advice on how to stay on top of repair and maintenance needs and minimize financial losses and legal problems with tenants. It discusses tenants' rights if you do not meet your legal responsibilities and the pros and cons of delegating repairs and maintenance to the tenant. *Every Landlord's Legal Guide* also includes chapters on landlords' liability for tenant injuries from defective housing conditions, such as a broken step or defective wiring; liability for environmental hazards such as asbestos and lead; and responsibility to provide secure premises and protect tenants from assault or criminal activities, such as drug dealing.

Clause 12. Repairs and Alterations by Tenant

a. Except as provided by law or as authorized by the prior written consent of Landlord, Tenant will not make any repairs or alterations to the premises, including nailing holes in the walls or painting the rental unit.

b. Tenant will not, without Landlord's prior written consent, alter, rekey, or install any locks to the premises or install or alter any security alarm system. Tenant will provide Landlord with a key or keys capable of unlocking all such rekeyed or new locks as well as instructions on how to disarm any altered or new security alarm system.

Clause 12 makes it clear that the tenant may not make alterations and repairs without your consent, including painting the unit or nailing holes in the walls.

And, to make sure you can take advantage of your legal right of entry in an emergency situation, Clause 12 specifically forbids the tenant from rekeying the locks or installing a security alarm system without your consent. If you do grant permission, make sure your tenant gives you duplicate keys or the name and phone number of the alarm company or instructions on how to disarm the alarm system so that you can enter in case of emergency.

The "except as provided by law" language in Clause 12 is a reference to the fact that, in certain situations and in certain states, tenants have a narrowly defined right to alter or repair the premises, regardless of what you've said in the lease or rental agreement. Examples include:

- **Alterations by a person with a disability, such as lowering countertops for a tenant who uses a wheelchair.** Under the federal Fair Housing Act, a disabled person may modify a living space to the extent necessary to make the space safe and comfortable, as long as the modifications will not make the unit unacceptable to the next tenant, or if the tenant with a disability agrees to undo the modification when the tenant leaves. (42 U.S.C. § 3604(f)(3)(A).)
- **Use of the "repair and deduct" procedure.** In most states, tenants have the right to repair defects or damage that makes the premises uninhabitable or substantially interferes with the tenant's safe use or enjoyment of the premises. The tenant must first notify you of the problem and give you a reasonable amount of time to fix it.
- **Installation of satellite dishes and antennas.** Federal law gives tenants limited rights to install wireless antennas and small satellite dishes. (47 C.F.R. § 1.4000.)
- **Specific alterations allowed by state statutes.** Some states allow tenants to install energy conservation measures (like removable interior storm windows) or burglary prevention devices without the landlord's prior consent. Check your state statutes or call your local rental property association for more information on these types of laws.

How to Fill In Clause 12

If you do not want the tenant to make any repairs without your permission, you do not need to add anything to this clause.

You may, however, want to go further and specifically prohibit certain repairs or alterations by adding details in Clause 22 (Additional Provisions). For example, you may want to make it clear that any "fixtures"—a legal term that describes any addition that is attached to the structure, such as bolted-in bookcases or built-in dishwashers—are your property and may not be removed by the tenant without your permission.

If you do authorize the tenant to make any repairs, provide enough detail so that the tenant knows exactly what is expected, how much repairs can cost, and who will pay. For example, if you decide to allow the tenant to take over the repair of any broken windows, routine plumbing jobs, or landscaping, give specific descriptions and limits to the tasks.

> ! CAUTION
> **Do not delegate to a tenant your responsibility for major maintenance of essential services.** The duty to repair and maintain heating, plumbing, and electrical and structural systems (the roof, for example) is yours. Absent unusual circumstances, and even then only after carefully checking state law, it's a mistake to try to delegate this responsibility to the tenant. Many courts have held that landlords cannot delegate to a tenant the responsibility for keeping the premises fit for habitation, fearing that the tenant will rarely be in the position, either

practically or financially, to do the kinds of repairs that are often needed to bring a structure up to par.

Clause 13. Prohibition Against Violating Laws and Causing Disturbances

> Tenant is entitled to quiet enjoyment of the premises. Tenant and guests or invitees will not use the premises or adjacent areas in such a way as to: (1) violate any law or ordinance, including laws prohibiting the use, possession, or sale of illegal drugs; (2) commit waste (severe property damage); or (3) create a nuisance by annoying, disturbing, inconveniencing, or interfering with the quiet enjoyment and peace and quiet of any other tenant or nearby resident.

This type of clause is found in most form leases and rental agreements. Although it contains some legal jargon, it's probably best to leave it as is, since courts have much experience in working with these terms. As courts define it, the "covenant of quiet enjoyment" amounts to an implied promise that you will not act (or fail to act) in a way that interferes with or destroys the ability of the tenant to use the rented premises.

Examples of landlord violations of the covenant of quiet enjoyment include:

- allowing garbage to pile up
- tolerating a major rodent infestation, or
- failing to control a tenant whose constant loud music makes it impossible for other tenants to sleep.

If you want more specific rules—for example, no loud music played after midnight—add them to Clause 18: Tenant Rules and Regulations, or to Clause 22: Additional Provisions.

How to Fill In Clause 13

You do not need to add anything to this clause.

How to Prevent Illegal Tenant Activity

There are several practical steps you can take, both to avoid trouble among your tenants and, in the event that hostilities do erupt, to limit your exposure to lawsuits:

- Screen tenants carefully and choose tenants who are likely to be law-abiding and peaceful citizens. (Chapter 2 recommends a comprehensive system for screening prospective tenants, including checking out references from past landlords and employers.)
- Establish a system to respond to tenants' complaints and concerns about other tenants, especially those involving drug dealing on the rental property.
- Make it clear that you will not tolerate tenants' disruptive behavior. An explicit lease or rental agreement provision such as Clause 13 prohibiting drug dealing and illegal activity is the most effective way to make this point. If a tenant does cause trouble, act swiftly. Some situations, such as drug dealing, call for prompt efforts to evict the troublemaker. Your failure to evict drug-dealing tenants can result in lawsuits from tenants injured or annoyed by drug dealers, and local, state, or federal authorities may choose to levy stiff fines for allowing the illegal activity to continue. In extreme cases, you may actually lose your property to the government under public nuisance abatement laws and forfeiture laws.

Waste and Nuisance: What Are They?

In legalese, committing **waste** means causing severe damage to real estate, including a house or an apartment unit—damage that goes way beyond ordinary wear and tear. Punching holes in walls, pulling out sinks and fixtures, and knocking down doors are examples of waste.

Nuisance means behavior that prevents neighbors from fully enjoying the use of their homes. Continuous loud noise and foul odors are examples of legal nuisances that may disturb nearby neighbors and affect their "quiet enjoyment" of the premises. So, too, is selling drugs or engaging in other illegal activities that greatly disturb neighbors.

Clause 14. Pets

No animal may be kept on the premises without Landlord's prior written consent, except animals needed by tenants who have a disability, as that term is understood by law, except for the following:

_____

_____

under the following conditions: _____

_____

_____ .

This clause prevents tenants from keeping pets without your written permission. If you want, you can have a flat "no pets" rule, though many landlords, in fact, report that pet-owning tenants are more appreciative, stable, and responsible than the norm. But it does provide you with a legal mechanism that will keep your premises from being waist-deep in Irish wolfhounds. Without this sort of provision, particularly if you use a longer-term lease that can't be terminated early save for a clear violation of one of its provisions, there's little to prevent your tenant from keeping multiple, dangerous, or nonhousebroken pets, except for city ordinances prohibiting tigers, and animal cruelty laws.

You have the right to prohibit all pets (including pets of guests), or to restrict the types of pets or dog breeds you allow, with the exception of trained dogs and some other animals used by people who have a mental or physical disability.

Renting to Pet Owners

The San Francisco Society for the Prevention of Cruelty to Animals (SPCA) is one of several humane societies across the country that seeks to encourage landlords to rent to pet-owning tenants. The SPCA offers a sample pet agreement and other resources for both landlords and tenants on their website, www.sfspca.org/resources/tenants-landlords.

Also, the national Humane Society's website at www.humanesociety.org has helpful resources for landlords and property managers, including recommended pet policies and a sample pet application form.

How to Fill in Clause 14

If you do not allow pets, simply delete the words "except for the following: _____ under the following conditions: _____ _____ ."

If you allow pets, be sure to identify the type and number of pets in the first blank—for example, "one cat" or "one dog under 20 pounds." It's also wise to spell out your pet rules in the second blank.

> **EXAMPLE:**
>
> Tenant must keep the grounds and street free of all animal waste. Tenant's pet must be well behaved and under Tenant's control at all times and will not pose a threat or apparent threat to the safety of other tenants, their guests, or other people on or near the premises.

Your tenant rules and regulations may be another place to spell out your pet rules—in which case, add this language in the second blank: Tenant must comply with pet rules included in the Tenant Rules and Regulations (Clause 18) attached to this agreement.

Should You Require a Separate Security Deposit for Pets?

Some landlords allow pets but require the tenant to pay a separate deposit to cover any damage caused by the pet. The laws of a few states specifically allow separate, nonrefundable pet deposits. In others, charging a designated pet deposit is legal only if the total amount you charge for deposits does not exceed the state maximum for all deposits. (See Clause 8 for details on security deposits.)

Even where allowed, separate pet deposits can often be a bad idea, because they limit how you can use that part of the security deposit. For example, if the pet is well-behaved but the tenant trashes your unit, you can't use the pet portion of the deposit to clean up after the human. If you want to protect your property from damage done by a pet, you are probably better off charging a slightly higher rent or security deposit to start with (assuming you are not restricted by rent control or the upper security deposit limits).

⊘ **CAUTION**
It is illegal to charge an extra pet deposit for people with trained service or companion animals.

Clause 15. Landlord's Right to Access

> Landlord or Landlord's agents may enter the premises in the event of an emergency, to make repairs or improvements, or to show the premises to prospective buyers or tenants. Landlord may also enter the premises to conduct an annual inspection to check for safety or maintenance problems. Except in cases of emergency, Tenant's abandonment of the premises, court order, or where it is impractical to do so, Landlord will give Tenant _____ notice before entering.

The tenant's duty to pay rent is typically conditioned on your having fulfilled your legal responsibility to properly repair and maintain the premises. This means that, of necessity, you have a legal responsibility to keep fairly close tabs on the condition of the property. For this reason, and because it makes good sense to allow landlords reasonable access to their property, nearly every state clearly recognizes the right of a landlord to legally enter rented premises while a tenant is still in residence under certain broad circumstances, such as to deal with an emergency and when the tenant gives permission.

Many states have access laws specifying the circumstances under which landlords may legally enter rented premises. Most access laws allow landlords to enter rental units to make repairs and inspect the property and to show property to prospective tenants and purchasers. (See "General Rules of Entry," below.) State access laws typically specify the amount of notice required for such entry—usually 24 hours (unless it is impractical to do so—for example, in cases of emergency). A few states simply require the landlord to provide "reasonable" notice, often presumed to be 24 hours.

General Rules of Entry

Here are the general circumstances under which landlords may legally enter rented premises. Except in cases of emergency, or where it is impractical to do so, you generally must enter only at reasonable times, and you must give at least the amount and type of notice required in your state.

Emergency. In all states, you can enter rental property to respond to a true emergency—such as a gas leak.

To make repairs or inspect the property. By law, many states allow you and your repairperson to enter the tenant's home to make necessary or agreed-upon repairs, decorations, alterations, or improvements, and to supply necessary or agreed-upon services—for example, when you need to fix a broken oven.

To show property. Most states with access laws allow a landlord to enter rented property to show it to prospective tenants toward the end of the tenancy or to prospective purchasers if the landlord wishes to sell the property. (See Chapter 2 for advice on renting property that's still occupied.)

With the permission of the tenant. You can always enter rental property, even without notice, if the tenant agrees.

Entry after the tenant has moved out. To state the obvious, you may enter the premises after the tenant has completely moved out— regardless of whether the tenant left voluntarily after giving back the key or involuntarily as a result of an eviction lawsuit. In addition, if you believe the tenant has abandoned the property—that is, skipped out without giving any notice or returning the key—you may legally enter.

Clause 15 makes it clear to the tenant that you have a legal right of access to the property to make repairs or to show the premises for sale or rental, provided you give the tenant reasonable notice. (The chart "State Laws on Landlord's Access to Rental Property" in Appendix A provides details on a landlord's right to entry and notice requirements.)

How to Fill In Clause 15

In the blank, indicate the amount of notice you will provide the tenant before entering—at least the minimum required in your state. If your state law simply requires "reasonable" notice or has no notice requirement, we suggest you provide at least 24 hours' notice.

Clause 16. Extended Absences by Tenant

Tenant will notify Landlord in advance if Tenant will be away from the premises for _____ or more consecutive days. During such absence, Landlord may enter the premises at times reasonably necessary to maintain the property and inspect for damage and needed repairs.

Several states give landlords the specific legal right to enter the rental unit during a tenant's extended absence to maintain the property as necessary and to inspect for damage and needed repairs. Extended absence is often defined as seven days or more. For example, if you live in a cold-weather place and temperatures take a dive, it makes sense to check the pipes in rental units (to make sure they haven't burst) when the tenant is away for winter vacation.

While many states do not address this issue, either by statute or court decision, you should be on safe legal ground to enter rental property during a tenant's extended absence, as long as you have a genuine reason to enter to protect the property from damage. You should enter only if something really needs to be done—that is, something the tenant would do if he were home as part of his obligation to keep the property clean, safe, and in good repair.

To protect yourself, include Clause 16, which requires that the tenant notify you when they will be gone for an extended time and alerts the tenant of your intent to enter the premises during these times, if necessary.

How to Fill In Clause 16

In the blank, fill in the length of the tenant's expected absence that will trigger your tenant's duty to notify you. Ten or 14 days is common.

Clause 17. Possession of the Premises

> *a. Tenant's failure to take possession.*
> If, after signing this Agreement, Tenant fails to take possession of the premises, Tenant will still be responsible for paying rent and complying with all other terms of this Agreement.
>
> *b. Landlord's failure to deliver possession.* If Landlord is unable to deliver possession of the premises to Tenant for any reason not within Landlord's control, including, but not limited to, partial or complete destruction of the premises, Tenant will have the right to terminate this Agreement upon proper notice as required by law. In such event, Landlord's liability to Tenant will be limited to the return of all sums previously paid by Tenant to Landlord.

The first part of this clause (Part a) explains that a tenant who chooses not to move in (take possession) after signing the lease or rental agreement will still be required to pay rent and satisfy other conditions of the agreement. This does not mean, however, that you can sit back and expect to collect rent for the entire lease or rental agreement term. (As we explain in Chapter 4, you generally must take reasonably prompt steps to re-rent the premises, and you must credit the rent you collect against the first tenant's rent obligation.)

The second part of the clause (Part b) protects you if you're unable, for reasons beyond your control, to turn over possession after having signed the agreement or lease—for example, if a fire spreads from next door and destroys the premises. It limits your financial liability to the new tenant to the return of any prepaid rent and security deposits (the "sums previously paid," in the language of the clause).

CAUTION

Clause 17 may not limit your liability if you cannot deliver possession because the old tenant is still on the premises—even if he is the subject of an eviction that you ultimately win. When a holdover tenant prevents the new tenant from moving in, landlords are often sued by the new tenant for not only the return of any prepaid rent and security deposits, but also the costs of temporary housing, storage costs, and other losses. In some states, an attempt in the lease to limit the new tenant's recovery to the return of prepaid sums alone would not hold up in court. To protect yourself, you will want to shift some of the financial liability to the holdover tenant. You'll have a stronger chance of doing this if the old tenant has given written notice of his intent to move out. (See Clause 4, above, which requires written notice.)

How to Fill In Clause 17

You do not need to add anything to this clause.

Clause 18. Tenant Rules and Regulations

> ☐ Tenant acknowledges receipt of, and has read a copy of, tenant rules and regulations, which are labeled Attachment A and attached to and incorporated into this Agreement by this reference. Tenant understands that serious or repeated violations of the rules may be grounds for termination. Landlord may change the rules and regulations without notice.

> ### What's Covered in Tenant Rules and Regulations
>
> Tenant rules and regulations typically cover issues such as:
>
> - elevator safety and use
> - pool rules
> - garbage disposal and recycling
> - vehicles and parking regulations—for example, restrictions of repairs on the premises or types of vehicles (such as no RVs)
> - lockout and lost key charges
> - pet rules
> - no smoking—either in common areas in multiunit buildings (including the hallways and lobby), or even in individual units
> - security system use
> - specific details on what's considered excessive noise
> - dangerous materials—nothing explosive should be on the premises
> - storage of bikes, baby strollers, and other equipment in halls, stairways, and other common areas
> - specific landlord and tenant maintenance responsibilities (such as stopped-up toilets or garbage disposals, broken windows, rodent and pest control, and lawn and yard maintenance)
> - use of the grounds and recreation areas
> - maintenance of balconies and decks (for instance, no drying clothes on balconies)
> - display of signs in windows
> - laundry room rules, and
> - waterbeds.

Many landlords don't worry about detailed rules and regulations, especially when they rent single-family homes or duplexes. However, in larger buildings with many tenants, rules are usually important to control the use of common areas and equipment—both for the convenience, safety, and welfare of the tenants and as a way to protect your property from damage. Rules and regulations also help avoid confusion and misunderstandings about day-to-day issues such as garbage disposal, lost key charges, and parking rules.

Not every minor rule needs to be incorporated in your lease or rental agreement. But it is a good idea to specifically incorporate important ones (especially those that are likely to be ignored by some tenants). Doing so gives you the authority to evict a tenant who persists in seriously violating your code of tenant rules and regulations. Also, to avoid charges of illegal discrimination, rules and regulations should apply equally to all tenants in your rental property.

Because tenant rules and regulations are often lengthy and may be revised occasionally, we suggest you prepare a separate attachment. (See "How to Prepare an Attachment Page," above.) Be sure the rules and regulations (including any revisions) are dated on each page and signed by both you and the tenant.

How to Fill In Clause 18

If you have a set of tenant rules and regulations, or your rental is in a community with homeowners' association or condo rules, check the box, and attach a copy to your lease or rental agreement. If you do not, simply delete this clause or write the words "N/A" or "Not Applicable."

Clause 19. Payment of Court Costs and Attorneys' Fees in a Lawsuit

> In any action or legal proceeding to enforce any part of this Agreement, the prevailing party ☐ shall not / ☐ shall recover reasonable attorneys' fees and court costs.

Many landlords assume that if they sue a tenant and win (or prevail, in legalese), the court will order the losing tenant to pay the landlord's court costs (filing fees, service of process charges, deposition costs, and so on) and attorneys' fees. This is not generally true. In most states, a court will order the losing tenant to pay your attorneys' fees only if a written agreement specifically provides for it.

If, however, you have an "attorneys' fees" clause in your lease, all this changes. If you hire a lawyer to bring a lawsuit and win, the judge will order your tenant to pay your costs and attorneys' fees. (In rare instances, a court will order the loser to pay costs and fees on its own if it finds that the behavior of the losing party was particularly egregious.)

But there's another important issue you need to know about: By law in many states, an attorneys' fees clause in a lease or a rental agreement works both ways, even if you haven't written it that way. That is, even if the lease states only that you are entitled to attorneys' fees if you win a lawsuit, your tenants will be entitled to collect their attorneys' fees from you if they prevail. The amount you would be ordered to pay would be whatever the judge decides is reasonable.

So, especially if you live in a state that will read a "one-way" attorneys' fees clause as a two-way street, give some thought to whether you want to bind both of you to paying for the winner's costs and fees. Remember, if you can't actually collect a judgment containing attorneys' fees from an evicted tenant (which often happens), the clause will not help you. But if the tenant prevails, you will be stuck paying the tenant's costs and fees. In addition, the presence of a two-way clause will make it far easier for a tenant to secure a willing lawyer for even a doubtful claim, because the source of the lawyer's fee (you, if you lose) will probably appear more financially solid than if the client were paying the bill himself or herself.

Especially if you intend to do all or most of your own legal work in any potential eviction or other lawsuit, you will almost surely be better off not to allow for attorneys' fees. Why? Because if the tenant wins, you will have to pay the tenant's fees; but if you win, the tenant will owe you nothing, since you didn't hire an attorney. You can't even recover for the long hours you spent preparing for and handling the case.

Finally, be aware that attorneys' fees clauses only cover lawsuits concerning the meaning or implementation of the lease—such as a dispute about rent, security deposits, or your right to access. An attorneys' fees clause would not apply in a personal injury or discrimination lawsuit.

> **CAUTION**
>
> **If your rental property is in Ohio, do not include the attorneys' fees clause**—it's prohibited by law in Ohio. (Ohio Rev. Code Ann. § 5321.13(c).)

How to Fill In Clause 19

If you don't want to allow for attorneys' fees, check the box before the words "shall not" and delete or cross out the word "shall."

If you want to be entitled to attorneys' fees and costs if you win—and you're willing to risk paying them if you lose—check the box before the word "shall" and delete or cross out the words "shall not."

Clause 20. Disclosures

> Tenant acknowledges that Landlord has made the following disclosures regarding the premises:
> ☐ *Disclosure of Information on Lead-Based Paint and/or Lead-Based Paint Hazards*
> ☐ Other disclosures: _____
> _____ .

Federal, state, or local laws may require you to make certain disclosures before a new tenant signs a lease or rental agreement or moves in.

Lead Disclosures

If your rental unit was built prior to 1978, before signing a lease or rental agreement you must tell new tenants about any known lead-based paint or lead-based paint hazards in the rental premises, including individual units and common areas, such as hallways, parking garages, or play areas. You must also give them an EPA pamphlet, *Protect Your Family From Lead in Your Home.* This is a requirement of the Residential Lead-Based Paint Hazard Reduction Act, commonly known as Title X (42 U.S.C. § 4852d), which is administered by the U.S. Environmental Protection Agency (EPA).

In addition, both you and the tenant must sign an EPA-approved form—*Disclosure of Information on Lead-Based Paint and/or Lead-Based Paint Hazards*—that will prove that you told your tenants what you know about these hazards on your premises. You must keep the disclosure form as part of your records for three years from the date of the start of the tenancy.

As discussed below, state laws on lead disclosure may also come into play.

FORM

Lead forms. You'll find copies of the *Disclosure of Information on Lead-Based Paint and/or Lead-Based Paint Hazards* form, and the EPA pamphlet *Protect Your Family From Lead in Your Home* (both in English and in Spanish) in Appendix C of this book. You can also download this form and pamphlet on the Nolo website; the link is included in Appendix B of this book.

CAUTION

Penalties are severe. Property owners who fail to comply with EPA regulations for disclosing lead-based paint hazards face penalties of up to $16,773 for each violation (24 C.F.R. 30.65) and treble (triple) damages if a tenant is injured by your willful noncompliance.

Rental Properties Exempt From Title X Regulations

Landlords who rent the following types of property are not required to comply with federal lead disclosure requirements:

- housing built after January 1978
- housing certified lead-free by an accredited lead inspector
- lofts, efficiencies, and studios
- short-term vacation rentals of 100 days or less
- a single room rented in a residential dwelling
- housing designed for persons with disabilities, unless children under age six are present, and
- retirement communities (housing designed for seniors, where one or more tenant is at least 62 years old), unless children under age six are present.

RESOURCE

Lead disclosure forms, copies of Title X regulations, and background information on the evaluation and control of lead may be obtained by calling the National Lead Information Center at 800-424-LEAD, or checking www.epa.gov/lead.

Many states have also addressed the lead issue by prohibiting the use of lead-based paint in residences and requiring the careful maintenance of existing lead-based building materials. Some states require property owners to disclose lead hazards to prospective tenants. If you are subject to a state statute, you must comply with it as well as federal law. Check with your state housing department or local office of the U.S. Department of Housing and Urban Development (www.hud.gov) to find out if this applies to you.

Other Disclosures

State laws may impose disclosure requirements, too, such as for known radon hazard risks, shared utility arrangements, or a history of bedbug problems. Local rent control ordinances often require disclosures, such as the name and address of the government agency or elected board that administers the ordinance. Some states require landlords to inform tenants of the name and address of the bank where their security deposit is being held. (Clause 8 covers security deposits.) (See "Required Landlord Disclosures" and "State Security Deposit Rules," in Appendix A.)

How to Fill In Clause 20

If your rental property was built before 1978, you must meet federal lead disclosure requirements, so check the first box and follow the advice above.

If you are legally required to make other disclosures as described above, check the second box and provide details in the blank space, adding pages as necessary.

Also, if there is a hidden (not obvious) problem with the property that could cause injury or substantially interfere with your tenant's safe enjoyment and use of the dwelling, and it is impossible to fix it, you are better off legally if you disclose the defective or dangerous condition before the tenant signs the lease. Examples include naturally occurring dangers, such as loose soil, and man-made dangers, such as steep stairs. (See "Disclosures of Hidden Defects," below, for more on the subject.)

Clause 21. Authority to Receive Legal Papers

The Landlord, any person managing the premises, and anyone designated by the Landlord are authorized to accept service of process and receive other notices and demands, which may be delivered to:

☐ The Landlord, at the following address:

_____

_____

☐ The manager, at the following address:

_____

_____

☐ The following person, at the following address:

_____

_____

It's the law in many states, and a good idea in all, to give your tenants information about everyone whom you have authorized to receive notices and legal papers, such as a tenant's notice that he or she is ending the tenancy or a tenant's court documents as part of an eviction defense. Of course, you may want to handle all of this yourself or delegate it to a manager or management company. Make sure the person you designate to receive legal papers is almost always available to receive tenant notices and legal papers. Also, be sure to keep your tenants up to date on any changes in this information.

How to Fill In Clause 21

Provide your name and street address or the name and address of someone else you authorize to receive notices and legal papers on your behalf, such as a property manager.

Disclosures of Hidden Defects

Landlords have a duty to warn tenants and others about naturally occurring dangers (such as loose soil) and human-made dangers (like low doorways or steep stairs) that are hidden but which you know (or should know) about. Disclose hidden defects in Clause 20 of your lease or rental agreement, so that it can never be claimed that a tenant was not warned of a potentially dangerous condition. For example, if the building contains asbestos insulation that could be dangerous if anyone made a hole in the wall, disclose this to your tenants. If appropriate, also post warning signs near hazards, such as a ramp that's slippery when wet or a tree that drops entire strips of bark during windy weather.

While disclosure doesn't guarantee that you won't be legally liable (also make sure your insurance protects you), it will likely help. Putting the tenant on notice that a problem exists will help prevent injuries and limit your liability should an injury occur from a defective condition in the rental unit or on the premises.

> **CAUTION**
>
> **Some problems need to be fixed, not merely disclosed.** Warning your tenants about a hidden defect does not absolve you of legal responsibility if the condition makes the dwelling uninhabitable or unreasonably dangerous. For example, you are courting liability if you rent an apartment with a gas heater that you know might blow up, even if you warn the tenant that the heater is faulty. Nor can you simply warn your tenants about prior crime on the premises and then fail to do anything (like installing dead bolts or an alarm system) to promote safety.

Clause 22. Additional Provisions

> Additional provisions are as follows: _____
> _____ .

In this clause, you may list any additional provisions or agreements that are unique to you and the particular tenant signing the lease or rental agreement, such as a provision that allows limited business use of the premises—for example, for occasional weekday piano lessons.

If you don't have separate tenant rules and regulations (see Clause 18, above), you may spell out a few rules under this clause—for example, regarding lost key charges, use of a pool on the property, or no-smoking rules.

How to Fill In Clause 22

List additional provisions or rules here or in an attachment. If there are no additional provisions, delete this clause or write "N/A" or "Not Applicable."

> **TIP**
>
> **There is no legal or practical imperative to put every small detail you want to communicate to the tenant into your lease or rental agreement.** Instead, prepare a welcoming, but no-nonsense, "move-in letter" that dovetails with the lease or rental agreement and highlights important terms of the tenancy—for example, how and where to report maintenance problems. You may also use a move-in letter to cover issues not included in the lease or rental agreement—for example, rules for use of a laundry room. (Chapter 3 covers move-in letters.)

> **CAUTION**
>
> **Do not include exculpatory ("If there's a problem, I'm not responsible") clauses or hold harmless ("If there's a problem, you are responsible")**

clauses. Many form leases include provisions that attempt to absolve you in advance from responsibility for your legal misdeeds. For example, one lease form generated by a popular software package contains a broad provision stating that you are not responsible for injuries to tenants and guests, even those you cause intentionally. Many exculpatory clauses are blatantly illegal: If a tenant is injured because of a dangerous condition you failed to fix for several months, no boilerplate lease provision will protect you from civil—and probably criminal—charges.

Clause 23. Validity of Each Part

> If any portion of this Agreement is held to be invalid, its invalidity will not affect the validity or enforceability of any other provision of this Agreement.

This clause is known as a "savings" clause, and it is commonly used in contracts. It means that, in the unlikely event that one of the other clauses in the Agreement is found to be invalid by a court, the remainder of the Agreement will remain in force.

How to Fill In Clause 23

You do not need to add anything to this clause.

Clause 24. Grounds for Termination of Tenancy

> The failure of Tenant or Tenant's guests or invitees to comply with any term of this Agreement, or the misrepresentation of any material fact on Tenant's rental application, is grounds for termination of the tenancy, with appropriate notice to the Tenant and procedures as required by law.

This clause states that any violation of the Agreement by the tenant, or by the tenant's business or social guests, is grounds for terminating the tenancy, according to the procedures established by your state or local laws. Making the tenant responsible for the actions of his guests can be extremely important—for example, if you discover that the tenant's family or friends are dealing illegal drugs on the premises or have damaged the property. Clause 24 also tells the tenant that if he or she has made false statements on a rental application concerning an important fact—such as his or her prior criminal history—you may terminate the tenancy and evict if necessary.

How to Fill In Clause 24

You do not need to add anything to this clause.

Clause 25. Entire Agreement

> This document constitutes the entire Agreement between the parties, and no promises or representations, other than those contained here and those implied by law, have been made by Landlord or Tenant. Any modifications to this Agreement must be in writing, signed by Landlord and Tenant.

This clause establishes that the lease or rental agreement and any attachments (such as tenant rules and regulations) constitute the entire agreement between you and your tenant. It means that oral promises (by you or the tenant) to do something different with respect to any aspect of the rental are not binding. Any changes or additions must be in writing. For example, if your lease prohibits pets, and your tenant wants to get a dog and you agree, you should amend the Pets clause of the lease accordingly. This will help assure that a casual conversation about pets doesn't lead the tenant to bringing in a dog without your permission. (Chapter 4 discusses how to modify signed rental agreements and leases.)

How to Fill In Clause 25

You do not need to add anything to this clause.

Instructions for Signing the Lease or Rental Agreement

After all terms are final, you're ready to sign. Make two copies of the lease or rental agreement, including all attachments. You and each tenant should sign both copies in the space at the end. Include your signature, street address, phone number, and email, or that of the person you authorize as your agent, such as a property manager. There's also space for the tenants' signatures and phone numbers.

Again, as stressed in Clause 1, make sure all adults living in the rental unit, including both members of a married couple, sign the lease or rental agreement. And check that the tenant's name and signature match his or her driver's license or other legal document.

If the tenant has a cosigner (see "About Cosigners," below), you'll need to add a line for the cosigner's signature.

If you alter our form by writing or typing in changes, be sure that you and all tenants initial the changes when you sign the document, so as to forestall any possibility that a tenant will claim you unilaterally inserted changes after the tenant signed.

> **CAUTION**
> **Don't sign a lease until all terms are final and the tenant understands all terms of the agreement and what's expected.** All of your

expectations should be written into the lease or rental agreement (or any attachments, such as tenant rules and regulations) before you and the tenant sign the document. Never sign an incomplete document assuming last-minute changes can be made later.

Give one copy of the signed lease or rental agreement to the tenant(s), and keep the other one for your files. (If you are renting to more than one tenant, you don't need to prepare a separate agreement for each cotenant. After the agreement is signed, cotenants may make their own copies of the signed document.)

> **TIP**
> **Help tenants understand the lease or rental agreement before they sign it.** Too many landlords thrust a lease or rental agreement at tenants and expect them to sign it unread. Far better to encourage tenants to ask questions about anything that's unclear, or to actually review each clause with new tenants. It will save you lots of hassles later on.
>
> If English is not a tenant's first language— especially if you regularly rent to people in the tenant's ethnic group—prepare and give the tenant a written translation. Appendix C includes a Spanish version of our lease and rental agreement, and a copy is available for download on this book's companion page on www. nolo.com. Some states require this. California, for example, requires landlords who discuss the lease or written rental agreement primarily in Spanish, Chinese, Tagalog, Vietnamese, or Korean to give the applicant an unsigned, translated version of the lease before asking the applicant to sign. This rule does not apply (that is, you may supply your English version only) if the tenant has supplied his or her own translator, someone who is not a minor and can fluently speak and read both languages. But even if it's not legally required, you want your tenants to know and follow the rules. Providing a written translation of your lease or rental agreement is a great way to establish rapport with tenants. Chapter 3 discusses how to get your new tenancy off to the right start.

About Cosigners

Some landlords require cosigners on rental agreements and leases, especially when renting to students who depend on parents for much of their income. The cosigner signs a separate agreement or the rental agreement or lease, under which the cosigner agrees to cover any rent or damage-repair costs the tenant fails to pay.

In practice, a cosigner's promise to guarantee the tenant's rent obligation may have less legal value than at first you might think. This is because the threat of eviction is the primary factor that motivates a tenant to pay the rent, and, obviously, you cannot evict a cosigner. Also, since the cosigner must be sued separately in either a regular civil lawsuit or in small claims court—for example, if a tenant stiffs you for a month's rent—actually doing so may be more trouble than it's worth. This is especially true if the cosigner lives in another state, since the amount of money you are out will rarely justify hiring a lawyer and collecting a judgment.

In sum, the benefits of having a lease or rental agreement cosigned by someone who won't be living on the property are largely psychological. But these benefits may still be worth something: A tenant who thinks you can (and will) notify and sue a cosigning relative or friend may be less likely to default on the rent. Similarly, a cosigner asked to pay the tenant's debts may persuade the tenant to pay.

Because of the practical difficulties associated with cosigners, many landlords refuse to consider them, which is legal in every situation but one: If a tenant with a disability who has insufficient income (but is otherwise suitable) asks you to accept a cosigner who will cover the rent if needed, you must relax your blanket rule at least to the extent of investigating the suitability of the proposed cosigner. If that person is solvent and stable, federal law requires you to accommodate the applicant by accepting the cosigner, in spite of your general policy. (*Giebeler v. M & B Associates*, 343 F.3d 1143 (9th Cir. 2003).)

If you decide to accept a cosigner, you should have that person fill out a separate rental application and agree to a credit check—after all, a cosigner who has no resources or connection to the tenant will be completely useless. Should the tenant and her prospective cosigner object to these inquiries and the costs of a credit check, you may wonder how serious they are about the guarantor's willingness to stand behind the tenant. Once you are satisfied that the cosigner can genuinely back up the tenant, add a line at the end of the lease or rental agreement for the dated signature, phone, and address of the cosigner.

> **CAUTION**
>
> **If you later amend the rental agreement or change the lease, have the cosigner sign the new version.** Generally speaking, a cosigner is bound only to the terms of the exact lease or rental agreement he cosigns.

Lease-Option Contracts (Rent-to-Buy)

Occasionally, landlords of single-family houses will agree to rent to tenants who would like to eventually own the house. In periods of economic downturn, especially, these arrangements are attractive to tenants who may not have the down payment money (or good credit required for a loan) to purchase the property outright, but expect their finances to improve over a period of one or more years. These tenants would like the option to buy their rented home, and would also like the opportunity to have some of their rent money applied toward the house purchase price.

Rent-to-buy can also be attractive for the landlord, who may intend to sell in the near future and would like to avoid the hassle and expense of putting the house on the market (selling to a resident tenant avoids staging costs and brokers' fees). In addition, a tenant who hopes to someday own the property will be motivated to take good care of it, and to honor other aspects of the lease.

If a landlord and tenant agree to a rent-to-buy (also called rent-to-own) arrangement, they sign an agreement (typically called a lease-option contract) that gives the tenant the right (the option) of buying the house in the future, providing certain conditions are met. The option agreement should be separate from the lease, but refer to it. The agreement covers issues like:

- the amount of the option fee and how it will be paid
- the date by which or the window of time the tenant has to exercise (or lose) the option
- how much (if any) of the monthly rent will be applied to the house purchase price, and
- the sale price of the home.

Many landlords are wary of rent-to-buy arrangements, for good reasons. The major drawback is that giving a tenant the option to buy the rental house ties the landlord down; you can't easily sell it to someone else, and you may find it difficult to use the property as collateral for a loan.

A second major disadvantage of agreeing to allow the tenant to buy the house is that in some states, purchase options trigger disclosures regarding the condition of the property and any defects, the same disclosures that sellers must make when engaging in a normal sale. Depending on the laws of your state, this might involve inspections and considerable work and expense.

When thinking about offering an option to buy, keep the following issues in mind.

Paying for the Option

An option curtails the ability of the owner to use the house for collateral. For example, if you want to finance your child's college education by getting a second mortgage on the property, you may have difficulty doing so. Because you are giving up a valuable right when granting the option, you can expect to be compensated. You'll need to negotiate how much the option right should cost; ideally, your tenant will pay you up front, though you may also agree to monthly payments, in addition to the rent.

Sales Price of the House

When you give a tenant an option to buy, you'll need to either name the price in your option contract or supply an objective way in which the price can be determined later. Naming the price now means that you risk misreading the market, and may specify a sale price that turns out to be less than actual market value at the time of sale.

You can avoid this risk by deferring the price, but you must set up a fail-safe method for arriving at it. For example, your contract might say, "Market value as determined by licensed brokers, one each chosen by landlord and tenant; and if the brokers cannot agree, the price to be determined by a third who will be chosen by the two brokers." If you simply say, "Fair market value at the time the option is exercised," or "Price to be negotiated at the time," and you and the tenant cannot agree on a price, you won't be able to go to court and get a judge to settle it for you. In other words, the option will fall apart.

When the Tenant Must Exercise the Option, and Under What Circumstances

You'll want to give the tenant a specific window of time, or a deadline, by which he must tell you that he's exercising the option. You may specify that the option be exercised within several months of the end of the underlying lease—this gives you time to begin planning for a sale or a successor tenant. Or, you could set a deadline (like the ending date of the lease), regardless of the amount of time left on the underlying lease (exercise of the option will terminate the lease).

You'll also need to decide whether the tenant must have been "squeaky clean" in order to take advantage of the option—whether any prior lease defaults will bar the exercise (current lease violations should give you grounds to refuse to honor the option, as explained below). For instance, you may not want a tenant who has a history of late rent to exercise the option, because a tenant who has trouble making timely rent payments will probably have a hard time making mortgage payments, too. You may also want to insist on certain financial criteria, such as a minimum credit score.

The manner in which you will accept the tenant's decision should be spelled out. Written notification is preferable and personal delivery is the best method (certified mail is a good second choice).

Tenant Improvements and Rent

Many tenants will want the ability to begin improving "their" home, with the value of the improvements credited against the selling price. If you agree, be sure to consider what will happen if the tenant decides not to buy the home—will you reimburse the tenant?

Similarly, tenants may ask you to apply a portion of the rent toward a down payment. As with improvements, you'll need to address what will happen if the tenant does not exercise the option, or if the sale does not go through.

What Happens If You Need to Evict?

Your option contract should not, if drafted properly, curtail your ability to terminate the underlying lease if the tenant fails to pay the rent, causes damage, or otherwise gives you solid legal grounds for ending the tenancy. The option contract should specify that the tenant may exercise the option only if he is in "good standing" with respect to the lease. A tenant who has been terminated or evicted is obviously not in good standing. Be sure you do not become obligated to return any option fees already paid.

"Right of Refusal" and "Right of Offer"

Instead of entering into a full-blown option contract, some landlords agree to give their tenants preferential treatment when and if the property goes on the market. In these situations, the landlord avoids some of the tricky issues mentioned above, but they are still not without drawbacks.

A "right of refusal" allows the tenant to match or improve on any deal the landlord hammers out with a third-party buyer. Once the landlord has secured a buyer, he must give the tenant an opportunity to buy the property on the same or better terms. These arrangements are nothing but a headache for a seller, because it means that any potential buyer runs the risk of having the tenant trump the deal that the buyer has painstakingly hammered out. Knowing this, buyers won't bother negotiating with these sellers, and seasoned brokers (on both sides) avoid these situations like the plague.

A "right of first refusal" is much milder. With this right, the landlord promises to give the tenant the first opportunity to buy the home at the price named by the landlord. If the tenant declines, the home goes on the market. The landlord must not artificially inflate the offering price, in order to get rid of the tenant—he must name a commercially reasonable price. But as many happy sellers find out, sometimes you don't really know what the house will go for, and selling at your named price might deprive you of a lucrative bidding war (which the tenant could always join, too).

Landlords do not give away rights of first refusal or offer—like options, these rights come at a price.

Get Legal Advice

Think long and hard about whether your interests would be served by giving tenants an option to buy, or even rights of first refusal or offer. If you decide to go ahead, be sure to consult an attorney who specializes in real estate law and a tax specialist before signing a lease-option contract. Remember, you're dealing with a very expensive investment—once the tenant exercises the option, it's the same as a sales contract. Structuring the option contract (or offer rights) in ways that do not protect your interests could be financially disastrous. You'll also need professional help in preparing a house sales contract.

Month-to-Month Residential Rental Agreement

Clause 1. Identification of Landlord and Tenant

This Agreement is entered into between _____ Marty Nelson _____

_____ [Tenant] and

_____ Alex Stevens _____ [Landlord].

Each Tenant is jointly and severally liable for the payment of rent and performance of all other terms of this Agreement.

Clause 2. Identification of Premises

Subject to the terms and conditions in this Agreement, Landlord rents to Tenant, and Tenant rents from Landlord, for residential purposes only, the premises located at _____ 137 Howell St., Philadelphia, Pennsylvania ____

_____ [the premises],

together with the following furnishings and appliances: _____

_____ .

Rental of the premises also includes _____

_____

_____ .

Clause 3. Limits on Use and Occupancy

The premises are to be used only as a private residence for Tenant(s) listed in Clause 1 of this Agreement, and their minor children. Occupancy by guests for more than _____ ten days every six months ____ is prohibited without Landlord's written consent and will be considered a breach of this Agreement.

Clause 4. Term of the Tenancy

The rental will begin on _____ September 15, 20xx _____ , and continue on a month-to-month basis. Landlord may terminate the tenancy or modify the terms of this Agreement by giving the Tenant _____ 30 _____ days' written notice. Tenant may terminate the tenancy by giving the Landlord _____ 30 _____ days' written notice.

Clause 5. Payment of Rent

Regular monthly rent

Tenant will pay to Landlord a monthly rent of $ _____ 1,800 _____ , payable in advance on the first day of each month, except when that day falls on a weekend or legal holiday, in which case rent is due on the next business day. Rent will be paid in the following manner unless Landlord designates otherwise:

Delivery of payment

Rent will be paid:

☑ by mail, to ___Alex Stevens, 28 Franklin St., Philadelphia, Pennsylvania 19120___

☐ in person, at _____

Form of payment

Landlord will accept payment in these forms:

☑ personal check made payable to ___Alex Stevens___

☑ cashier's check made payable to ___Alex Stevens___

☐ credit card

☑ money order

☐ automatic credit card debit

☐ electronic funds transfer

☐ cash

Prorated first month's rent

For the period from Tenant's move-in date, ___September 15, 20xx___ , through the end of the

month, Tenant will pay to Landlord the prorated monthly rent of $___900___ . This amount will be

paid on or before the date the Tenant moves in.

Clause 6. Late Charges

If Tenant fails to pay the rent in full before the end of the ___third___ day after it's due, Tenant will pay

Landlord a late charge as follows: ___$10 plus $5 for each additional day that the rent remains unpaid.___

___The total late charge for any one month will not exceed $45___ .

Landlord does not waive the right to insist on payment of the rent in full on the date it is due.

Clause 7. Returned Check and Other Bank Charges

If any check offered by Tenant to Landlord in payment of rent or any other amount due under this Agreement is

returned for lack of sufficient funds, a "stop payment," or any other reason, Tenant will pay Landlord a returned

check charge of $___15___ .

Clause 8. Security Deposit

On signing this Agreement, Tenant will pay to Landlord the sum of $___1,800___ as a security

deposit. Tenant may not, without Landlord's prior written consent, apply this security deposit to the last

month's rent or to any other sum due under this Agreement. Within ___30 days___

after Tenant has vacated the premises, returned keys, and provided Landlord with a forwarding address,

Landlord will return the deposit in full or give Tenant an itemized written statement of the reasons for, and the

dollar amount of, any of the security deposit retained by Landlord, along with a check for any deposit balance.

[optional clauses here, if any]

The security deposit of $1,800 will be held at: _____

_____ Federal Bank _____

_____ 1 Federal Street _____

_____ Philadelphia, PA 19120 _____

Clause 9. Utilities

Tenant will pay all utility charges, except for the following, which will be paid by Landlord:

_____ garbage and water _____

_____.

Clause 10. Prohibition of Assignment and Subletting

Tenants will not sublet any part of the premises or assign this Agreement without the prior written consent of Landlord.

☐ a. Tenants shall not sublet or rent any part of the Premises for short-term stays of any duration, including but not limited to vacation rentals.

☐ b. Short-stay rentals are prohibited except as authorized by law. Any short-stay rental is expressly conditioned upon the tenants' following all regulations, laws, and other requirements as a condition to offering a short-stay rental. Failure to follow all laws, ordinances, regulations, and other requirements, including any registration requirement, will be deemed a material, noncurable breach of this Agreement and will furnish cause for termination.

Clause 11. Tenant's Maintenance Responsibilities

Tenant will: (1) keep the premises clean, sanitary, and in good condition and, upon termination of the tenancy, return the premises to Landlord in a condition identical to that which existed when Tenant took occupancy, except for ordinary wear and tear; (2) immediately notify Landlord of any defects or dangerous conditions in and about the premises of which Tenant becomes aware; and (3) reimburse Landlord, on demand by Landlord, for the cost of any repairs to the premises damaged by Tenant or Tenant's guests or business invitees through misuse or neglect.

Tenant has examined the premises, including appliances, fixtures, carpets, drapes, and paint, and has found them to be in good, safe, and clean condition and repair, except as noted in the Landlord-Tenant Checklist.

Clause 12. Repairs and Alterations by Tenant

a. Except as provided by law, or as authorized by the prior written consent of Landlord, Tenant will not make any repairs or alterations to the premises, including nailing holes in the walls or painting the rental unit.

b. Tenant will not, without Landlord's prior written consent, alter, rekey, or install any locks to the premises or install or alter any security alarm system. Tenant will provide Landlord with a key or keys capable of unlocking all such rekeyed or new locks as well as instructions on how to disarm any altered or new security alarm system.

Clause 13. Prohibition Against Violating Laws and Causing Disturbances

Tenant is entitled to quiet enjoyment of the premises. Tenant and guests or invitees will not use the premises or adjacent areas in such a way as to: (1) violate any law or ordinance, including laws prohibiting the use, possession, or sale of illegal drugs; (2) commit waste (severe property damage); or (3) create a nuisance by annoying, disturbing, inconveniencing, or interfering with the quiet enjoyment and peace and quiet of any other tenant or nearby resident.

Clause 14. Pets

No animal may be kept on the premises without Landlord's prior written consent, except animals needed by tenants who have a disability, as that term is understood by law, except for the following: _____ one dog under 20 pounds _____

under the following conditions: Tenant complies with rules set out in "Attachment 1, Addition to Clause 14, Pets," attached to this agreement _____ .

Clause 15. Landlord's Right to Access

Landlord or Landlord's agents may enter the premises in the event of an emergency, to make repairs or improvements, or to show the premises to prospective buyers or tenants. Landlord may also enter the premises to conduct an annual inspection to check for safety or maintenance problems. Except in cases of emergency, Tenant's abandonment of the premises, court order, or where it is impractical to do so, Landlord will give Tenant _____ 24 hours' _____ notice before entering.

Clause 16. Extended Absences by Tenant

Tenant will notify Landlord in advance if Tenant will be away from the premises for _____ seven _____ or more consecutive days. During such absence, Landlord may enter the premises at times reasonably necessary to maintain the property and inspect for damage and needed repairs.

Clause 17. Possession of the Premises

a. *Tenant's failure to take possession.*

If, after signing this Agreement, Tenant fails to take possession of the premises, Tenant will still be responsible for paying rent and complying with all other terms of this Agreement.

b. *Landlord's failure to deliver possession.*

If Landlord is unable to deliver possession of the premises to Tenant for any reason not within Landlord's control, including, but not limited to, partial or complete destruction of the premises, Tenant will have the right to terminate this Agreement upon proper notice as required by law. In such event, Landlord's liability to Tenant will be limited to the return of all sums previously paid by Tenant to Landlord.

Clause 18. Tenant Rules and Regulations

☑ Tenant acknowledges receipt of, and has read a copy of, tenant rules and regulations, which are labeled Attachment A and attached to and incorporated into this Agreement by this reference. Tenant understands that serious or repeated violations of the rules may be grounds for termination. Landlord may change the rules and regulations without notice.

Clause 19. Payment of Court Costs and Attorneys' Fees in a Lawsuit

In any action or legal proceeding to enforce any part of this Agreement, the prevailing party ☐ shall not / ☑ shall recover reasonable attorneys' fees and court costs.

Clause 20. Disclosures

Tenant acknowledges that Landlord has made the following disclosures regarding the premises:

☑ *Disclosure of Information on Lead-Based Paint and/or Lead-Based Paint Hazards*

☐ Other disclosures: _____

_____

_____

_____ .

Clause 21. Authority to Receive Legal Papers

The Landlord, any person managing the premises, and anyone designated by the Landlord are authorized to accept service of process and receive other notices and demands, which may be delivered to:

☑ The Landlord, at the following address: 28 Franklin St., Philadelphia, Pennsylvania 19120

_____ .

☐ The manager, at the following address: _____

_____ .

☐ The following person, at the following address: _____

_____ .

Clause 22. Additional Provisions

Additional provisions are as follows: _____

_____

_____

_____

_____ .

Clause 23. Validity of Each Part

If any portion of this Agreement is held to be invalid, its invalidity will not affect the validity or enforceability of any other provision of this Agreement.

Clause 24. Grounds for Termination of Tenancy

The failure of Tenant or Tenant's guests or invitees to comply with any term of this Agreement, or the misrepresentation of any material fact on Tenant's rental application, is grounds for termination of the tenancy, with appropriate notice to Tenant and procedures as required by law.

Clause 25. Entire Agreement

This document constitutes the entire Agreement between the parties, and no promises or representations, other than those contained here and those implied by law, have been made by Landlord or Tenant. Any modifications to this Agreement must be in writing, signed by Landlord and Tenant.

Sept. 1, 20xx	*Alex Stevens*	Landlord
Date	Landlord or Landlord's Agent	Title

28 Franklin Street		
Street Address		

Philadelphia	Pennsylvania	19120	215-555-1578
City	State	Zip Code	Phone

Alex@Alex.com		
Email		

Sept. 1, 20xx	*Marty Nelson*	215-555-8751
Date	Tenant	Phone

Date	Tenant	Phone

Date	Tenant	Phone

Choosing Tenants:
Your Most Important Decision

Choosing tenants is the most important decision any landlord makes. To do it well and stay out of legal trouble, you need a good system. Follow the steps in this chapter to maximize your chances of selecting tenants who will pay their rent on time, keep their units in good condition, and not cause you any legal or practical problems later.

TIP

Before you advertise your property for rent, make a number of basic decisions—including how much rent to charge, whether to offer a fixed-term lease or a month-to-month tenancy, how many tenants can occupy each rental unit, how big a security deposit to require, and whether you'll allow pets. Making these important decisions should dovetail with writing your lease or rental agreement (see Chapter 1).

How to Advertise Rental Property

You can advertise rental property in many ways:

- posting a notice online on Craigslist (see "Craigslist and Online Services," below, for details)
- putting an "Apartment for Rent" sign in front of the building or in one of the windows
- taking out an ad in a local newspaper
- posting flyers on neighborhood bulletin boards
- listing with a local real estate broker that handles rentals
- buying ads in apartment rental guides or magazines, or
- hiring a property management company that will advertise your rentals as part of the management fee.

Craigslist and Online Services

Dozens of online services now make it easy to reach potential tenants, whether they already live in your community or are from out of state.

Craigslist and other online community posting boards allow you to list your rentals at no or low charge and are a good place to start. Craigslist, the most established community board, has local sites for every major metropolitan area. Check out www.craigslist.org for details.

National apartment listing services are also available, with the largest ones representing millions of apartment units in the United States. Some of the most established are:

- www.rentals.com
- www.apartments.com
- www.apartmentsearch.com
- www.forrent.com
- www.zumper.com
- www.rent.com, and
- www.apartmentguide.com.

These national sites offer a wide range of services, from simple text-only ads that provide basic information on your rental (such as the number of bedrooms) to full-scale virtual tours and floor plans of the rental property. Services typically include mobile apps, too. Prices vary widely depending on the type of ad, how long you want it to run, and any services you purchase (some websites provide tenant-screening services).

Before you use any online apartment rental service, make sure it's reputable. Find out how long the company has been in business and how they handle problems with apartment listings. Check for any consumer complaints, and avoid paying any hefty fee without thoroughly checking out a company and its services.

What will work best depends on a number of factors, including the characteristics of the particular rental property (such as rent, size, and amenities), its location, your budget, and whether you are in a hurry to rent. Many smaller landlords find that instead of advertising widely and having to screen many potential tenants in an effort to sort the good from the bad, it makes better sense to market their rentals through word of mouth—telling friends, colleagues, neighbors, current tenants, and social media contacts.

But no matter how you let people know about the availability of your rental units, you want to follow these simple rules and stay out of legal hot water:

Describe the rental unit accurately. As a practical matter, you should avoid abbreviations and real estate jargon in your ad. Include basic details, such as:

- rent and deposit
- size—particularly number of bedrooms and baths
- location—either the general neighborhood or street address
- move-in date and term—fixed-term lease or month-to-month rental agreement
- special features—such as fenced-in yard, view, washer/dryer, fireplace, remodeled kitchen, furnished, garage parking, doorman, hardwood floors, or wall-to-wall carpeting
- pets (whether you allow or not, and any restrictions, such as dog breeds your insurance prohibits)
- phone number, email, or website for more details (unless you're going to show the unit only at an open house and don't want to take calls), and
- date and time of any open house.

If you have any important rules (legal and non-discriminatory, of course), such as no smoking, put them in your ad. Letting prospective tenants know about your important policies can save you from talking to a lot of unsuitable people.

Be sure your ad can't be construed as discriminatory. The best way to do this is to focus on only the rental property—not on any particular type of tenant. Specifically, ads should never mention sex, race, religion, disability, or age (unless yours is legally recognized senior citizens housing). And ads should never imply through words, photographs, or illustrations that you prefer to rent to people because of their age, sex, or race. (See "Avoiding Illegal Discrimination," below, for more on the subject.)

Quote an honest price in your ad. Or, put another way, if a tenant who is otherwise acceptable (has a good credit history and impeccable references and meets all the criteria explained below) shows up promptly, and agrees to all the terms set out in your ad, he or she should be able to rent your property for the price you have advertised. By contrast, if you suddenly find a reason why it will cost significantly more, you are likely to be in violation of your state's false advertising laws. This doesn't mean you are always legally required to rent at your advertised price, however. If a tenant asks for more services or significantly different lease terms that you feel require more rent, it's fine to bargain and raise your price, as long as your proposed increase doesn't violate any local rent control laws.

Don't advertise something you don't have. Some large landlords, management companies, and rental services have advertised units that weren't really available in order to produce a large number of prospective tenants who could then be directed to higher-priced or inferior units. Such bait-and-switch advertising is clearly illegal under consumer fraud laws, and many property owners have been prosecuted for such practices.

Don't overhype security measures. Don't exaggerate your written or oral description of security measures. Not only will you have begun the landlord-tenant relationship on a note of insincerity, but your descriptions of security may legally obligate you to actually provide what you have portrayed. Or, if you fail to do so, or fail to conscientiously maintain promised security measures in working order (such as outdoor lighting or an electronic gate on the parking garage), a court or jury may find your failure to be a material factor allowing a crime to occur on the premises. And, if this happens, chances are good you will be held liable for a tenant's losses or injuries.

Ads That Invite Lawsuits

Advertisements like the following will come back to haunt you if a crime occurs on your rental property:

- "No one gets past our mega-security systems. A highly trained guard is on duty at all times."
- "We provide highly safe, highly secure buildings."
- "You can count on us. We maintain the highest apartment security standards in the business."

Again, the point is not that you shouldn't provide good security—or even that you shouldn't tell prospective tenants about it—but that it's best to do so in a calm, straightforward way.

Renting Property That's Still Occupied

Often, you can wait until the old tenant moves out to show a rental unit to prospective tenants. This gives you the chance to refurbish the unit and avoids problems such as promising the place to a new tenant, only to have the existing tenant not move out on time or leave the place a mess.

To eliminate any gap in rent, however, you may want to show a rental unit while its current tenants are still there. This can create a conflict; in most states, you have a right to show the still-occupied property to prospective tenants, but your current tenants are still entitled to a reasonable level of privacy. (For details, see Clause 15 of the lease and rental agreement in Chapter 1.)

To minimize disturbing your current tenant, follow these guidelines:

- Before implementing your plans to find a new tenant, discuss them with outgoing tenants so you can be as accommodating as possible.
- Give current tenants as much notice as possible before entering and showing a rental unit to prospective tenants.
- Try to limit the number of times you show the unit in a given week, and make sure your current tenants agree to any evening and weekend visits.
- Consider reducing the rent slightly for the existing tenant if showing the unit really will be an imposition.
- If possible, avoid putting a sign on the rental property itself, since this almost guarantees that your existing tenants will be bothered by strangers. Or, if you can't avoid putting up a sign, make sure any sign clearly warns against disturbing the occupant and includes a telephone number for information. Something on the order of "For Rent: Shown by Appointment Only. Call 555-1700. Do Not Disturb Occupants" should work fine.

If, despite your best efforts to protect their privacy, the current tenants are uncooperative or hostile, it really is best to avoid legal hassles and wait until they leave before showing the unit. Also, if the current tenant is a complete slob or has damaged the place, you'll be far better off to apply paint and elbow grease before trying to rerent it.

Accepting Rental Applications

It's good business, as well as a sound way to protect yourself from future legal problems, to carefully screen prospective tenants. To avoid legal problems and choose the best tenant, ask all prospective tenants to fill out a written rental application that includes information on the applicant's employment, income, credit, and rental housing history, including up-to-date references. It's legal and a good idea to ask for the applicant's Social Security and driver's license numbers or other identifying information. For example, instead of a Social Security number, you could accept an ITIN (Individual Taxpayer Identification Number), which is issued by the IRS to persons who are required to file income taxes but who can't obtain a Social Security number (SSN). ITINs are issued to nonimmigrants (people who are in the United States legally but don't have the right to live here permanently). Almost anyone planning on staying in the United States long enough to rent an apartment (like someone with a student visa) will have an ITIN. If you refuse to rent to someone who has an ITIN but not an SSN, you may be courting a fair housing claim. You can also ask if the applicant has declared bankruptcy, been evicted, or been convicted of a crime. (You'll also get much of this information from a credit report, as discussed below.)

FORM

Rental Application form. You'll find a Rental Application in Appendix C of this book. You can also download this form on the Nolo website; the link is included in Appendix B of this book. A filled-in sample rental application is shown below.

Before giving prospective tenants a rental application, complete the box at the top, filling in the property address, the first month's rent, the rental term, and any deposit or credit check fee that tenants must pay before moving in.

(Credit check fees are discussed later in this chapter.) If you're charging any other fee, such as a nonrefundable cleaning deposit, note this as well—if you are sure that the nonrefundable fee is legal in your state. (See "Don't Charge Nonrefundable Fees" in Chapter 1 for details.)

Here are some basic guidelines for accepting rental applications:

- Each prospective tenant—everyone age 18 or older who wants to live in your rental property—should completely fill out and sign a separate written application. This is true whether you're renting to a married couple or to unrelated roommates, a complete stranger, or the cousin of your current tenant.

- Always make sure that prospective tenants complete the entire rental application, including Social Security number, driver's license or other identifying information (such as a passport number), current employment, bank, and emergency contacts. You may need this information later to track down a tenant who skips town leaving unpaid rent or abandoned property. Also, you may need the Social Security number or other identifying information, such as a passport, to request an applicant's credit report.

- Request proof of identity and immigration status. In these security-sensitive times, many landlords ask prospective tenants to show their driver's license or other photo identification as a way to verify that the applicant is using his real name. Except in California (Cal. Civ. Code § 1940.3) and New York City (NYC Admin. Code § 8-107(5)(a)), you may also ask applicants for proof of identity and eligibility to work under U.S. immigration laws, such as a work permit, a passport, or a naturalization certificate, using Form I-9 (*Employment Eligibility Verification*) from the U.S. Citizenship and Immigration Services, or

Rental Application

Separate application required from each applicant age 18 or older.

Date and time received by landlord _____

THIS SECTION TO BE COMPLETED BY LANDLORD

Address of Property to Be Rented: _____ 178 West 81st St., Apt. 4F, NYC _____

Rental Term: ☐ month-to-month ☑ lease from _____ March 1, 20xx _____ to _____ February 28, 20xx _____

Amounts Due Prior to Occupancy

First month's rent:	$ 3,000
Security deposit:	$ 3,000
Credit-check fee:	$ 38
Other (specify): _____	$ _____
TOTAL	$ 6,038

Applicant

Full Name—include all names you use(d): _____ Hannah Silver _____

Home Phone: _____ 609-555-3789 _____ Work Phone: _____ 609-555-4567 _____ Cell Phone: _____ 609-555-3790 _____

Email: _____ hannah@coldmail.com _____ Fax:* _____

Social Security Number: _____ 123-00-4567 _____ Driver's License Number/State: _____ D123456/New Jersey _____

Other Identifying Information: _____

Vehicle Make: _____ Toyota _____ Model: _____ Corolla _____ Color: _____ White _____ Year: _____ 2015 _____

License Plate Number/State: _____ NJ1234567/New Jersey _____

Additional Occupants

List everyone, including minor children, who will live with you:

Full Name	Relationship to Applicant
Dennis Olson	Husband

Rental History

FIRST-TIME RENTERS: ATTACH A DESCRIPTION OF YOUR HOUSING SITUATION FOR THE PAST FIVE YEARS.

Current Address: _____ 39 Maple St., Princeton, NJ 08540 _____

Dates Lived at Address: _____ May 2011–date _____ Rent $ _____ 2,000 _____ Security Deposit $ _____ 4,000 _____

Landlord/Manager: _____ Jane Tucker _____ Landlord/Manager's Phone: _____ 609-555-7523 _____

Reason for Leaving: _____ New job in NYC _____

* By providing this fax number I agree to receive facsimile advertisements from the Landlord or management company.

Previous Address: ___1215 Middlebrook Lane, Princeton, NJ 08540___

Dates Lived at Address: ___June 2008–May 2011___ Rent $ _1,800_ Security Deposit $ _1,000_

Landlord/Manager: ___Ed Palermo___ Landlord/Manager's Phone: ___609-555-3711___

Reason for Leaving: ___Better apartment___

Previous Address: ___1527 Highland Dr., New Brunswick, NJ 08444___

Dates Lived at Address: ___Jan. 2007–June 2008___ Rent $ _800_ Security Deposit $ _800_

Landlord/Manager: ___Millie & Joe Lewis___ Landlord/Manager's Phone: ___609-555-9999___

Reason for Leaving: ___Wanted to live closer to work___

Employment History

SELF-EMPLOYED APPLICANTS: ATTACH TAX RETURNS FOR THE PAST TWO YEARS.

Name and Address of Current Employer: ___Argonworks, 54 Nassau St., Princeton, NJ___

___ Phone: (609) _555-2333_

Name of Supervisor: ___Tom Schmidt___ Supervisor's Phone: (609) _555-2333_

Dates Employed at This Job: ___2008–date___ Position or Title: _Marketing Director_

Name and Address of Previous Employer: ___Princeton Times___

___13 Junction Rd., Princeton, NJ___ Phone: (609) _555-1111_

Name of Supervisor: ___Dory Krossber___ Supervisor's Phone: (609) _555-2366_

Dates Employed at This Job: ___Jan. 2007–June 2008___ Position or Title: _Marketing Associate_

ATTACH PAY STUBS FOR THE PAST TWO YEARS, FROM THIS EMPLOYER OR PRIOR EMPLOYERS.

Income

1. Your gross monthly employment income (before deductions): $ _8,000_

2. Average monthly amounts of other income (specify sources): $ ___

   Note: This does not include my husband's income. See his application. $ ___

   ___ $ ___

   TOTAL: $ _8,000_

Bank/Financial Accounts

	Account Number	Bank/Institution	Branch
Savings Account: ___	1222345	N.J. Federal	Trenton, NJ
Checking Account: ___	789101	Princeton S&L	Princeton, NJ
Money Market or Similar Account: ___	234789	City Bank	Princeton, NJ

Credit Card Accounts

Major Credit Card: ☑ VISA ☐ MC ☐ Discover Card ☐ Am Ex ☐ Other: _____

Issuer: _____City Bank_____   Account No. _____1234 5555 6666 7777_____

Balance $ _____1,000_____   Average Monthly Payment $ _____1,000_____

Major Credit Card: ☐ VISA ☐ MC ☐ Discover Card ☐ Am Ex ☑ Other: _____Dept. Store_____

Issuer: _____City Bank_____   Account No. _____2345 0000 9999 8888_____

Balance $ _____1,000_____   Average Monthly Payment $ _____1,000_____

Loans

Type of Loan (mortgage, car, student loan, etc.)	Name of Creditor	Account Number	Amount Owed	Monthly Payment

Other Major Obligations

Type	Payee	Amount Owed	Monthly Payment

Miscellaneous

Describe the number and type of pets you want to have in the rental property: _____None now, but we might_____ _____want to get a cat some time_____ .

Describe water-filled furniture you want to have in the rental property: _____None_____ .

Do you smoke?   ☐ yes ☑ no

Have you ever:

	Filed for bankruptcy?	☐ yes ☑ no	How many times _____
	Been sued?	☐ yes ☑ no	How many times _____
	Sued someone else?	☐ yes ☑ no	How many times _____
	Been evicted?	☐ yes ☑ no	How many times _____
	Been convicted of a crime?	☐ yes ☑ no	How many times _____

Explain any "yes" listed above: _____

_____

_____

_____

References and Emergency Contact

Personal Reference: _Joan Stanley_   Relationship: _Friend, coworker_

Address: _785 Spruce St., Princeton, NJ 08540_

     Phone: (609) _555-4578_

Personal Reference: _Marnie Swatt_   Relationship: _Friend_

Address: _82 East 59th St., #12B, NYC_

     Phone: (212) _555-8765_

Contact in Emergency: _Connie & Martin Silver_   Relationship: _Parents_

Address: _7852 Pierce St., Somerset, NJ 08321_

     Phone: (609) _555-7878_

Source

Where did you learn of this vacancy? _Ryan Cowell, Broker_

I certify that all the information given above is true and correct and understand that my lease or rental agreement may be terminated if I have made any material false or incomplete statements in this application. I authorize verification of the information provided in this application from my credit sources, credit bureaus, current and previous landlords and employers, and personal references. This permission will survive the expiration of my tenancy.

Hannah Silver   _February 15, 20xx_

Applicant   Date

Notes (Landlord/Manager): _____

USCIS, a bureau of the U.S. Department of Homeland Security. This form (and instructions for completing it) are available from the USCIS website at www.uscis.gov/i-9, or by phone at 800-375-5283. Under federal fair housing laws, you may not selectively ask for such immigration information—that is, you must ask all prospective tenants, not just those you suspect may be in the country illegally. It is illegal to discriminate on the basis of race, color, or national origin, although you may reject someone on the basis of immigration status.

- Be sure all potential tenants sign the rental application, authorizing you to verify the information and references and to run a credit report. (Some employers and banks require written authorization before they will talk to you.) You may also want to prepare a separate authorization, signed and dated by the applicant, so that you don't need to copy the entire application and send it off every time a bank or employer wants proof that the tenant authorized you to verify the information.

Finally, note that this application does not ask applicants for their dates of birth (DOB). Many fair housing experts believe that doing so is risky, should a disappointed applicant attempt to challenge your rejection as an instance of age discrimination—having the date on the application at least establishes that you knew of the applicant's age. Some landlords still ask for the DOB, responding to credit reporting companies' requests for this information. You should be able to order a credit report and a screening report using the applicant's Social Security number; if vendors balk, you may want to ask for the DOB.

Consent to Contact References and Perform Credit Check

I authorize ___Jan Gold_____

to obtain information about me from my credit sources, current and previous landlords, employers, and personal

references, to enable ___Jan Gold_____ to

evaluate my rental application.

I give permission for the landlord or its agent to obtain a consumer report about me for the purpose of this

application, to ensure that I continue to meet the terms of the tenancy, for the collection and recovery of any

financial obligations relating to my tenancy, or for any other permissible purpose.

_Michael Clark_____
Applicant Signature
___Michael Clark_____
Printed Name
___123 State Street, Chicago, Illinois_____
Address
___312-555-9876_____
Phone Number
___February 2, 20xx_____
Date

FORM

Reference and Credit Check Consent form. You'll find a copy of the Consent to Contact References and Perform Credit Check in Appendix C of this book. You can download this form on the Nolo website; the link is included in Appendix B of this book. A filled-in sample consent form is shown below.

Checking References, Credit History, and More

If an application looks good, your next step is to follow up thoroughly. The time and money you spend are some of the most cost-effective expenditures you'll ever make.

CAUTION

Be consistent in your screening. You risk a charge of illegal discrimination if you screen certain categories of applicants more stringently than others—for example, only requiring credit reports from racial minorities. (See "Avoiding Illegal Discrimination," below, for more on the subject.)

Here are six elements of a very thorough screening process. You should always go through at least the first three to check out the applicant's previous landlords and income and employment, and run a credit check.

Check With Current and Previous Landlords and Other References

Always call current and previous landlords or managers for references—even if you have a written letter of reference from them. It's worth the time if it helps you weed out a tenant who may cause problems down the road. Also call employers and personal references listed on the application.

To organize the information you gather from these calls, use the Tenant References

form, which lists key questions to ask landlords, employers, and other references.

TIP

Check out pets, too. If the prospective tenant has a dog or cat, be sure to ask previous landlords if the pet caused any damage or problems for other tenants or neighbors. It's also a good idea to meet the dog or cat, so you can make sure that it's well-groomed and well-behaved, before you make a final decision. You must, however, accommodate a mentally or physically disabled applicant whose pet serves as a support animal—no matter how mangy-looking the pet might be. (See the discussion of pet rules in Chapter 1, Clause 14.)

Be sure to take notes of all your conversations and keep them on file. You may indicate your reasons for refusing an individual on the Tenant References form—for example, negative credit information, bad references from a previous landlord, or your inability to verify information. You'll want a record of this information so that you can survive a fair housing challenge if a disappointed applicant files a discrimination complaint against you.

FORM

Tenant References form. You'll find a copy of the Tenant References screening form in Appendix C of this book. You can also download this form on the Nolo website; the link is included in Appendix B of this book. A filled-in sample Tenant References form is shown below.

Verify Income and Employment

Obviously, you want to make sure that all tenants have the income to pay the rent each month. Call the prospective tenant's employer to verify income and length of employment. Make notes on the Tenant References form, discussed above.

Tenant References

Name of Applicant: _____Michael Clark_____

Address of Rental Unit: _____123 State Street, Chicago, Illinois_____

Previous Landlord or Manager

Contact (name, property owner or manager, address of rental unit): _Kate Steiner, 345 Mercer St., Chicago, Illinois;_

_____(312) 555-5432_____

Date: _____February 4, 20xx_____

Questions

When did tenant rent from you (move-in and move-out dates)? _____December 2012 to date_____

What was the monthly rent? ___$1,250_____   Did tenant pay rent on time?   ☐ Yes ☑ No

If rent was not paid on time, did you have to give tenant a legal notice demanding the rent?   ☐ Yes ☑ No

If rent was not paid on time, provide details _____He paid rent a week late a few times_____

_____

Did you give tenant notice of any lease violation for other than nonpayment of rent?   ☐ Yes ☑ No

If you gave a lease violation notice, what was the outcome? _____

Was tenant considerate of neighbors—that is, no loud parties and fair, careful use of common areas?

_____Yes, considerate_____

_____

Did tenant have any pets?   ☑ Yes ☐ No   If so, were there any problems? _____He had a cat, contrary to

_____rental agreement_____

Did tenant make any unreasonable demands or complaints?   ☐ Yes ☑ No   If so, explain: _____

_____

Why did tenant leave? _____He wants to live someplace that allows pets_____

_____

Did tenant give the proper amount of notice before leaving?   ☑ Yes ☐ No

Did tenant leave the place in good condition? Did you need to use the security deposit to cover damage?

_____No problems_____

Any particular problems you'd like to mention? _____No_____

_____

Would you rent to this person again? _____Yes, but without pets_____

_____

Other comments: _____

_____

Employment Verification

Contact (name, company, position): ____Brett Field, Manager, Chicago Car Company____

Date: ____February 5, 20xx____   Salary $____80,000 + bonus____

Dates of Employment: ____March 2011 to date____

Comments: ____No problems. Fine employee. Michael is responsible and hard-working.____

Personal Reference

Contact (name and relationship to applicant): ____Sandy Cameron, friend____

Date: ____February 5, 20xx____   How long have you known the applicant? ____Five years____

Would you recommend this person as a prospective tenant? ____Yes____

Comments: ____Michael is very neat and responsible. He's reliable and will be a great tenant.____

Credit and Financial Information

____Mostly fine—see attached credit report.____

Notes, Including Reasons for Rejecting Applicant

____Applicant had a history of late rent payments and kept a cat, contrary to the rental agreement.____

Before providing this information, some employers require written authorization from the employee. You will need to send the employer a signed copy of the release included at the bottom of the rental application form or the separate Consent to Contact References and Perform Credit Check form. If for any reason you question the income information you get by telephone—for example, you suspect a buddy of the applicant is exaggerating on his behalf—you may also ask applicants for copies of recent paycheck stubs.

It's also reasonable to require documentation of other sources of income, such as Social Security, disability payments, workers' compensation, welfare, child support, or alimony.

How much income is enough? Think twice before renting to someone if the rent will take more than one-third of their income, especially if they have a lot of debts.

Obtain a Credit Report

Private credit reporting agencies collect and sell credit files and other information about consumers. Many landlords find it essential to check a prospective tenant's credit history with at least one credit reporting agency to see how responsible the person is about managing money. Jot your findings down on the Tenant References form, discussed above.

How to Get a Credit Report

A credit report contains a gold mine of information on a prospective tenant. You can find out, for example, if a particular person has a history of paying rent or bills late or has gone through bankruptcy, been convicted of a crime, or ever been evicted. (Your legal right to get information on evictions, however, may vary from state to state.) Credit reports usually cover the past seven to ten years. Depending on the type of report

you order, you may also get an applicant's credit, the most popular being the "FICO," score, a number that purports to indicate the risk that an individual will default on payments.

To run a credit check, you'll normally need a prospective tenant's name, address, and Social Security number, or ITIN (Individual Taxpayer Identification Number). Three credit bureaus have cornered the market on credit reports:

- Equifax, www.equifax.com
- Experian, www.experian.com, and
- TransUnion, www.transunion.com.

You cannot order a credit report directly from the big three bureaus. Instead, you'll need to work through a credit reporting agency or tenant screening service (type "tenant screening" or "credit reporting agency" into your browser's search box, or look in the yellow pages). Look for a company that operates in your area, has been in business for a while, and provides you with a sample report that's clear and informative. Your state or local apartment association may also offer credit reporting services. With credit reporting agencies, you can often obtain a credit report the same day it's requested. Fees depend on how many reports you order each month.

Tenants who are applying for more than one rental are understandably dismayed at the prospect of paying each landlord to pull the same credit report. They may obtain their own report, make copies, and ask you to accept their copy. Federal law does not require you to accept an applicant's copy—that is, you may require applicants to pay a credit check fee for you to run a new report. Wisconsin and Washington are exceptions: State law in Wisconsin forbids landlords from charging for a credit report if, before the landlord asks for a report, the applicant offers one from a consumer reporting agency and the report is less than 30 days old. (Wis. Adm. Code ATCP 134.05(4)(b).) In Washington, landlords must advise tenants whether they will accept a screening report done by a consumer reporting agency (in which case the landlord may not charge the tenant a fee for a screening report). Landlords who maintain a website that advertises residential rentals must include this information on the home page. (Wash. Rev. Code Ann. § 59.18.257.)

Credit Check Fees

It's legal in most states to charge prospective tenants a fee for the cost of the credit report itself and for your time and trouble. Any credit check fee should be reasonably related to the cost of the credit check—$20 to $30 is common. Check your state law for any limits. California, for example, sets a maximum screening fee per applicant and requires landlords to provide an itemized receipt when accepting a credit check fee. (Cal. Civ. Code § 1950.6.)

Some landlords don't charge credit check fees, preferring to absorb the cost as they would any other cost of business. For low-end units, charging an extra fee can be a barrier to getting tenants in the first place, and a tenant who pays a fee, but is later rejected, is likely to be annoyed and possibly more apt to claim that you have rejected him or her for a discriminatory reason.

The rental application form in this book informs prospective tenants if you charge a credit check fee. Be sure prospective tenants understand that paying a credit check fee does not guarantee the tenant will get the rental unit.

TIP

It's a mistake to collect a credit check fee from lots of people. If you expect a large number of applicants, you'd be wise not to accept fees from everyone. Instead, read over the applications first and do a credit check only on applicants you're seriously considering. That way, you won't waste your time (and prospective tenants' money) collecting fees from unqualified applicants.

CAUTION

It is generally illegal to charge a credit check fee if you do not use it for the stated purpose and pocket it instead. Return any credit check fees you don't use for that purpose.

What You're Looking for in a Credit Report

It makes sense to be leery of applicants with lots of debts—this clearly includes people whose monthly payments plus the rent obligation exceed 40% of their after-tax income. Also, look at the person's bill-paying habits, and, of course, pay attention to lawsuits and evictions.

Sometimes, your only choice is to rent to someone with poor or fair credit—or even no credit (for example, a student or recent graduate). If that's your situation, you should still adopt sensible screening requirements such as these:

- positive references from previous landlords and employers
- a creditworthy cosigner of the lease (see the discussion on cosigners at the end of Chapter 1)
- a good-sized deposit—as much as you can collect under state law and the market will bear (see Clause 8 of the form agreements in Chapter 1), and
- proof of specific steps taken to improve bad credit—for example, enrollment in a debt counseling group.

CAUTION

Take special care to store credit reports in a safe place, where only you and those who "need to know" have access to them. In fact, under the "Disposal Rule" of the Fair and Accurate Credit Transactions Act, you must destroy the report when you have reviewed it and no longer need it. Use a shredder or burn the credit report, and delete any reports kept on your computer or phone.

Verify Bank Account Information

If an individual's credit history raises questions about financial stability, you may want to double-check the bank accounts listed on the rental application. If so, you'll probably need an authorization form such as the one included at the bottom of the rental application, or the separate Consent to Contact References and Perform Credit Check form (discussed above). Banks differ as to the type of information they will provide over the phone. Generally, without a written authorization, banks will only confirm that an individual has an account there and that it is in good standing.

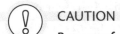 CAUTION

Be wary of an applicant who has no checking or savings account. Tenants who offer to pay cash or with a money order should be viewed with extreme caution. Perhaps the individual bounced so many checks that the bank dropped the account or the income comes from a shady or illegitimate source—for example, from drug dealing.

Review Court Records

If your prospective tenant has previously lived in your area, you may want to review local court records to see if collection or eviction lawsuits have ever been filed against him. Checking court records may seem like overkill, since some of this information may be available on credit reports, but now and then it's an invaluable tool, and it's not a violation of antidiscrimination laws as long as you check the records of every applicant who reaches this stage of your screening process. Because court records are kept for many years, this kind of information can supplement references from recent landlords. Talk to the court

clerk at the local court that handles eviction cases for information on how to check court records.

Use Megan's Law to Check State Databases of Sex Offenders

Not surprisingly, most landlords do not want tenants with criminal records, particularly convictions for violent crimes or crimes against children. Checking a prospective tenant's credit report, as recommended above, is one way to find out about a person's criminal history. Self-reporting is another: Rental applications, such as the one in this book, typically ask whether the prospective tenant has ever been convicted of a crime.

"Megan's Law" may also be a useful source of information. Named after a young girl who was killed by a convicted child molester who lived in her neighborhood, this federal crime prevention law charges the FBI with keeping a nationwide database of persons convicted of sexual offenses against minors and violent sexual offenses against anyone. (42 U.S.C. §§ 14071 and following.) Every state has its own version of Megan's Law that requires certain convicted sexual offenders to register with local law enforcement officials who keep a database on their whereabouts.

For information on your access to this type of database, and restrictions on your use of information derived from a Megan's Law database, contact your local law enforcement agency. California landlords may not access their state's database unless they are doing so to protect a person "at risk." This means that routine checking is not legal. (Cal. Penal Code § 290.46(j)(1).) Massachusetts, Nevada, and New Jersey have some restrictions, too. To find out how to access your state's sex offender registry, you can also contact the Parents for Megan's Law (PFML) Hotline at 888-ASK-PFML, or check this organization's website at www.parentsformeganslaw.org.

Avoiding Illegal Discrimination

Federal and state antidiscrimination laws limit what you can say and do in the tenant selection process. Basically, you need to keep in mind three important points:

1. You are legally free to choose among prospective tenants as long as your decisions are based on legitimate business criteria. You are entitled to reject people for the following reasons:
   - poor credit history
   - income that you reasonably regard as insufficient to pay the rent
   - negative references from previous landlords indicating problems—such as property damage or consistently late rent payments—that make someone a bad risk
   - convictions for criminal offenses
   - inability to meet the legal terms of a lease or rental agreement, such as someone who can't come up with the security deposit or who wants to keep a pet and your policy is no pets, or
   - more people than you want to live in the unit—assuming that your limit on the number of tenants is clearly tied to health and safety or legitimate business needs. (See Clause 3 discussion of occupancy limits in Chapter 1.)

2. Antidiscrimination laws specify clearly illegal reasons to refuse to rent to a

---

The Rights of Tenants With Disabilities

The Fair Housing Act requires that landlords *accommodate* the needs of tenants with disabilities, at the landlord's own expense. (42 U.S.C. § 3604(f)(3)(B).) You are expected to adjust your rules, procedures, or services in order to give a person with a disability an equal opportunity to use and enjoy a dwelling unit or a common space. Accommodations include such things as providing a close-in, spacious parking space for a tenant who uses a wheelchair (assuming you provide parking). Your duty to accommodate tenants with disabilities does not mean that you must bend every rule and change every procedure at the tenant's request. You are expected to accommodate "reasonable" requests, but need not undertake changes that would seriously impair your ability to run your business.

The Fair Housing Act also requires landlords to allow tenants with disabilities to make reasonable *modifications* of their living unit at their expense if that is what is needed for the person to comfortably and safely live in the unit. (42 U.S.C. § 3604(f)(3)(A).) For example, a person with a disability has the right to modify the living space to the extent necessary to make the space safe and comfortable, as long as the modifications will not make the unit unacceptable to the next tenant or the tenant with a disability agrees to undo the modification when the tenant leaves. An example of a modification undertaken by a tenant with a disability is lowering countertops for a tenant who uses a wheelchair.

You are not obliged to allow a tenant with a disability to modify his unit at will, without your prior approval. You are entitled to ask for a reasonable description of the proposed modifications, proof that they will be done in a workmanlike manner, and evidence that the tenant is obtaining any necessary building permits. Moreover, if a tenant proposes to modify the unit in such a manner that will require restoration when the tenant leaves (such as the repositioning of lowered kitchen counters), you may require that the tenant pay into an interest-bearing escrow account the amount estimated for the restoration. (The interest belongs to the tenant.)

tenant. The federal Fair Housing Act and Fair Housing Amendments Act (42 U.S.C. §§ 3601–3619, 3631) prohibit discrimination on the basis of race or color, religion, national origin, gender, age, familial status (pregnancy or children), and physical or mental disability (including recovering alcoholics and people with a past drug addiction). Many states and cities also prohibit discrimination based on marital status, source of income, military status, sexual orientation, or gender identity.

RESOURCE

More on housing discrimination rules. For more information on the rules and regulations of the Fair Housing Act, contact HUD's Housing Discrimination Hotline at 800-669-9777 or check the HUD website at www.hud.gov. You can also contact a local HUD office.

For information on state and local housing discrimination laws, contact your state fair housing agency. For a list of state agencies and contact information, see the HUD website at www.hud.gov.

3. Consistency is crucial when dealing with prospective tenants. If you don't treat all tenants more or less equally—for example, if you arbitrarily set tougher standards (such as a higher income level or proof of legal status, such as legal papers) for renting to a member of an ethnic minority—you are violating federal laws and opening yourself up to expensive lawsuits and the possibility of being hit with large judgments. On the other hand, if you require all prospective tenants to meet the same income standard and to supply satisfactory proof of their legal eligibility to work (as well as meet your other criteria), you will get the needed information, but in a nondiscriminatory way.

CAUTION

Show the property to and accept applications from everyone who's interested. Even if, after talking to someone on the phone, you doubt that a particular tenant can qualify, it's best to politely take all applications. Unless you can point to something in writing that clearly disqualifies a tenant, you are always on shaky legal ground. Refusing to take an application may unnecessarily anger a prospective tenant, and may make him or her more likely to look into the possibility of filing a discrimination complaint. Make decisions later about who will rent the property. Be sure to keep copies of all applications. (See discussion of record keeping in Chapter 3.)

Choosing—and Rejecting— an Applicant

After you've collected applications and done some screening, you can start sifting through the applicants, using the basic criteria discussed above for evaluating and choosing tenants. Start by eliminating the worst risks: people with negative references from previous landlords, a history of nonpayment of rent, or poor credit or recent and numerous evictions. Then make your selection.

Assuming you choose the best-qualified candidate (based on income, credit history, and references), you have no legal problem. But what if you have a number of more or less equally qualified applicants? Can you safely choose an older white man over a young black woman? The answer is a qualified "yes." If two people rate equally, you can legally choose either one without legal risk in any particular situation. But be extra careful not to take the further step of always selecting a person of the same sex, age, or ethnicity. For example, if you are a larger landlord who is frequently faced with tough choices and who always avoids an equally qualified minority or disabled applicant, you are exposing yourself to charges of discrimination.

Information You Should Keep on Rejected Applicants

A crucial use of any tenant-screening system is to document how and why you chose a particular tenant.

Be sure to note your reasons for rejection—such as poor credit history, pets (if you don't accept pets), or a negative reference from a previous landlord—on the tenant references form or other document so that you have a paper trail if a tenant ever accuses you of illegal discrimination. You want to be able to back up your reason for rejecting the person. Keep organized files of applications and other materials and notes on prospective tenants for at least three years after you rent a particular unit. (See "Organize Your Tenant Records" in Chapter 3.) Keep in mind that if a rejected applicant files a complaint with a fair housing agency or files a lawsuit, your file will be made available to the applicant's lawyers. Knowing that, choose your words carefully, avoiding the obvious (slurs and exaggerations) and being scrupulously truthful.

Information You Must Provide Rejected Applicants

If you do not rent to someone because of an insufficient credit report or negative information in the report, you must give the applicant the name and address of the agency that reported the negative information or furnished the insufficient report. This is a requirement of the federal Fair Credit Reporting Act (FCRA). (15 U.S.C. §§ 1681 and following.) The notices are known as "adverse action reports."

In these cases, you must tell the applicant that he or she has a right to obtain a copy of the file from the agency that reported the negative information, by requesting it within the next 60 days, or by asking within one year of having asked for their last free report. You must also tell the rejected applicant that the credit reporting agency did not make the decision to reject them and cannot explain the reason for the rejection. Finally, you must tell applicants that they can dispute the accuracy of their credit report and add their own consumer statement to their report. The law doesn't require you to communicate an applicant's right to disclosure in writing, but it's a good idea to do so (and to keep a copy of the rejection letter in your files). That way, you'll have irrefutable proof that you complied with the law if you're ever challenged in court. Use the Notice of Denial Based on Credit Report or Other Information form, shown below, to comply with the federal Fair Credit Reporting Act when you reject an applicant because of an insufficient credit report or negative information in the report.

FORM

Rejection letter form. You'll find a copy of the Notice of Denial Based on Credit Report or Other Information form in Appendix C of this book. You can also download this form on the Nolo website; the link is included in Appendix B of this book. A filled-in sample notice of denial form is shown below.

Exceptions: The federal requirements do not apply if you reject someone based on information that the applicant furnished or that you or an employee learned on your own.

Conditional Acceptances

You may want to make an offer to an applicant but condition that offer on the applicant paying more rent or a higher security deposit (one that's within any legal limits, of course), supplying a cosigner, or agreeing to a different rental term than you originally advertised. If your decision to impose the condition resulted from information you gained from a credit report or a report from a tenant screening service, you have to accompany

Notice of Denial Based on Credit Report or Other Information

To: Ryan Paige
Applicant

1 Mariner Square
Street Address

Seattle, Washington 98101
City, State, and Zip Code

Your rights under the Fair Credit Reporting Act and Fair and Accurate Credit Transactions (FACT) Act of 2003. (15 U.S.C. §§ 1681 and following.)

THIS NOTICE is to inform you that your application to rent the property at 75 Starbucks Lane, Seattle, WA 98108

[rental property address] has been denied because of [*check all that apply*]:

☑ Insufficient information in the credit report provided by:

Credit reporting agency: ABC Credit Bureau

Address, phone number, URL: 310 Griffey Way, Seattle, WA 98140; Phone: 206-555-1212; www.abccredit.com

☐ Negative information in the credit report provided by:

Credit reporting agency: _____

Address, phone number, URL: _____

☑ The credit score supplied on the credit report, 511, was used in whole or in part when making the selection.

☑ The consumer credit reporting agency noted above did not make the decision not to offer you this rental. It only provided information about your credit history. You have the right to obtain a free copy of your credit report from the consumer credit reporting agency named above, if your request is made within 60 days of this notice or if you have not requested a free copy within the past year. You also have the right to dispute the accuracy or completeness of your credit report. The agency must reinvestigate within a reasonable time, free of charge, and remove or modify inaccurate information. If the reinvestigation does not resolve the dispute to your satisfaction, you may add your own "consumer statement" (up to 100 words) to the report, which must be included (or a clear summary) in future reports.

☐ Information supplied by a third party other than a credit reporting agency or you and gathered by someone other than myself or any employee. You have the right to learn of the nature of the information if you ask me in writing within 60 days of the date of this notice.

Jason McGuire
Landlord/Manager

10-01-20xx
Date

Notice of Conditional Acceptance Based on Credit Report or Other Information

To: __William McGee__
     Applicant

     __1257 Bay Avenue__
     Street Address

     __Anytown, FL 12345__
     City, State, and Zip Code

Your application to rent the property at ____37 Ocean View Drive, #10-H, Anytown, FL 12345____

_____ [rental property address] has been accepted, conditioned on your

willingness and ability to: _____Supply a cosigner that is acceptable to the landlord_____

_____

Your rights under the Fair Credit Reporting Act and Fair and Accurate Credit Transactions (FACT) Act of 2003. (15 U.S.C. §§ 1681 and following.)

Source of information prompting conditional acceptance

My decision to conditionally accept your application was prompted in whole or in part by:

☑ Insufficient information in the credit report provided by

   Credit reporting agency: _____Mountain Credit Bureau_____

   Address, phone number, URL: ___75 Baywood Drive, Anytown, FL 12345. 800-123-4567;___
      ___www.mountaincredit.com___

☐ Negative information in the credit report provided by:

   Credit reporting agency: _____

   Address, phone number, URL: _____

   _____

☑ The consumer credit reporting agency noted above did not make the decision to offer you this conditional acceptance. It only provided information about your credit history. You have the right to obtain a free copy of your credit report from the consumer credit reporting agency named above, if your request is made within 60 days of this notice or if you have not requested a free copy within the past year. You also have the right to dispute the accuracy or completeness of your credit report. The agency must reinvestigate within a reasonable time, free of charge, and remove or modify inaccurate information. If the reinvestigation does not resolve the dispute to your satisfaction, you may add your own "consumer statement" (up to 100 words) to the report, which must be included (or a clear summary) in future reports.

☐ Information supplied by a third party other than a credit reporting agency or you and gathered by someone other than myself or any employee. You have the right to learn of the nature of the information if you ask me in writing within 60 days of the date of this notice.

Jane Thomas _____   _May 15, 20xx_ _____
Landlord/Manager   Date

the offer with an adverse action report (described in the section immediately above). Use the Notice of Conditional Acceptance Based on Credit Report or Other Information, shown below.

FORM

Conditional acceptance form. You'll find a copy of the Notice of Conditional Acceptance Based on Credit Report or Other Information in Appendix C of this book. You can also download this form on the Nolo website; the link is included in Appendix B of this book. A filled-in sample notice of conditional acceptance form is shown above.

Choosing a Tenant-Manager

Many landlords hire a manager to handle all the day-to-day details of running a rental property, including fielding tenants' routine repair requests and collecting the rent. If you hire a resident manager, make sure he or she (like all other tenants) completes a rental application and that you check references and other information carefully. If you use a property management company, it will do this work for you. (See below.)

The person you hire as a manager will occupy a critical position in your business. Your manager will interact with every tenant and will often have access to her personal files and her home. Legally, you have a duty to protect your tenants from injuries caused by employees you know (or should know) pose a risk of harm to others. If someone gets hurt or has property stolen or damaged by a manager whose background you didn't check carefully, you could be sued, so it's crucial that you be especially vigilant when hiring a manager.

When you hire a manager, you should sign two separate agreements:

- an employment agreement that covers manager responsibilities, hours, and pay, and that can be terminated at any time for any reason by either party, and

- a month-to-month rental agreement that can be terminated by either of you with the amount of written notice, typically 30 days, required under state law.

Whether or not you compensate a manager with reduced rent or regular salary, be sure you comply with your legal obligations as an employer, such as following laws governing minimum wage and overtime.

RESOURCE

More legal resources for landlords. *Every Landlord's Legal Guide,* by Marcia Stewart, Ralph Warner, and Janet Portman (Nolo), provides detailed advice on hiring a manager, including how to prepare a property manager agreement, and your legal obligations as an employer, such as following laws governing minimum wage and overtime.

The Employer's Legal Handbook, by Fred S. Steingold (Nolo), is a complete guide to the latest workplace laws and regulations. It covers everything you need to know about hiring and firing employees, personnel policies, employee benefits, discrimination, and other laws affecting small business practices.

Property Management Companies

Property management companies are often used by owners of large apartment complexes and by absentee owners too far away from the property to be directly involved in everyday details. Property management companies generally take care of renting units, collecting rent, taking tenant complaints, arranging repairs and maintenance, and evicting troublesome tenants. Of course, some of these responsibilities may be shared with or delegated to resident managers who, in some instances, may work for the management company.

A variety of relationships between owners and management companies is possible, depending on your wishes and how the particular management company chooses to do business. For example, if you own one or more big buildings, the management company will probably recommend hiring a resident manager. But if your rental property has only a few units, or you own a number of small buildings spread over a good-sized geographical area, the management company will probably suggest simply responding to tenant requests and complaints from its central office.

One advantage of working with a management company is that you avoid all the legal hassles of being an employer: paying payroll taxes, buying workers' compensation insurance, and withholding income tax. The management company is an independent contractor, not an employee. It hires and pays the people who do the work. Typically, you sign a contract spelling out the management company's duties and fees. Most companies charge a fixed percentage—about 6% to 12%—of the total rent collected. (The salary of any resident manager is additional.) This gives the company a good incentive to keep the building filled with rent-paying tenants.

Another advantage is that management companies are usually well informed about the law, keep good records, and are adept at staying out of legal hot water in such areas as discrimination, invasion of privacy, and returning deposits.

The primary disadvantage of hiring a management company is the expense. For example, if you pay a management company 10% of the $14,000 you collect in rent each month from tenants in a 12-unit building, this amounts to $1,400 a month and $16,800 per year. While many companies charge less than 10%, it's still quite an expense—even if you adjust for the fact that the property manager's fee is tax deductible. Also, if the management company works from a central office with no one on-site, tenants may feel that management is too distant and unconcerned with their day-to-day needs.

Management companies have their own contracts, which you should read thoroughly and understand before signing. Be sure you understand how the company is paid and its exact responsibilities.

Getting the Tenant Moved In

Legal disputes between landlords and tenants can be almost as emotional as divorce court battles. While some may be inevitable, many disputes could be defused at the start if tenants were better educated as to their legal rights and responsibilities. A clearly written and easy-to-understand lease or rental agreement that details a tenant's obligations and is signed by all adult occupants of your rental unit is the key to starting a tenancy. (See Chapter 1.) But there's more that can be done to help establish a positive relationship when new tenants move in. Most important, you should:

- inspect the property, fill out a landlord-tenant checklist with the tenant, and photograph the rental unit, and
- prepare a move-in letter highlighting important terms of the tenancy and your expectations, such as how to report repair problems.

Inspect and Photograph the Unit

To eliminate the possibility of all sorts of future arguments, it is absolutely essential that you (or your representative) and prospective tenants (together, if possible) check the place over for damage and obvious wear and tear before the tenant moves in. The best way to document what you find is to jointly fill out a landlord-tenant checklist form and take photographs of the rental unit.

Use a Landlord-Tenant Checklist

A landlord-tenant checklist, inventorying the condition of the rental property at the beginning and end of the tenancy, is an excellent device to protect both you and your tenant when the tenant moves out and wants the security deposit returned. Without some record as to the condition of the unit, the tenant is all too likely to make unreasonable demands. For example, is

there a landlord alive who has not been falsely told that a stained rug or a cracked mirror or broken stove was already damaged when the tenant moved in?

The checklist will provide good evidence as to why you withheld all or part of a security deposit. Coupled with a system to regularly keep track of the rental property's condition, the checklist will also be extremely useful to you if a tenant withholds rent, breaks the lease and moves out, or sues you outright, claiming the unit needs substantial repairs.

 FORM

Landlord-Tenant Checklist form. You'll find a copy of the Landlord-Tenant Checklist in Appendix C. You can also download this form on the Nolo website; the link is included in Appendix B of this book. A filled-in sample Landlord-Tenant Checklist is shown below.

> ### States That Require a Landlord-Tenant Checklist
>
> A number of states require landlords to give new tenants a written statement on the condition of the rental premises at move-in time, including a comprehensive list of existing damages. Check "Required Landlord Disclosures" in Appendix A for the exact requirements in your state, including the type of inspection required at the end of the tenancy.

How to Fill Out the Checklist

You and the tenant should fill out the checklist together. If that's impossible, complete the form and then make a copy and give it to the tenant to review. You should ask the tenant to note any disagreement promptly and return the checklist to you within a few days.

Landlord-Tenant Checklist

GENERAL CONDITION OF RENTAL UNIT AND PREMISES

572 Fourth St.		Apt. 11	Washington, DC
Street Address		Unit No. City	

	Condition on Arrival	Condition on Departure	Estimated Cost of Repair/ Replacement
Living Room			
Floors & Floor Coverings	OK		
Drapes & Window Coverings	Miniblinds discolored		
Walls & Ceilings	OK		
Light Fixtures	OK		
Windows, Screens, & Doors	Window rattles		
Front Door & Locks	OK		
Fireplace	OK		
Other			
Other			
Kitchen			
Floors & Floor Coverings	Cigarette burn hole		
Walls & Ceilings	OK		
Light Fixtures	OK		
Cabinets	OK		
Counters	Stained		
Stove/Oven	Burners filthy (grease)		
Refrigerator	OK		
Dishwasher	N/A		
Garbage Disposal	OK		
Sink & Plumbing	OK		
Windows, Screens, & Doors	OK		
Other			
Other			
Dining Room			
Floors & Floor Covering	OK		
Walls & Ceilings	Crack in ceiling		
Light Fixtures	OK		
Windows, Screens, & Doors	OK		
Other			

	Condition on Arrival		Condition on Departure		Estimated Cost of Repair/ Replacement
Bathroom(s)	Bath #1	Bath #2	Bath #1	Bath #2	
Floors & Floor Coverings	OK				
Walls & Ceilings	Wallpaper peeling				
Windows, Screens, & Doors	OK				
Light Fixtures	OK				
Bathtub/Shower	Tub chipped				
Sink & Counters	OK				
Toilet	Base of toilet very dirty				
Other					
Other					
Bedroom(s)	Bdrm #1	Bdrm #2	Bdrm #3	Bdrm #1	Bdrm #2	Bdrm #3
Floors & Floor Coverings	OK	OK				
Windows, Screens, & Doors	OK	OK				
Walls & Ceilings	OK	OK				
Light Fixtures	Dented	OK				
Other	Water stains in closet					
Other						
Other						
Other						
Other Areas					
Heating System	OK				
Air Conditioning	OK				
Lawn/Garden	OK				
Stairs and Hallway	OK				
Patio, Terrace, Deck, etc.	N/A				
Basement	OK				
Parking Area	OK				
Other					
Other					
Other					
Other					
Other					

☑ Tenants acknowledge that all smoke detectors were tested in their presence and found to be in working order, and that the testing procedure was explained to them. Tenants agree to promptly notify Landlord in writing should any smoke detector appear to be malfunctioning or inoperable. Tenants will not refuse Landlord access for the purpose of inspecting, maintaining, repairing, or installing legally-required smoke detectors.

FURNISHED PROPERTY

	Condition on Arrival			Condition on Departure			Estimated Cost of Repair/ Replacement
Living Room							
Coffee Table	Two scratches on top						
End Tables	OK						
Lamps	OK						
Chairs	OK						
Sofa	OK						
Other							
Other							
Kitchen							
Broiler Pan	N/A						
Ice Trays	N/A						
Other							
Other							
Dining Room							
Chairs	OK						
Stools	N/A						
Table	Leg bent slightly						
Other							
Other							
Bathroom(s)	Bath #1	Bath #2		Bath #1	Bath #2		
Mirrors	OK						
Shower Curtain	Torn						
Hamper	N/A						
Other							
Bedroom(s)	Bdrm #1	Bdrm #2	Bdrm #3	Bdrm #1	Bdrm #2	Bdrm #3	
Beds (single)	OK	N/A					
Beds (double)	N/A	OK					
Chairs	OK	OK					
Chests	N/A	N/A					
Dressing Tables	OK	N/A					
Lamps	OK	OK					
Mirrors	OK	OK					
Night Tables	OK	N/A					

	Condition on Arrival			Condition on Departure			Estimated Cost of Repair/ Replacement
Other	N/A	N/A					
Other	N/A	N/A					
Other Areas							
Bookcases							
Desks							
Pictures	Hallway picture frame chipped						
Other							
Other							

Use this space to provide any additional explanation:

_____

_____

_____

_____

_____

_____

_____

_____

_____

Landlord-Tenant Checklist completed on moving in on ____May 1, 20xx_____ and approved by:

*Bernard Cohen*_____ and *Maria Crouse*_____
Landlord/Manager   Tenant

                                                         *Sandra Martino*_____
                                                         Tenant

                                                         _____
                                                         Tenant

Landlord-Tenant Checklist completed on moving out on _____ and approved by:

_____ and _____
Landlord/Manager   Tenant

                                                         _____
                                                         Tenant

                                                         _____
                                                         Tenant

The checklist is in two parts. The first part covers the general condition of each room, such as the kitchen floor. The second part covers furnishings, such as a living room lamp or bathroom shower curtain. You should simply mark "Not Applicable" or "N/A" in most of these boxes if your unit is not furnished or does not have a particular item listed, such as a fireplace, or delete particular items.

If your rental property has rooms or furnishings not listed on the form, note them in the rows labelled "Other," or cross out something that you don't have and write in the changes. If you download the form from Nolo website, you can simply add items or rooms. If you are renting out a large house or apartment or providing many furnishings, you should attach a separate sheet of furnishings. Use the same headings (Condition on Arrival and so on).

In the Condition on Arrival column, mark "OK" in the space next to items that are in satisfactory condition. Make a note—as specific as possible—on items that are not working or are dirty, worn, scratched, or simply not in the best condition. For example, don't simply note that the refrigerator "needs fixing" if an ice maker doesn't work—it's just as easy to write "ice maker broken, should not be used." This way, if the tenant uses the ice maker anyway and causes water damage in the unit below, he cannot claim that you failed to tell him. Be sure to note any mildew, pest, or rodent problems. (Better yet, fix problems before the new tenant moves in.)

The last two columns—Condition on Departure and Estimated Cost of Repair/Replacement—are for use when the tenant moves out and, ideally, the two of you inspect the unit again. At that time, the checklist will document your need to make deductions from the security deposit for repairs or cleaning or to replace missing items. (Chapter 4 discusses returning security deposits and using the checklist as part of your final inspection.) If you don't know what it will cost

to fix or replace something, simply write in "Cost will be documented by Landlord."

CAUTION

As part of your move-in procedures, make sure you test all smoke detectors and fire extinguishers in the tenant's presence and show them to be in good working order. Clearly explain to the tenant how to test the smoke detectors and point out the signs—for example, a beeping noise—of a failing detector. Alert tenants to their responsibility to regularly test smoke detectors, and explain how to replace the battery when necessary. Be sure the tenant checks the box on the bottom of the second page of the checklist acknowledging that the smoke detector was tested in his presence and shown to be in working order. By doing this, you'll limit your liability if the smoke detector fails and results in fire damage or injury. Do the same for any carbon monoxide detectors (required in some states, such as California).

After you and the tenant agree on all of the particulars on the rental unit, you each should sign and date the checklist, as well as any attachments (such as a separate list of furnishings), on both sides. Keep the original checklist for yourself and attach a copy to the tenant's lease or rental agreement. (This checklist is referred to in Clause 11 of the form agreements in Chapter 1.)

Be sure to keep the checklist up to date if you repair, replace, add, or remove items or furnishings after the tenant moves in. Both you and the tenant should initial and date any changes on the original, signed checklist.

Photograph the Rental Unit

Taking photos or videos of the unit before the tenant moves in is another excellent way to avoid disputes over a tenant's responsibility for damage and dirt. In addition to the checklist, you'll be able to compare "before" and "after" pictures when a tenant leaves. This should help refresh your tenant's memory and may result in her being more reasonable. Certainly, if you end up in mediation or court for not returning the full security deposit, being able to document your point of view with photos will be invaluable. In addition, photos or a video can also help if you have to sue a former tenant for cleaning and repair costs above the deposit amount.

Whether you take a photo with your phone or use a separate camera, print out two sets of the photos as soon as possible. Give one set to your tenant. Each of you should date and sign both sets of photos. If you make a video, clearly state the date and time when the video was made.

If possible, you should repeat this process after the tenant leaves, as part of your standard move-out procedure. (Chapter 4 discusses how to prepare a move-out letter.)

Send New Tenants a Move-In Letter

A move-in letter should dovetail with the lease or rental agreement and provide basic information, such as your or a manager's phone number and office hours.

You can also use a move-in letter to explain any procedures and rules that are too detailed or numerous to include in your lease or rental agreement. (Alternatively, large landlords may use a set of tenant rules and regulations to cover some of these issues. See Clause 18 of the form agreements in Chapter 1.)

Here are some items you may want to cover in a move-in letter:

- how and where to report maintenance and repair problems
- any lock-out or rekey fees
- use of grounds and garage
- your policy regarding rent increases for additional roommates
- location of garbage cans, available recycling programs, and trash pickup days

- maintenance dos and don'ts, such as how to avoid overloading circuits and use the garbage disposal properly
- renters' insurance, and
- other issues, such as pool hours, elevator operation, building access during evening hours, and use of a laundry room and storage space, should be covered as needed.

Because every rental situation is at least a little different, we cannot supply you with a generic move-in letter that will work for everyone. We can, however, give you a template for a move-in letter that you can easily fill in with your own details. You can use the sample shown here as a model in preparing your own move-in letter.

We recommend that you make a copy of each tenant's move-in letter for yourself and ask him to sign the last page, indicating that he has read it.

Be sure to update the move-in letter from time to time as necessary.

FORM

Move-In Letter form. You'll find a copy of the Move-In Letter in Appendix C of this book. You can also download this form on the Nolo website; the link is included in Appendix B. A filled-in sample move-in letter is shown below.

Cash Rent and Security Deposit Checks

Every landlord's nightmare is a new tenant whose first rent or deposit check bounces and who must be dislodged with time-consuming and expensive legal proceedings.

To avoid this, never sign a rental agreement, or let a tenant move furniture into your property or give the tenant a key, until you have the tenant's cash, certified check, or money order for the first month's rent and security deposit. An alternative is to cash the tenant's check at the bank before the move-in date. (While you have the tenant's

Move-In Letter

Date September 1, 20xx

Tenant Frank O'Hara

Street Address 139 Porter Street

City and State Madison, Wisconsin 53704

Dear Frank   ,

              Tenant

Welcome to Apartment 45 B at Happy Hill Apartments

_____ (address of rental unit). We hope you will enjoy living here. This letter is to explain what you can expect from the management and what we'll be looking for from you.

1. Rent: Rent is due on the first day of the month. There is no grace period for the payment of rent. (See Clauses 5 and 6 of your rental agreement for details, including late charges.) Also, we don't accept postdated checks.

2. New Roommates: If you want someone to move in as a roommate, please contact us first. If your rental unit is big enough to accommodate another person, we will arrange for the new person to fill out a rental application. If it's approved, all of you will need to sign a new rental agreement. Depending on the situation, there may be a rent increase to add a roommate. Note that under our written agreement, you may not sublet without our prior approval. This includes short-term vacation rentals through Airbnb or similar services.

3. Notice to End Tenancy: To terminate your month-to-month tenancy, you must give at least 28 days' written notice. We have a written form available for this purpose. We may also terminate the tenancy, or change its terms, on 28 days' written notice. If you give less than 28 days' notice, you will still be financially responsible for rent for the balance of the 30-day period.

4. Deposits: Your security deposit will be applied to costs of cleaning, damages, or unpaid rent after you move out. You may not apply any part of the deposit toward any part of your rent in the last month of your tenancy. (See Clause 8 of your rental agreement.)

5. Manager: Sophie Beauchamp (Apartment #15, phone 555-1234) is your resident manager. You should pay your rent to her at that address and promptly let her know of any maintenance or repair problems (see #7, below) and any other questions or problems. She's in her office every day from 8 a.m. to 10 a.m. and from 4 p.m. to 6 p.m. and can be reached by phone at other times.

6. Landlord-Tenant Checklist: By now, Sophie Beauchamp should have taken you on a walk-through of your apartment to check the condition of all walls, drapes, carpets, and appliances and to test the smoke alarms and fire extinguisher. These are all listed on the Landlord-Tenant Checklist, which you should have reviewed carefully and signed. When you move out, we will ask you to check each item against its original condition as described on the Checklist.

7. Maintenance/Repair Problems: We are determined to maintain a clean, safe building in which all systems are in good repair. To help us make repairs promptly, we will give you Maintenance/Repair Request forms to report to the manager any problems in your apartment, such as a broken garbage disposal, or on the building or grounds, such a burned-out light in the garage. (Extra copies are available from the manager.) In an emergency, or when it's not convenient to use this form, please call the manager at 555-1234.

8. Semiannual Safety and Maintenance Update: To help us keep your unit and the common areas in excellent condition, we'll ask you to fill out a form every six months updating any problems on the premises or in your rental unit. This will allow you to report any potential safety hazards or other problems that otherwise might be overlooked.

9. Annual Safety Inspection: Once a year, we will ask to inspect the condition and furnishings of your rental unit and update the Landlord-Tenant Checklist. In keeping with state law, we will give you reasonable notice before the inspection, and you are encouraged to be present for it.

10. Insurance: We highly recommend that you purchase renters' insurance. The building property insurance policy will not cover the replacement of your personal belongings if they are lost due to fire, theft, or accident. In addition, you could be found liable if someone is injured on the premises you rent as a result of your negligence. If you damage the building itself—for example, if you start a fire in the kitchen and it spreads—you could be responsible for large repair bills.

11. Moving Out: It's a little early to bring up moving out, but please be aware that we have a list of items that should be cleaned before we conduct a move-out inspection. If you decide to move, please ask the manager for a copy of our Move-Out Letter, explaining our procedures for inspection and returning your deposit.

12. Telephone Number Changes: Please notify us if your home or work phone number changes, so we can reach you promptly in an emergency.

Please let us know if you have any questions.

Sincerely,

Tom Guiliano
_____   September 1, 20xx
Landlord/Manager   Date

I have read and received a copy of this statement.

Frank O'Hara
_____   September 1, 20xx
Tenant   Date

first check, photocopy it for your records. The information on it can be helpful if you ever need to sue to collect a judgment from the tenant.) Be sure to give the tenant a signed receipt for the deposit.

Clause 5 of the form lease and rental agreements in Chapter 1 requires tenants to pay rent on the first day of each month. If the move-in date is other than the first day of the month, rent is prorated between that day and the end of that month.

Organize Your Tenant Records

A good system to record all significant tenant complaints and repair requests will provide a valuable paper trail should disputes develop later—for example, regarding your right to enter a tenant's unit to make repairs, or the time it took for you to fix a problem. Without good records, the outcome of a dispute may come down to your word against your tenant's—always a precarious situation.

Set up a file folder on each property with individual files for each tenant. Include the following documents:

- tenant's rental application, credit report, and references, including information about any cosigners
- a signed lease or rental agreement, plus any changes made along the way
- Landlord-Tenant Checklist and photos or video made at move-in (or a note as to where to find these online), and
- signed move-in letter.

CAUTION

Don't keep copies of tenant credit reports. Under the "Disposal Rule" of the Fair and Accurate Credit Transactions Act of 2003, you must destroy the report when you have reviewed it and no longer need it. Use a shredder or burn the credit report, or delete it from your computer or phone. For more information, search "Disposal Rule" on www.ftc.gov.

After a tenant moves in, add these documents to the individual's file:

- your written requests for entry
- rent increase notices
- records of repair requests and details of how and when they were handled. If you keep repair records on the computer, you should regularly print out and save files from past months; if you have a master system to record all requests and complaints in one log, you would save that log separately, not necessarily put it in every tenant's file
- safety and maintenance updates and inspection reports, and
- correspondence and other relevant information, including copies of important emails.

Your computer can also be a valuable tool to keep track of tenants. Set up a simple database for each tenant with spaces for the following information:

- address or unit number
- move-in date
- home phone number
- name, address, and phone number of employer
- credit information, including up-to-date information as to where tenant banks
- monthly rent amount and rent due date
- amount and purpose of deposits plus any information your state requires on location of deposit and interest payments
- vehicle make, model, color, year, and license plate number, and
- emergency contacts, and whatever else is important to you.

Once you enter the information into your database, you can sort the list by address or other variables and easily print labels for rent increases or other notices.

If you own many rental properties, you should check into one of the property management software programs that allow you to keep track of every aspect of your business, from the tracking of rents to the follow-up on repair requests.

Organize Income and Expenses for Schedule E

If you've been in the landlording business for any length of time, you will be used to reporting your income and expenses on Schedule E (assuming you file IRS Form 1040 to pay your taxes). The Schedule is relatively simple. For each address (which may include multiple rental units), you report the year's rent and list enumerated expenses (the first page of Schedule E is reproduced below). You can download a fillable version of Schedule E from www.irs.gov.

Many landlords find it easiest to use *QuickBooks* or another accounting software package to track their income and expenses. There are also programs designed specifically for completing Schedule E, notably *Quicken Rental Property Manager*, which allows you to track income, expenses, and tax deductions and converts the information into a Schedule E at tax time. You can also design your own spreadsheet using *Excel* or a similar program to keep track of rental income and expenses. Finally, there's always the old-fashioned way of making your own paper ledger of income and expenses.

Of course, the system you use to track income and expenses is only as good as the information you enter. To maximize tax deductions, keep receipts and records of all rental-property–related expenses, such as interest payments on mortgage loans, property taxes, professional fees (your accountant, attorney, property management), insurance, repairs, advertising and tenant screening, and membership fees, plus all income from rent, late fees, and the like.

RESOURCE

For detailed information on completing Schedule E and valuable tax advice for landlords, see *Every Landlord's Tax Deduction Guide*, by Stephen Fishman (Nolo). For personalized advice, consult an accountant or tax professional (and remember, buying this book, or consulting with a tax pro, are both tax-deductible expenses).

SCHEDULE E
(Form 1040)

Department of the Treasury
Internal Revenue Service (99)

Supplemental Income and Loss

(From rental real estate, royalties, partnerships, S corporations, estates, trusts, REMICs, etc.)

▶ Attach to Form 1040, 1040NR, or Form 1041.

▶ Information about Schedule E and its separate instructions is at *www.irs.gov/schedulee.*

OMB No. 1545-0074

20**16**

Attachment
Sequence No. **13**

Name(s) shown on return

Your social security number

Part I	Income or Loss From Rental Real Estate and Royalties

Note: If you are in the business of renting personal property, use **Schedule C** or **C-EZ** (see instructions). If you are an individual, report farm rental income or loss from **Form 4835** on page 2, line 40.

A Did you make any payments in 2016 that would require you to file Form(s) 1099? (see instructions) ☐ Yes ☐ No
B If "Yes," did you or will you file required Forms 1099? ☐ Yes ☐ No

1a Physical address of each property (street, city, state, ZIP code)

A
B
C

1b	Type of Property (from list below)	2	For each rental real estate property listed above, report the number of fair rental and personal use days. Check the **QJV** box only if you meet the requirements to file as a qualified joint venture. See instructions.		Fair Rental Days	Personal Use Days	QJV
A				A			☐
B				B			☐
C				C			☐

Type of Property:

1 Single Family Residence   3 Vacation/Short-Term Rental   5 Land   7 Self-Rental
2 Multi-Family Residence   4 Commercial   6 Royalties   8 Other (describe)

Income:	Properties:		A	B	C
3 Rents received	**3**				
4 Royalties received	**4**				
Expenses:					
5 Advertising	**5**				
6 Auto and travel (see instructions)	**6**				
7 Cleaning and maintenance	**7**				
8 Commissions	**8**				
9 Insurance	**9**				
10 Legal and other professional fees	**10**				
11 Management fees	**11**				
12 Mortgage interest paid to banks, etc. (see instructions)	**12**				
13 Other interest	**13**				
14 Repairs	**14**				
15 Supplies	**15**				
16 Taxes	**16**				
17 Utilities	**17**				
18 Depreciation expense or depletion	**18**				
19 Other (list) ▶	**19**				
20 Total expenses. Add lines 5 through 19	**20**				
21 Subtract line 20 from line 3 (rents) and/or 4 (royalties). If result is a (loss), see instructions to find out if you must file **Form 6198**	**21**				
22 Deductible rental real estate loss after limitation, if any, on **Form 8582** (see instructions)	**22**	(	)(	)(	)

23a	Total of all amounts reported on line 3 for all rental properties	**23a**	
b	Total of all amounts reported on line 4 for all royalty properties	**23b**	
c	Total of all amounts reported on line 12 for all properties	**23c**	
d	Total of all amounts reported on line 18 for all properties	**23d**	
e	Total of all amounts reported on line 20 for all properties	**23e**	
24	**Income.** Add positive amounts shown on line 21. **Do not** include any losses	**24**	
25	**Losses.** Add royalty losses from line 21 and rental real estate losses from line 22. Enter total losses here	**25**	( )
26	**Total rental real estate and royalty income or (loss).** Combine lines 24 and 25. Enter the result here. If Parts II, III, IV, and line 40 on page 2 do not apply to you, also enter this amount on Form 1040, line 17, or Form 1040NR, line 18. Otherwise, include this amount in the total on line 41 on page 2	**26**	

For Paperwork Reduction Act Notice, see the separate instructions.   Cat. No. 11344L   Schedule E (Form 1040) 2016

Changing or Ending a Tenancy

Sometime after you've signed a lease or rental agreement, you may want to make changes—perhaps you need to increase the rent, or you agree to let the tenant bring in a roommate or keep a small pet. This chapter shows how to modify a signed lease or rental agreement. It also discusses how you—or your tenant—may end a tenancy, and offers tips on how to take steps to try and avoid problems, such as a tenant giving inadequate notice and breaking the lease. This chapter also summarizes basic rules for returning security deposits when a tenant leaves.

RELATED TOPIC

If you haven't done so already, see the following chapters for related discussions:

- writing clear lease and rental agreement provisions on notice required to end a tenancy: Chapter 1
- how to advertise and rent property before a current tenant leaves: Chapter 2, and
- highlighting notice requirements in a move-in letter to the tenant: Chapter 3.

How to Modify Signed Rental Agreements and Leases

All amendments to your lease or rental agreement should be in writing and signed by both you and the tenant.

Amending a Fixed-Term Lease

If you use a fixed-term lease, you cannot unilaterally alter the terms of the tenancy. For the most part, the lease fixes the terms of the tenancy for the length of the lease. You can't raise the rent or change the terms of the lease until the end of the lease period unless the lease allows it or the tenant agrees. If the tenant agrees to changes, however, simply follow the directions below for amending the rental agreement.

Amending a Month-to-Month Rental Agreement

If you want to change one or more clauses in a month-to-month rental agreement, there is no legal requirement that you get the tenant's consent. Legally, you need simply to send the tenant a notice of the change.

Most states require 30 days' advance notice (subject to any rent control ordinances) to change a month-to-month tenancy—for example, to increase the rent. (See the "State Rules on Notice Required to Change or Terminate a Month-to-Month Tenancy" chart in Appendix A for a list of each state's notice requirements, and Clause 4 of the rental agreement in Chapter 1.) You'll need to consult your state statutes for the specific information on how you must deliver a 30-day notice to the tenant. (Most allow you to use first-class mail.)

TIP

Contact the tenant and explain the changes. It makes good personal and business sense for you or your manager to contact the tenant personally and tell him about a rent increase or other changes before you follow up with a written notice. If the tenant is opposed to your proposal, your personal efforts will allow you to explain your reasons.

You don't generally need to redo the rental agreement in order to make a change or two. Just keep a copy of the change with the rental agreement. In some cases, however, you may want the tenant to sign a new rental agreement—for example, if the tenant initiates a change. If the change is small and simply alters part of an existing clause—such as increasing the rent or making the rent payable every 14 days instead of every 30 days—you can cross out the old language, write in the new, and sign in the margin next to the new words. Make sure the tenant also signs next to the change. Be sure to add the date, in case there is a dispute later as to when the change became effective.

Preparing a New Lease or Rental Agreement

If you're adding a clause or making several changes to your lease or rental agreement, you will probably find it easiest to substitute a whole new agreement for the old one. If you prepare an entire new agreement, be sure that you and the tenant write "Canceled by mutual consent, effective (date)" on the old one, and sign it. In order to avoid the possibility of two inconsistent agreements operating at the same time, be sure that there is no time overlap between the old and new agreements. Similarly, so that the tenant is always subject to a written agreement, do not allow any gap between the cancellation date of the old agreement and the effective date of the new one.

TIP

A new tenant should mean a new agreement. Even if a new tenant is filling out the rest of a former tenant's lease term under the same conditions, it is never wise to allow her to operate under the same lease or rental agreement. Start over and prepare a new agreement in the new tenant's name. (See Clause 10 of the form agreements in Chapter 2.)

Ending a Month-to-Month Tenancy

This section discusses a landlord's and a tenant's responsibilities to end a month-to-month tenancy.

Giving Notice to the Tenant

If you want a tenant to leave, you can end a month-to-month tenancy simply by giving the proper amount of notice. You don't usually have to state a reason, unless state or local law requires it. In most places, all you need to do is give the tenant a simple written notice that complies with your state's minimum notice requirement and states the date on which the tenancy will end. After that date, the tenant no longer has the legal right to occupy the premises.

In most states, and for most rentals, a landlord who wants to terminate a month-to-month tenancy must provide the same amount of notice as a tenant —typically 30 days (discussed below). But this is not true everywhere. For example, in Georgia, landlords must give 60 days' notice to terminate a month-to-month tenancy, while tenants need only give 30 days' notice. (See the "State Rules on Notice Required to Change or Terminate a Month-to-Month Tenancy" chart in Appendix A.) State and local rent control laws can also impose notice requirements on landlords. Things are different if you want a tenant to move because he or she has violated a material term of the rental agreement— for example, by failing to pay rent. If so, notice requirements are commonly greatly shortened, sometimes to as little as three days.

Each state (and even some cities) has its own very detailed rules and procedures for preparing and serving termination notices, and it is impossible for this book to provide all specific forms and instructions. Consult a landlords' association or local rent control board and your state statutes for information and sample forms. Once you understand how much notice you must give, how the notice must be delivered, and any other requirements, you'll be in good shape to handle this work yourself—usually with no lawyer needed.

RESOURCE

California resource for terminating tenancies. If you are a California landlord, see *The California Landlord's Law Book: Evictions*, by David Brown, Janet Portman, and Nils Rosenquest (Nolo). It covers rules and procedures and contains forms for serving termination notices in California. See www. nolo.com for details.

Restrictions to Ending a Tenancy

The general rules for terminating a tenancy described in this chapter often don't apply in the following situations:

- **Rent control ordinances.** Many rent control cities require "just cause" (a good reason) to end a tenancy, which typically includes moving in a close relative and refurbishing the unit. You will likely have to state your legal reason in the termination notice you give the tenant.

- **Discrimination.** It is illegal to end a tenancy because of a tenant's race, religion, or sex; because they have children; or for any other reason constituting illegal discrimination.

- **Retaliation.** You cannot legally terminate a tenancy to retaliate against a tenant for exercising any right under the law, such as the tenant's right to complain to governmental authorities about defective housing conditions or, in many states, to withhold rent because of a health or safety problem the landlord has failed to correct. Chapter 16 of *Every Landlord's Legal Guide*, by Marcia Stewart, Ralph Warner, and Janet Portman (Nolo), covers how to avoid tenant retaliation claims.

How Much Notice the Tenant Must Give

In most states, the tenant who decides to move out must give you at least 30 days' notice. Some states allow less than 30 days' notice in certain situations—for example, because a tenant must leave early due to military orders or health problems. And, in some states, tenants who pay rent more frequently than once a month can give notice to terminate that matches their rent payment interval—for example, tenants who pay rent every two weeks would have to give 14 days' notice. If your tenant joins the military and wants to terminate a rental agreement, federal law specifies the maximum amount of notice you may require. But if state law requires less notice, you must follow state rules. (See "Special Rules for Active Military Tenants," below.)

To educate your tenants as to what they can expect, make sure your rental agreement includes your state's notice requirements for ending a tenancy. (See Clause 4 of the form agreements in Chapter 1.) It is also wise to list termination notice requirements in the move-in letter (discussed in Chapter 3) you send to new tenants.

For details on your state, see the "State Rules on Notice Required to Change or Terminate a Month-to-Month Tenancy" table in Appendix A.

You Should Insist on a Tenant's Written Notice of Intent to Move

In many states, a tenant's notice must be in writing and give the exact date the tenant plans to move out. Even if it is not required by law, it's a good idea to insist that the tenant give you notice in writing (as does Clause 4 of the form agreements in Chapter 1). Why bother, especially if the tenant politely calls you to say she will be out on a particular date?

Insisting on written notice will prove essential should the tenant not move as planned after you have signed a lease or rental agreement with a new tenant. Not only will this be true if, at the last minute, the tenant tries to claim that she didn't really set a firm move-out date, but it will also be invaluable if a new tenant sues you to recover the costs of temporary housing or storage fees for her belongings because you could not deliver possession of the unit. In turn, you will want to sue the old (holdover) tenant for causing the problem by failing to move out. Should this be necessary, you will have a much stronger case against the holdover tenant if you can produce a written promise to move on a specific date instead of your version of a conversation (which will undoubtedly be disputed by the tenant).

A sample tenant's notice of intent to move out form is shown below. Give a copy of this form to any tenant who tells you he or she plans to move.

FORM

Tenant's Intent to Move Out form.
You'll find a copy of the Tenant's Notice of Intent to Move Out in Appendix C of this book. You can also download this form on the Nolo website; the link is included in Appendix B of this book. A filled-in sample Tenant's Notice of Intent to Move Out form is shown below.

Special Rules for Active Military Tenants

Tenants who are in the active military, or who enter military service after signing a lease or rental agreement, may terminate when they receive permanent change of station orders or are deployed to a new location for 90 days or more. (War and National Defense Servicemembers Civil Relief Act, 50 App. U.S.C. §§ 3901 and following.) Tenants must mail written notice of their intent to terminate their tenancy for military reasons to the landlord or manager.

Rental agreements. Once the notice is mailed or delivered, the tenancy will terminate 30 days after the day that rent is next due. For example, if rent is due on the first of June and the tenant mails a notice on May 28, the tenancy will terminate on July 1. This rule takes precedence over any longer notice periods that might be specified in your rental agreement or by state law. If state law or your agreement provides for shorter notice periods, however, the shorter notice will control. Recently, many states have passed laws that offer the same or greater protections to members of the state militia or National Guard.

Leases. A tenant who enters military service after signing a lease may terminate the lease by following the procedure for rental agreements, above. For example, suppose a tenant signs a one-year lease in April, agreeing to pay rent on the first of the month. The tenant enlists October 10 and mails you a termination notice on October 11. In this case, you must terminate the tenancy on December 1, 30 days after the first time that rent is due (November 1) following the mailing of the notice. This tenant will have no continuing obligation for rent past December 1, even though this is several months before the lease expires.

Tenant's Notice of Intent to Move Out

Date ___ April 3, 20xx _____

Tenant ___ Anne Sakamoto _____

Street Address ___ 888 Mill Avenue _____

City and State ___ Nashville, Tennessee 37126 _____

Dear ___ Ms. Sakamoto _____ ,
                              Landlord

This is to notify you that the undersigned tenants, ___ Patti and Joe Ellis _____

_____ , will be moving from

___ 999 Brook Lane, Apartment Number 11 _____ ,

on ___ May 3, 20xx _____ , ___ 30 days _____ from today. This

provides at least _____ 30 days' _____ written notice as required in our rental

agreement.

Sincerely,

Patti Ellis _____
Tenant
Joe Ellis _____
Tenant
_____
Tenant

Preparing a Move-Out Letter

Chapter 3 explains how a move-in letter can help get a tenancy off to a good start. Similarly, a move-out letter can also help reduce the possibility of disputes, especially over the return of security deposits. Send the letter as soon as you receive notice of the tenant's intent to leave. Your move-out letter should explain the following to the tenant:

- how you expect the rental unit to be left, including specific cleaning requirements
- details on your final inspection procedures and how you will determine what cleaning and damage repair is necessary, requiring a deduction from the tenant's security deposit
- what kinds of deposit deductions you may legally make, and
- when and how you will send any refund that is due.

See below for more detail on returning security deposits and on final inspection procedures.

 FORM

Tenant's Move-Out Letter form. You'll find a copy of the Move-Out Letter in Appendix C of this book. You can also download this form on the Nolo website; the link is included in Appendix B of this book. A filled-in sample move-out letter form is shown below.

Accepting Rent After a 30-Day Notice Is Given

If you accept rent for any period beyond the date the tenant told you he is moving out, this likely cancels the termination notice and creates a new tenancy. An exception would be where a tenant pays you past-due rent and you document this in writing.

Suppose, after giving notice, the tenant asks for a little more time in which to move out. Assuming no new tenant is moving in and you are willing to accommodate this request, prepare a written agreement setting out what you have agreed to in detail, and have the tenant sign it. See the sample letter, below, extending the tenant's move-out date.

 CAUTION

If you collected the "last month's rent" when the tenant moved in, do not accept rent for the last month of the tenancy. You are legally obligated to use this money for the last month's rent. Accepting an additional month's rent may extend the tenant's tenancy.

When the Tenant Doesn't Give the Required Notice

All too often, a tenant will send or give you a "too short" notice of intent to move. And it's not unheard of for a tenant to move out with no notice or with a wave as he tosses the keys on your doorstep.

A tenant who leaves without giving enough notice has lost the right to occupy the premises but is still obligated to pay rent through the end of the required notice period. For example, if the notice period is 30 days, but the tenant moves out after telling you 20 days ago that he intended to move, he still owes you rent for the remaining ten days.

In most states, you have a legal duty to try to rerent the property before you can charge the tenant for giving you too little notice, but few courts expect a landlord to accomplish this in less than a month. (This rule, called the landlord's duty to mitigate damages, is discussed below.) You can also use the security deposit to cover unpaid rent (also discussed below).

Move-Out Letter

Date _____July 5, 20xx_____

Tenant _____Jane Wasserman_____

Street Address _____123 North Street, Apartment #23_____

City and State_____Atlanta, Georgia 30360_____

Dear _____Jane_____ ,
                               Tenant

We hope you have enjoyed living here. In order that we may mutually end our relationship on a positive note, this move-out letter describes how we expect your unit to be left and what our procedures are for returning your security deposit.

Basically, we expect you to leave your rental unit in the same condition it was when you moved in, except for normal wear and tear. To refresh your memory on the condition of the unit when you moved in, I've attached a copy of the Landlord-Tenant Checklist you signed at the beginning of your tenancy. I'll be using this same form to inspect your unit when you leave.

Specifically, here's a list of items you should thoroughly clean before vacating:

- ☑ Floors
    - ☑ sweep wood floors
    - ☑ vacuum carpets and rugs (shampoo if necessary)
    - ☑ mop kitchen and bathroom floors
- ☑ Walls, baseboards, ceilings, and built-in shelves
- ☑ Kitchen cabinets, countertops and sink, stove and oven—inside and out
- ☑ Refrigerator—clean inside and out, empty it of food, and turn it off, with the door left open
- ☑ Bathtubs, showers, toilets, and plumbing fixtures
- ☑ Doors, windows, and window coverings
- ☑ Other _____

   _Microwave oven—clean inside and out_____

   _____

   _____

   _____

   _____

If you have any questions as to the type of cleaning we expect, please let me know.

Please don't leave anything behind—that includes bags of garbage, clothes, food, newspapers, furniture, appliances, dishes, plants, cleaning supplies, or other items that belong to you.

Please be sure you have disconnected phone and utility services, canceled all newspaper subscriptions, and sent the post office a change of address form.

Once you have cleaned your unit and removed all your belongings, please call me at ___555-1234___ to arrange for a walk-through inspection and to return all keys. Please be prepared to give me your forwarding address where we may mail your security deposit.

It's our policy to return all deposits either in person or at an address you provide within ___one month___ _____ after you move out. If any deductions are made—for past-due rent or because the unit is damaged or not sufficiently clean—they will be explained in writing.

If you have any questions, please contact me at ___555-1234___ .

Sincerely,

Denise Parsons
Landlord/Manager

When You or Your Tenant Violates the Rental Agreement

If you seriously violate the rental agreement and fail to fulfill your legal responsibilities—for example, by not correcting serious health or safety problems—a tenant may be able to legally move out with no written notice or by giving less notice than is otherwise required. Called a "constructive eviction," this doctrine typically applies only when living conditions are intolerable—for example, if the tenant has had no heat for an extended period in the winter, or if a tenant's use and enjoyment of the property has been substantially impaired because of drug dealing in the building.

What exactly constitutes a constructive eviction varies slightly under the laws of different states. Generally, if you are on notice that a rental unit has serious habitability problems for an extended time, the tenant is entitled to move out on short notice or, in extreme cases, without giving notice.

Along the same lines, a landlord may evict a tenant who violates a lease or rental agreement. For example, you may give a "notice to quit" to a tenant who fails to pay rent or damages the premises with less notice than is normally required to end a tenancy (typically three to five days, rather than 30 days). And, in the case of drug dealing, many states provide for expedited eviction procedures. Because of the wide state-by-state variations on eviction rules and procedures, the details of how to evict a tenant are beyond the scope of this book.

How Fixed-Term Leases End

A lease lasts for a fixed term, typically one year. As a general rule, neither you nor the tenant may unilaterally terminate the tenancy or change a material condition during the period of the lease, unless the other party has violated the terms of the lease. (There's an exception for tenants who join the military and want to terminate a lease, as explained in "Special Rules for Active Military Tenants," above.)

If you and the tenant both live up to your promises, the lease simply ends of its own accord at the end of the lease term, and the tenant moves out. Alternatively, you may sign a new lease, with the same or different terms. As every landlord knows, however, life is not always so simple. Sooner or later, a tenant will stay beyond the end of the term without signing a new lease, or leave before the lease term ends without any legal right to do so.

Giving Notice to the Tenant

Because a lease clearly states when it will expire, you may not think it's necessary to remind the tenants of the expiration date. But doing so is a very good practice, and some states or cities (especially those with rent control) actually require it.

We suggest giving the tenant at least 60 days' written notice that the lease is going to expire. This reminder has several advantages:

- **Getting the tenant out on time.** Two months' notice allows plenty of time for the tenant to look for another place if he doesn't—or you don't—want to renew the lease.

- **Giving you time to renegotiate the lease.** If you would like to continue renting to your present tenant but also want to change some lease terms or increase the rent, your notice serves to remind the tenant that the terms of the old lease will not automatically continue. Encourage the tenant to stay, but mention that you need to make some changes to the lease.

- **Getting a new tenant in quickly.** If you know a tenant is going to move, you can show the unit to prospective tenants ahead of time and minimize the time the space is vacant. You must still respect the current tenant's privacy. (Chapter 2 discusses showing the unit to prospective tenants.)

Sample Letter Extending Tenant's Move-Out Date

June 20, 20xx

Kalinda Blake
777 Broadway Terrace, Apartment #3
Richmond, Virginia 23233

Dear Kalinda:

On June 1, you gave me a 30-day notice of your intent to move out on July 1. You have since requested to extend your move-out to July 18 because of last-minute problems with closing escrow on your new house. This letter is to verify our understanding that you will move out on July 18, instead of July 1, and that you will pay prorated rent for 18 days (July 1 through July 18). Prorated rent for 18 days, based on your monthly rent of $1,200 or $40 per day, is $720.

Please sign below to indicate your agreement to these terms.

Sincerely,

Fran Moore, Landlord

Agreed to by Kalinda Blake, Tenant:

Signature ___*Kalinda Blake*_____

Date ___June 20, 20xx_____

RENT CONTROL

Your options may be limited in a rent control area. If your property is subject to rent control, you may be limited in your ability to end your relationship with a current tenant. Many ordinances require "just cause" for refusing to renew a lease, which generally means that only certain reasons (such as the tenant's failure to pay rent, or your desire to move in a close relative) justify nonrenewal. If your city requires "just cause," and if your decision not to renew does not meet the city's test, you may end up with a perpetual month-to-month tenant. Check your city's rent control ordinance carefully.

If the Tenant Remains After the Lease Expires

It's fairly common for a tenant to remain in a unit even though the lease has run out. If this happens, you have a choice: You can continue renting to the tenant, or you can take legal steps to get the tenant out.

If a tenant stays beyond the end of the lease, and you accept rent money without signing a new lease, in most states you will have created a new, month-to-month tenancy on the same terms as applied for the old lease. In a few states, you may create a new lease for the same term—such as one year. In other words, you'll be stuck with the terms and rent in the old lease, at least for the first 30 days and possibly longer. If you want to change the terms in a new lease, you must abide by the law regarding giving notice for a month-to-month tenancy (discussed above). It will usually take you at least a month while you go about giving notice to your now month-to-month tenant.

To avoid problems of tenants staying longer than you want, be sure to notify the tenant that you expect him to leave at the lease expiration date, and don't accept rent after this date. If a tenant just wants to stay an extra few days after a lease expires and you agree, it is wise to put your understanding on this arrangement in a letter.

(See the sample letter extending the tenant's move-out date, above.)

If the Tenant Leaves Early

A tenant who leaves (with or without notifying you beforehand) before a fixed-term lease expires and refuses to pay the remainder of the rent due under the lease is said to have "broken the lease." Once the tenant leaves for good, you have the legal right to take possession of the premises and rerent to another tenant.

A key question that arises is, how much does a tenant with a lease owe if she walks out early? Let's start with the general legal rule. A tenant who signs a lease agrees at the outset to pay a fixed amount of rent: the monthly rent multiplied by the number of months of the lease. The tenant is obligated to pay this amount in monthly installments over the term of the lease. The fact that payments are made monthly doesn't change the tenant's responsibility to pay rent for the entire lease term. And the fact that a tenant who breaks a lease gives you notice of her intention to leave early changes nothing—you are still owed the money for the rest of the term. As discussed below, depending on the situation, you may use the tenant's security deposit to cover part of the shortfall, or sue the tenant for rent owed.

TIP

Require tenants to notify you of extended absences. Clause 16 of the form lease and rental agreements (Chapter 2) requires tenants to inform you when they will be gone for an extended time, such as two or more weeks.

By requiring tenants to notify you of long absences, you'll know whether property has been abandoned or the tenant is simply on vacation. In addition, if you have such a clause and, under its authority, enter an apparently abandoned unit only to be confronted later by an indignant tenant, you can defend yourself by pointing out that the tenant violated the lease.

When Leaving Early Is Justified

There are some important exceptions to the blanket rule that a tenant who breaks a lease owes you the rent for the entire lease term. A tenant who leaves early may *not* owe if:

- **Your rental unit is unsafe or otherwise uninhabitable.** If you don't live up to your obligations to provide habitable housing—for example, if you fail to maintain the unit in accordance with health and safety codes—a court will conclude that you have "constructively evicted" the tenant. That releases the tenant from further obligations under the lease.

- **You have rented—or could rent—the unit to someone else.** Most courts require landlords to try to soften ("mitigate") the ex-tenant's liability for the remaining rent by attempting to find a new rent-paying tenant as soon as possible. The new tenant's rent is credited against what the former tenant owed. (This "mitigation of damages" rule is discussed below.)

- **State law allows the tenant to leave early.** A few states have laws that list allowable reasons to break a lease. For example, in Delaware, a tenant need only give 30 days' notice to end a long-term lease if he needs to move because his present employer relocated or because health problems (of the tenant or a family member) require a permanent move. (Del. Code Ann. tit. 25 § 5314.) In many states, a victim of domestic violence, sexual assault, or stalking may terminate a lease with several or more days' notice. In all states, tenants who enter active military duty after signing a lease must be released after delivering proper notice. (See "Special Rules for Active Military Tenants," above.) If your tenant has a good reason for a sudden move, you may want to research your state's law to see whether or not he's still on the hook for rent.

- **The rental unit is damaged or destroyed.** If a tenant's home is significantly damaged—either by natural disaster or any other reason beyond his control—he has the right to consider the lease at an end and to move out. State laws vary on the extent of the landlord's responsibility, depending on the cause of the damage. If a fire, flood, tornado, earthquake, or other natural disaster makes the dwelling unlivable, or if a third party is the cause of the destruction (for instance, a fire due to an arsonist), your best bet is to look to your insurance policy for help in repairing or rebuilding the unit and to assist your tenants in resettlement.

Your Duty to Mitigate Your Loss If the Tenant Leaves Early

If a tenant breaks the lease and moves out without legal justification, you can't just sit back and wait until the end of the term of the lease, and then sue the departed tenant for the total amount of your lost rent. In most states, you must try to rerent the property reasonably quickly and subtract the rent you receive from the amount the original tenant owed you.

Even if this isn't the legal rule in your state, trying to rerent is obviously a sound business strategy. It's much better to have rent coming in every month than to wait, leaving a rental unit vacant for months, and then try to sue (and collect from) a tenant who may be long gone, broke, or otherwise difficult to collect from.

If you don't make an attempt (or make an inadequate one) to rerent, and instead sue the former tenant for the whole rent, you will collect only what the judge thinks is the difference between the fair rental value of the property had you rerented it and the original tenant's promised rent. This can depend on how easy it is to rerent in your area. Also, a judge is sure to give you some time (probably at least 30 days) to find a new tenant.

How to Mitigate Your Damages

When you're sure that a tenant has left permanently, then you can turn your attention to rerenting the unit.

You do not need to relax your standards for acceptable tenants—for example, you are entitled to reject applicants with poor credit or rental histories. Also, you need not give the suddenly available property priority over other rental units that you would normally attend to first.

You are not required to rent the premises at a rate substantially below its fair market value. Keep in mind, however, that refusing to rent at less than the original rate may be foolish. If you are unable to ultimately collect from the former tenant, you will get *no* income from the property instead of less. You will have ended up hurting no one but yourself.

The Tenant's Right to Find a Replacement Tenant

A tenant who wishes to leave before the lease expires may offer to find a suitable new tenant, so that the flow of rent will remain uninterrupted, and he will be off the hook for future rent payments. Unless you have a new tenant waiting, you have nothing to lose by cooperating. And refusing to cooperate could hurt you: If you refuse to accept an excellent new tenant and then withhold the lease-breaking tenant's deposit or sue

for unpaid rent, you may wind up losing in court because, after all, you turned down the chance to reduce your losses (mitigate your damages).

Keep Good Records

If you end up suing a former tenant, you will want to be able to show the judge that you acted reasonably in your attempts to rerent the property. Don't rely on your memory and powers of persuasion to convince the judge. Keep detailed records, including:

- the original lease
- receipts for cleaning and painting, with photos of the unit showing the need for repairs, if any
- your expenses for storing or properly disposing of any belongings the tenant left
- receipts for advertising the property and bills from credit reporting agencies investigating potential renters
- a log of the time you spent showing the property, and the value of that time
- a log of any people who offered to rent and, if you rejected them, documentation as to why, and
- if the current rent is less than what the original tenant paid, a copy of the new lease.

Of course, if the rental market is really tight in your area, you may be able to lease the unit easily at a higher rent, or you may already have an even better prospective tenant on your waiting list. In that case, you won't care if a tenant breaks the lease, and you may not be interested in any new tenant he provides.

If you and the outgoing tenant agree on a replacement tenant, you and the new tenant should sign a new lease.

When You Can Sue

If a tenant leaves prematurely, you may need to go to court and sue for your rerental costs and the difference between the original and the replacement rent. (Obviously, you should first use the tenant's deposit, if possible, to cover these costs, as discussed below.)

Deciding *where* to sue is usually easy: Small claims court is usually the court of choice, because it's fast and affordable and doesn't require a lawyer. The only exception is in states where small claims courts have very low dollar limits and you are owed lots more.

Knowing *when* to sue is trickier. You may be eager to start legal proceedings as soon as the original tenant leaves, but, if you do, you won't know the extent of your losses, because you might find another tenant who will make up part of the lost rent. Must you wait until the end of the original tenant's lease? Or can you bring suit when you rerent the property?

The standard approach, and one that all states allow, is to go to court after you rerent the property. At this point, your losses—your expenses and the rent differential, if any—are known and final. The disadvantage is that you have had no income from that property since the original tenant left, and the original tenant may be long gone and not, practically speaking, worth chasing down.

RESOURCE

Nolo's book on small claims court. *Everybody's Guide to Small Claims Court* (National Edition), by Ralph Warner, provides detailed advice on bringing or defending a small claims court case, preparing evidence and witnesses for court, and collecting your court judgment when you win. *Everybody's Guide to Small Claims Court* will also be useful in defending yourself against a tenant who sues you in small claims court—for example, claiming that you failed to return a cleaning or security deposit.

Returning Security Deposits When a Tenancy Ends

Most states set very specific rules for the return of security deposits when a tenant leaves—whether voluntarily or by your ending the tenancy. A landlord's failure to return security deposits as legally required can result in substantial financial penalties if a tenant files suit.

Alerting Tenants to Final Inspection Procedures

Many landlords do a final inspection of the rental unit on their own and simply send the tenant an itemized statement with any remaining balance of the deposit. If at all possible, you should make the inspection with the tenant who's moving out, rather than by yourself. Because state laws can be quite detailed as to rules and procedures for itemizing and returning security deposits, be sure to check your state statutes. (See "State Security Deposit Rules" in Appendix A.)

Inspecting the Unit When a Tenant Leaves

After the tenant leaves, you will need to inspect the unit to assess what cleaning and damage repair is necessary. At the final inspection, check the condition of each item—for example, bathroom walls—on the Landlord-Tenant Checklist (described in Chapter 3) or a similar document that you and the tenant signed when the tenant moved in. If you did not use a Landlord-Tenant Checklist or a similar form to inventory the condition of the rental property at move-in, you should still do a walk-through inspection when the tenant moves out. You won't have the benefit of the "before" documentation, but you can still review the condition of the unit together and identify items that need cleaning, repair, or replacement. It's a good idea (and the law in some states) to involve the tenants in the final inspection. (See "Alerting Tenants to Final Inspection Procedures," above.)

CAUTION

California has special rules and procedures for move-out inspections. California tenants are entitled to a pre–move-out inspection, when you tell the tenant what defects, if any, need to be corrected in order for the tenant to optimize the security deposit refund. California landlords must notify the tenant in writing of the right to request an initial inspection, at which the tenant has a right to be present. (Cal. Civ. Code § 1950.5 (f).) For details, see *The California Landlord's Law Book: Rights & Responsibilities*, by David Brown, Janet Portman, and Nils Rosenquest (Nolo).

Basic Rules for Returning Deposits

You are generally entitled to deduct from a tenant's security deposit whatever amount you need to fix damaged or dirty property (outside of "ordinary wear and tear") or to make up unpaid rent. But you must make your deductions and return deposits correctly. While the specific rules vary from state to state, you usually have between 14 and 30 days after the tenant leaves to return the deposit. (See "State Security Deposit Rules" in Appendix A.)

State security deposit statutes typically require you to mail the following within the time limit to the tenant's last known address (or forwarding address if you have one):

- the tenant's entire deposit with interest if required, and
- a written itemized accounting of deductions, including back rent and costs of cleaning and damage repair, together with payment for any deposit balance, including any interest that is required. The statement should list each deduction and briefly explain what it's for.

Even if there is no specific time limit in your state or law requiring itemization, promptly presenting the tenant with a written itemization of all deductions and a clear reason why each was made is an essential part of a savvy landlord's overall plan to avoid disputes with tenants. In general, we recommend three to four weeks as a reasonable time to return deposits.

Penalties for Violating Security Deposit Laws

If you don't follow state security deposit laws to the letter, you may pay a heavy price if a tenant sues you and wins. In addition to whatever amount you wrongfully withheld, you may have to pay the tenant extra or punitive damages (penalties imposed when the judge feels that the defendant has acted especially outrageously) and court costs. In many states, if you "willfully" (deliberately and not through inadvertence) violate the security deposit statute, you may forfeit your right to retain any part of the deposit and may be liable for two or three times the amount wrongfully withheld, plus attorneys' fees and costs.

If the Deposit Doesn't Cover Damage and Unpaid Rent

If the security deposit doesn't cover what a tenant owes you for back rent, cleaning, or repairs, you may wish to file a small claims lawsuit against the former tenant.

RESOURCE

More information on deposits. *Every Landlord's Legal Guide*, by Marcia Stewart, Ralph Warner, and Janet Portman (Nolo), provides complete details on state laws and sample forms for returning and itemizing security deposits.

State Landlord-Tenant Law Charts

How to Use the State Landlord-Tenant Law Charts

The State Landlord-Tenant Law Charts are comprehensive 50-state charts that give you two kinds of information:

- the state rules, such as notice periods and deposit limits (what the statutes and cases say), and
- specific citations for key statutes and cases, which you can use if you want to read the law yourself or look for more information.

When you're looking for information for your state, simply find your state along the left-hand list on the chart, and read to the right—you'll see the statute or case, and the rule.

RESOURCE

Where to find your state laws. For more information (the actual language of a particular state law), you can check your state statute online. You can find it by going to Nolo's website at www.nolo.com/legal-research and choosing the State Law Resources link.

State Landlord-Tenant Statutes

Here are some of the key statutes pertaining to landlord-tenant law in each state. In some states, important legal principles are contained in court opinions, not codes or statutes. Court-made law and rent stabilization—rent control—laws and regulations are not reflected in this chart.

State	Statute	State	Statute
Alabama	Ala. Code §§ 35-9-1 to 35-9-100; 35-9A-101 to 35-9A-603	Montana	Mont. Code Ann. §§ 70-24-101 to 70-27-117
Alaska	Alaska Stat. §§ 34.03.010 to 34.03.380	Nebraska	Neb. Rev. Stat. §§ 76-1401 to 76-1449
Arizona	Ariz. Rev. Stat. Ann. §§ 12-1171 to 12-1183; 33-1301 to 33-1381; 33-301 to 33-381	Nevada	Nev. Rev. Stat. Ann. §§ 118A.010 to 118A.530; 40.215 to 40.425
Arkansas	Ark. Code Ann. §§ 18-16-101 to 18-16-306; 18-16-501 to 18-16-509; 18-17-101 to 18-17-913	New Hampshire	N.H. Rev. Stat. Ann. §§ 540:1 to 540:29; 540-A:1 to 540-A:8; 540-B:1 to 540-B:10
California	Cal. Civ. Code §§ 1925 to 1954.1; 1961 to 1995.340	New Jersey	N.J. Stat. Ann. §§ 46:8-1 to 46:8-50; 2A:42-1 to 42-96
Colorado	Colo. Rev. Stat. §§ 38-12-101 to 38-12-104; 38-12-301 to 38-12-302; 38-12-501 to 38-12-511; 13-40-101 to 13-40-123	New Mexico	N.M. Stat. Ann. §§ 47-8-1 to 47-8-51
Connecticut	Conn. Gen. Stat. Ann. §§ 47a-1 to 47a-74; §§ 16-51-1 to 16-51-3	New York	N.Y. Real Prop. Law §§ 220 to 238; Real Prop. Acts §§ 701 to 853; Mult. Dwell. Law (all); Mult. Res. Law (all); Gen. Oblig. Law §§ 7-101 to 7-109
Delaware	Del. Code Ann. tit. 25, §§ 5101 to 5907	North Carolina	N.C. Gen. Stat. §§ 42-1 to 42-14.2; 42-25.6 to 42-76
Dist. of Columbia	D.C. Code Ann. §§ 42-3201 to 42-3610; D.C. Mun. Regs., tit. 14, §§ 300 to 311	North Dakota	N.D. Cent. Code §§ 47-16-01 to 47-16-41
Florida	Fla. Stat. Ann. §§ 83.40 to 83.683	Ohio	Ohio Rev. Code Ann. §§ 5321.01 to 5321.19
Georgia	Ga. Code Ann. §§ 44-7-1 to 44-7-81	Oklahoma	Okla. Stat. Ann. tit. 41, §§ 101 to 136
Hawaii	Haw. Rev. Stat. §§ 521-1 to 521-82	Oregon	Or. Rev. Stat. §§ 90.100 to 91.225
Idaho	Idaho Code §§ 6-301 to 6-324; §§ 55-208 to 55-308	Pennsylvania	68 Pa. Cons. Stat. Ann. §§ 250.101 to 399.18
Illinois	735 Ill. Comp. Stat. §§ 5/9-201 to 321 & 765 Ill. Comp. Stat. §§ 705/0.01 to 742/30	Rhode Island	R.I. Gen. Laws §§ 34-18-1 to 34-18-57
Indiana	Ind. Code Ann. §§ 32-31-1-1 to 32-31-9-15	South Carolina	S.C. Code Ann. §§ 27-40-10 to 27-40-940
Iowa	Iowa Code Ann. §§ 562A.1 to 562A.37	South Dakota	S.D. Codified Laws Ann. §§ 43-32-1 to 43-32-32
Kansas	Kan. Stat. Ann. §§ 58-2501 to 58-2573	Tennessee	Tenn. Code Ann. §§ 66-28-101 to 66-28-521
Kentucky	Ky. Rev. Stat. Ann. §§ 383.010 to 383.715	Texas	Tex. Prop. Code Ann. §§ 91.001 to 92.355
Louisiana	La. Rev. Stat. Ann. §§ 9:3251 to 9:3261.1; La. Civ. Code Ann. art. 2668 to 2729	Utah	Utah Code Ann. §§ 57-17-1 to 57-17-5, 57-22-1 to 57-22-7
Maine	Me. Rev. Stat. Ann. tit. 14, §§ 6000 to 6046	Vermont	Vt. Stat. Ann. tit. 9, §§ 4451 to 4469a
Maryland	Md. Code Ann. [Real Prop.] §§ 8-101 to 8-604	Virginia	Va. Code Ann. §§ 55-217 to 55-248.40
Massachusetts	Mass. Gen. Laws Ann. ch. 186, §§ 1A to 29; ch. 186a, §§ 1 to 6	Washington	Wash. Rev. Code Ann. §§ 59.04.010 to 59.18.912
Michigan	Mich. Comp. Laws §§ 554.131 to 554.201 & 554.601 to 554.641	West Virginia	W.Va. Code §§ 37-6-1 to 37-6A-6
Minnesota	Minn. Stat. Ann. §§ 504B.001 to 504B.471	Wisconsin	Wis. Stat. Ann. §§ 704.01 to 704.95; Wis. Admin. Code ATCP §§ 134.01 to 134.10
Mississippi	Miss. Code Ann. §§ 89-7-1 to 89-8-29		
Missouri	Mo. Rev. Stat. §§ 441.005 to 441.880; §§ 535.010 to 535.300	Wyoming	Wyo. Stat. §§ 1-21-1201 to 1-21-1211; 34-2-128 to 34-2-129

State Rules on Notice Required to Change or Terminate a Month-to-Month Tenancy

Except where noted, the amount of notice a landlord must give to increase rent or change another term of the rental agreement in month-to-month tenancy is the same as that required to end a month-to-month tenancy. Be sure to check state and local rent control laws, which may have different notice requirements.

State	Tenant	Landlord	Statute	Comments
Alabama	30 days	30 days	Ala. Code § 35-9A-441	No state statute on the amount of notice required to change rent or other terms
Alaska	30 days	30 days	Alaska Stat. § 34.03.290(b)	
Arizona	30 days	30 days	Ariz. Rev. Stat. Ann. § 33-1375	
Arkansas	30 days	30 days	Ark. Code Ann. § 18-17-704	No state statute on the amount of notice required to change rent or other terms
California	30 days	30 or 60 days	Cal. Civ. Code §§ 1946; 827a	30 days to change rental terms, but if landlord is raising the rent, tenant gets 60 days' notice if the sum of this and all prior rent increases during the previous 12 months is more than 10% of the lowest rent charged during that time. 60 days to terminate (landlord), 30 days (tenant).
Colorado	7 days	7 days	Colo. Rev. Stat. § 13-40-107	
Connecticut		3 days	Conn. Gen. Stat. Ann. § 47a-23	Landlord must provide 3 days' notice to terminate tenancy. Landlord is not required to give a particular amount of notice of a proposed rent increase unless prior notice was previously agreed upon.
Delaware	60 days	60 days	Del. Code Ann. tit. 25, §§ 5106, 5107	After receiving notice of landlord's proposed change of terms, tenant has 15 days to terminate tenancy. Otherwise, changes will take effect as announced.
District of Columbia	30 days	30 days	D.C. Code Ann. § 42-3202	No state statute on the amount of notice required to change rent or other terms
Florida	15 days	15 days	Fla. Stat. Ann. § 83.57	No state statute on the amount of notice required to change rent or other terms
Georgia	30 days	60 days	Ga. Code Ann. § 44-7-6 & -7	No state statute on the amount of notice required to change rent or other terms
Hawaii	28 days	45 days	Haw. Rev. Stat. §§ 521-71, 521-21(d)	
Idaho	One month	One month	Idaho Code §§ 55-208, 55-307	Landlords must provide 15 days' notice to increase rent or change tenancy.
Illinois	30 days	30 days	735 Ill. Comp. Stat. § 5/9-207	
Indiana	One month	One month	Ind. Code Ann. §§ 32-31-1-1, 32-31-5-4	Unless agreement states otherwise, landlord must give 30 days' written notice to modify written rental agreement.
Iowa	30 days	30 days	Iowa Code Ann. §§ 562A.34, 562A.13(5)	To end or change a month-to-month agreement, landlord must give written notice at least 30 days before the next time rent is due (not including any grace period).
Kansas	30 days	30 days	Kan. Stat. Ann. § 58-2570	No state statute on the amount of notice required to change rent or other terms

State Rules on Notice Required to Change or Terminate a Month-to-Month Tenancy (continued)				
State	**Tenant**	**Landlord**	**Statute**	**Comments**
Kentucky	30 days	30 days	Ky. Rev. Stat. Ann. § 383.695	
Louisiana	10 days	10 days	La. Civ. Code Art. 2728	No state statute on the amount of notice required to change rent or other terms
Maine	30 days	30 days	Me. Rev. Stat. Ann. tit. 14, §§ 6002, 6015	Landlord must provide 45 days' notice to increase rent.
Maryland	One month	One month	Md. Code Ann. [Real Prop.] § 8-402(b)(3), (b)(4)	Two months' notice required in Montgomery County (single family rentals excepted) and Baltimore City.
Massachusetts	See comments	See comments	Mass. Gen. Laws Ann. ch. 186, § 12	Interval between days of payment or 30 days, whichever is longer.
Michigan	One month	One month	Mich. Comp. Laws § 554.134	
Minnesota	See comments	See comments	Minn. Stat. Ann. § 504B.135	For terminations, interval between time rent is due or three months, whichever is less; no state statute on the amount of notice required to change rent or other terms.
Mississippi	30 days	30 days	Miss. Code Ann. § 89-8-19	No state statute on the amount of notice required to change rent or other terms
Missouri	One month	One month	Mo. Rev. Stat. § 441.060	No state statute on the amount of notice required to change rent or other terms
Montana	30 days	30 days	Mont. Code Ann. §§ 70-24-441, 70-26-109	Landlord may change terms of tenancy with 15 days' notice
Nebraska	30 days	30 days	Neb. Rev. Stat. § 76-1437	No state statute on the amount of notice required to change rent or other terms
Nevada	30 days	30 days	Nev. Rev. Stat. Ann. §§ 40.251, 118A.300	Landlords must provide 45 days' notice to increase rent. Tenants 60 years old or older, or physically or mentally disabled, may request an additional 30 days' possession, but only if they have complied with basic tenant obligations as set forth in Nev. Rev. Stat. Chapter 118A (termination notices must include this information).
New Hampshire	30 days	30 days	N.H. Rev. Stat. Ann. §§ 540:2, 540:3	Landlord may terminate only for just cause.
New Jersey	One month	One month	N.J. Stat. Ann. § 2A:18-56	Landlord may terminate only for just cause.
New Mexico	30 days	30 days	N.M. Stat. Ann. §§ 47-8-37, 47-8-15(F)	Landlord must deliver rent increase notice at least 30 days before rent due date.
New York	One month	One month	N.Y. Real Prop. Law § 232-b	No state statute on the amount of notice required to change rent or other terms
North Carolina	7 days	7 days	N.C. Gen. Stat. § 42-14	No state statute on the amount of notice required to change rent or other terms
North Dakota	30 days	30 days	N.D. Cent. Code §§ 47-16-07, 47-16-15	Tenant may terminate with 25 days' notice if landlord has changed the terms of the lease.
Ohio	30 days	30 days	Ohio Rev. Code Ann. § 5321.17	No state statute on the amount of notice required to change rent or other terms
Oklahoma	30 days	30 days	Okla. Stat. Ann. tit. 41, § 111	No state statute on the amount of notice required to change rent or other terms

State Rules on Notice Required to Change or Terminate a Month-to-Month Tenancy (continued)

State	Tenant	Landlord	Statute	Comments
Oregon	30 days or 72 hours (lack of bedroom exit only)	Landlord may not increase the rent during the first year, and must give 90 days' notice for any rent increases thereafter.	Or. Rev. Stat. §§ 91.070, 90.427, 90.460	To terminate, 30 days for occupancies of one year or less; 60 days for occupancies of more than one year (but only 30 days if the property is sold and other conditions are met). Tenant may terminate on 72 hours' notice if landlord's failure to provide proper bedroom emergency exit, properly noticed, has not been corrected. Temporary occupants are not entitled to notice (Or. Rev. Stat. § 90.275).
Pennsylvania			No statute	
Rhode Island	30 days	30 days	R.I. Gen. Laws §§ 34-18-16.1, 34-18-37	Landlord must provide 30 days' notice to increase rent.
South Carolina	30 days	30 days	S.C. Code Ann. § 27-40-770	No state statute on the amount of notice required to change rent or other terms
South Dakota	One month	One month	S.D. Codified Laws Ann. §§ 43-8-8, 43-32-13	If tenant (or spouse or minor child) is in active duty in the military, landlord must give two months' notice, in the absence of tenant misconduct, sale of the property, or passing of the property into the landlord's estate.
Tennessee	30 days	30 days	Tenn. Code Ann. § 66-28-512	No state statute on the amount of notice required to change rent or other terms
Texas	One month	One month	Tex. Prop. Code Ann. § 91.001	Landlord and tenant may agree in writing to different notice periods, or none at all. No state statute on the amount of notice required to change rent or other terms
Utah		15 days	Utah Code Ann. § 78B-6-802	No state statute on the amount of notice required to change rent or other terms
Vermont	One rental period, unless written lease says otherwise	30 days	Vt. Code Ann. tit. 9, §§ 4467, 4456(d)	If there is no written rental agreement, for tenants who have continuously resided in the unit for two years or less, 60 days' notice to terminate; for those who have resided longer than two years, 90 days. If there is a written rental agreement, for tenants who have lived continuously in the unit for two years or less, 30 days; for those who have lived there longer than two years, 60 days.
Virginia	30 days	30 days	Va. Code Ann. §§ 55-248.37, 55-248.7	Rental agreement may provide for a different notice period. No state statute on the amount of notice required to change rent or other terms, but landlord must abide by notice provisions in the rental agreement, if any.
Washington	20 days	20 days	Wash. Rev. Code Ann. §§ 59.18.200, 59.18.140	Landlord must give 30 days' notice to change rent or other lease terms.
West Virginia	One month	One month	W.Va. Code § 37-6-5	No state statute on the amount of notice required to change rent or other terms
Wisconsin	28 days	28 days	Wis. Stat. Ann. § 704.19	No state statute on the amount of notice required to change rent or other terms
Wyoming			No statute	

State Rent Rules

Here are citations for statutes that set out rent rules in each state. When a state has no statute, the space is left blank. (See the "Notice Required to Change or Terminate a Month-to-Month Tenancy" chart in this appendix for citations to raising rent.)

State	When Rent Is Due	Grace Period	Where Rent Is Due	Late Fees
Alabama	Ala. Code § 35-9A-161(c)		Ala. Code § 35-9A-161(c)	
Alaska	Alaska Stat. § 34.03.020(c)		Alaska Stat. § 34.03.020(c)	
Arizona	Ariz. Rev. Stat. Ann. §§ 33-1314(C), 33-1368(B)		Ariz. Rev. Stat. Ann. § 33-1314(C)	Ariz. Rev. Stat. Ann. § 33-1368(B) [1]
Arkansas	Ark. Code Ann. § 18-17-401	Ark. Code Ann. §§ 18-17-701 & 18-17-901	Ark. Code Ann. § 18-17-401	
California	Cal. Civil Code § 1947		Cal. Civil Code § 1962	*Orozco v. Casimiro*, 121 Cal. App.4th Supp. 7 (2004) [2]
Colorado	No statute.			
Connecticut	Conn. Gen. Stat. Ann. § 47a-3a	Conn. Gen. Stat. Ann. § 47a-15a	Conn. Gen. Stat. Ann. § 47a-3a	Conn. Gen. Stat. Ann. §§ 47a-4(a)(8), 47a-15a [3]
Delaware	Del. Code Ann. tit. 25, § 5501(b)		Del. Code Ann. tit. 25, § 5501(b)	Del. Code Ann. tit. 25, § 5501(d) [4]
Disrtict of Columbia		D.C. Code Ann. § 42-3501.31		D.C. Code Ann. § 42-3501.31 [5]
Florida	Fla. Stat. Ann. § 83.46(1)			
Georgia	No statute.			
Hawaii	Haw. Rev. Stat. § 521-21(b)		Haw. Rev. Stat. § 521-21(b)	
Idaho	No statute.			
Illinois	735 Ill. Comp. Stat. Ann. § 5/9-218		735 Ill. Comp. Stat. Ann. § 5/9-218	
Indiana	*Watson v. Penn*, 108 Ind. 21 (1886), 8 N.E. 636 (1886)			
Iowa	Iowa Code Ann. § 562A.9(3)		Iowa Code Ann. § 562A.9(3)	Iowa Code Ann. § 562A.9 [6]
Kansas	Kan. Stat. Ann. § 58-2545(c)		Kan. Stat. Ann. § 58-2545(c)	

[1] Late fees must be set forth in a written rental agreement and be reasonable. (Arizona)

[2] Late fees will be enforced only if specified language is included in a written lease or rental agreement. (California)

[3] Landlords may not charge a late fee until 9 days after rent is due. (Connecticut)

[4] To charge a late fee, landlord must maintain an office in the county where the rental unit is located at which tenants can pay rent. If a landlord doesn't have a local office for this purpose, tenant has 3 extra days (beyond the due date) to pay rent before the landlord can charge a late fee. Late fee cannot exceed 5% of rent and cannot be imposed until the rent is more than 5 days late. (Delaware)

[5] Fee policy must be stated in the lease, and cannot exceed 5% of rent due, nor be imposed until rent is five days late (or later, if lease so provides). Landlord cannot evict for failure to pay late fee (may deduct unpaid fees from security deposit at end of tenancy).

[6] When rent is $700 per month or less, late fees cannot exceed $12 per day, or a total amount of $60 per month; when rent is more than $700 per month, fees cannot exceed $20 per day or a total amount of $100 per month. (Iowa)

	State Rent Rules (continued)			
State	**When Rent Is Due**	**Grace Period**	**Where Rent Is Due**	**Late Fees**
Kentucky	Ky. Rev. Stat. Ann. § 383.565(2)		Ky. Rev. Stat. Ann. § 383.565(2)	
Louisiana	La. Civ. Code Ann. art. 2703		La. Civ. Code Ann. art. 2703	
Maine		Me. Rev. Stat. Ann. tit. 14, § 6028		Me. Rev. Stat. Ann. tit. 14, § 6028 [7]
Maryland				Md. Code Ann. [Real Prop.] § 8-208(d)(3) [8]
Massachusetts		Mass. Gen. Laws Ann. ch. 186, § 15B(1)(c); ch. 239, § 8A		Mass. Gen. Laws Ann. ch. 186, § 15B(1)(c) [9]
Michigan	*Hilsendegen v. Scheich*, 21 N.W. 894 (1885)			
Minnesota				Minn. Stat. Ann. § 504B.177 [10]
Mississippi	No statute.			
Missouri	Mo. Rev. Stat. § 535.060			
Montana	Mont. Code Ann. § 70-24-201(2)(c)		Mont. Code Ann. § 70-24-201(2)(b)	
Nebraska	Neb. Rev. Stat. § 76-1414(3)		Neb. Rev. Stat. § 76-1414(3)	
Nevada	Nev. Rev. Stat. Ann. § 118A.210		Nev. Rev. Stat. Ann. § 118A.210	Nev. Rev. Stat. Ann. § 118A.200(3)(g), (4)(c) [11]
New Hampshire	No statute.			
New Jersey		N.J. Stat. Ann. § 2A:42-6.1	N.J. Stat. Ann. § 2A:42-6.1	N.J. Stat. Ann. § 2A:42-6.1 [12]
New Mexico	N.M. Stat. Ann. § 47-8-15(B)		N.M. Stat. Ann § 47-8-15(B)	N.M. Stat. Ann § 47-8-15(D) [13]
New York	No statute.			

[7] Late fees cannot exceed 4% of the amount due for 30 days. Landlord must notify tenants, in writing, of any late fee at the start of the tenancy, and cannot impose it until rent is 15 days late. (Maine)

[8] Late fees cannot exceed 5% of the rent due. (Maryland)

[9] Late fees, including interest on late rent, may not be imposed until the rent is 30 days late. (Massachusetts)

[10] Late fee policy must be agreed to in writing, and may not exceed 8% of the overdue rent payment. The "due date" for late fee purposes does not include a date earlier than the usual rent due date, by which date a tenant earns a discount. (Minnesota)

[11] A court will presume that there is no late fee provision unless it is included in a written rental agreement, but the landlord can offer evidence to overcome that presumption. (Nevada)

[12] Landlord must wait 5 days before charging a late fee, but only when the premises are rented or leased by senior citizens receiving Social Security Old Age Pensions, Railroad Retirement Pensions, or other governmental pensions in lieu of Social Security Old Age Pensions; or when rented by recipients of Social Security Disability Benefits, Supplemental Security Income, or benefits under Work First New Jersey. (New Jersey)

[13] Late fee policy must be in the lease or rental agreement and may not exceed 10% of the rent specified per rental period. Landlord must notify the tenant of the landlord's intent to impose the charge no later than the last day of the next rental period immediately following the period in which the default occurred. (New Mexico)

		State Rent Rules (continued)		
State	**When Rent Is Due**	**Grace Period**	**Where Rent Is Due**	**Late Fees**
North Carolina		N.C. Gen. Stat. § 42-46		N.C. Gen. Stat. § 42-46 [14]
North Dakota	N.D. Cent. Code § 47-16-20			
Ohio	No statute.			
Oklahoma	Okla. Stat. Ann. tit. 41, § 109	Okla. Stat. Ann. tit. 41, § 132(B)	Okla. Stat. Ann. tit. 41, § 109	*Sun Ridge Investors, Ltd. v. Parker*, 956 P.2d 876 (1998) [15]
Oregon	Or. Rev. Stat. § 90.220	Or. Rev. Stat. § 90.260	Or. Rev. Stat. § 90.220	Or. Rev. Stat. § 90.260 [16]
Pennsylvania	No statute.			
Rhode Island	R.I. Gen. Laws § 34-18-15(c)	R.I. Gen. Laws § 34-18-35	R.I. Gen. Laws § 34-18-15(c)	
South Carolina	S.C. Code Ann. § 27-40-310(c)		S.C. Code Ann. § 27-40-310(c)	
South Dakota	S.D. Codified Laws Ann. § 43-32-12			
Tennessee	Tenn. Code Ann. § 66-28-201(c)	Tenn. Code Ann. § 66-28-201(d)	Tenn. Code Ann. § 66-28-201(c)	Tenn. Code Ann. § 66-28-201(d) [17]
Texas		Tex. Prop. Code Ann. § 92.019		Tex. Prop. Code Ann. § 92.019 [18]
Utah	No statute.			
Vermont	Vt. Stat. Ann. tit. 9, § 4455			
Virginia	Va. Code Ann. § 55-248.7(C)		Va. Code Ann. § 55-248.7(C)	
Washington	No statute.			
West Virginia	No statute.			
Wisconsin	No statute.			
Wyoming	No statute.			

[14] Late fee when rent is due monthly cannot be higher than $15 or 5% of the rental payment, whichever is greater (when rent is due weekly, may not be higher than $4.00 or 5% of the rent, whichever is greater); and may not be imposed until the rent is 5 days late. A late fee may be imposed only one time for each late rental payment. A late fee for a specific late rental payment may not be deducted from a subsequent rental payment so as to cause the subsequent rental payment to be in default. (North Carolina)

[15] Preset late fees are invalid. (Oklahoma)

[16] Landlord must wait 4 days after the rent due date before imposing a late fee, and must disclose the late fee policy in the rental agreement. A flat fee must be "reasonable." A daily late fee may not be more than 6% of a reasonable flat fee, and cannot add up to more than 5% of the monthly rent. (Oregon)

[17] Landlord can't charge a late fee until the rent is 5 days late (the day rent is due is counted as the first day). If day five is a Sunday or legal holiday, landlord cannot impose a fee if the rent is paid on the next business day. Fee can't exceed 10% of the amount past due. (Tennessee)

[18] Late fee provision must be included in a written lease and cannot be imposed until the rent remains unpaid one full day after the date it is due. The fee is valid only if it is a reasonable estimate of uncertain damages to the landlord that are incapable of precise calculation. Landlord may charge an initial fee and a daily fee for each day the rent is late. (Texas)

State Security Deposit Rules

Here are the statutes and rules that govern a landlord's collection and retention of security deposits. Many states require landlords to disclose, at or near the time they collect the deposit, information about how deposits may be used, as noted in the Disclosure or Requirement section. Required disclosures of other issues, such as a property's history of flooding, are in the chart, "Required Landlord Disclosures."

Alabama

Ala. Code § 35-9A-201

Exemption: Security deposit rules do not apply to a resident purchaser under a contract of sale (but do apply to a resident who has an option to buy), nor to the continuation of occupancy by the seller or a member of the seller's family for a period of not more than 36 months after the sale of a dwelling unit or the property of which it is a part.

Limit: One month's rent, except for pet deposits, deposits to cover undoing tenant's alterations, deposits to cover tenant activities that pose increased liability risks.

Deadline for Landlord to Itemize and Return Deposit: 60 days after termination of tenancy and delivery of possession.

Alaska

Alaska Stat. § 34.03.070

Limit: Two months' rent, unless rent exceeds $2,000 per month. Landlord may ask for an additional month's rent as deposit for a pet that is not a service animal, but may use it only to remedy pet damage.

Disclosure or Requirement: Orally or in writing, landlord must disclose the conditions under which landlord may withhold all or part of the deposit.

Separate Account: Required.

Advance Notice of Deduction: Not required.

Deadline for Landlord to Itemize and Return Deposit: 14 days if the tenant gives proper notice to terminate tenancy; 30 days if the tenant does not give proper notice or if landlord has deducted amounts needed to remedy damage caused by tenant's failure to maintain the property (Alaska Stat. § 34.03.120)

Arizona

Ariz. Rev. Stat. Ann. § 33-1321

Exemption: Excludes, among others, occupancy under a contract of sale of a dwelling unit or the property of which it is a part, if the occupant is the purchaser or a person who succeeds to his interest; occupancy by an employee of a landlord as a manager or custodian whose right to occupancy is conditional upon employment in and about the premises.

Limit: One and one-half months' rent.

Disclosure or Requirement: If landlord collects a nonrefundable fee, its purpose must be stated in writing. All fees not designated as nonrefundable are refundable.

Advance Notice of Deduction: Not required.

Deadline for Landlord to Itemize and Return Deposit: 14 days; tenant has the right to be present at final inspection.

Arkansas

Ark. Code Ann. §§ 18-16-303 to 18-16-305

Exemption: Excludes, among others, occupancy under a contract of sale of a dwelling unit or the property of which it is a part, if the occupant is the purchaser or a person who succeeds to his or her interest; occupancy by an employee of a landlord whose right to occupancy is conditional upon employment in and about the premises; and landlord who owns five or fewer rental units, unless these units are managed by a third party for a fee.

Limit: Two months' rent.

Advance Notice of Deduction: Not required.

Deadline for Landlord to Itemize and Return Deposit: 60 days.

California

Cal. Civ. Code §§ 1950.5, 1940.5(g)

Limit: Two months' rent (unfurnished); 3 months' rent (furnished). Add extra one-half month's rent for waterbed.

Advance Notice of Deduction: Required.

Deadline for Landlord to Itemize and Return Deposit: 21 days.

State Security Deposit Rules (continued)

Colorado

Colo. Rev. Stat. §§ 38-12-102 to 38-12-104

Limit: No statutory limit.

Advance Notice of Deduction: Not required.

Deadline for Landlord to Itemize and Return Deposit: One month, unless lease agreement specifies longer period of time (which may be no more than 60 days); 72 hours (not counting weekends or holidays) if a hazardous condition involving gas equipment requires tenant to vacate.

Connecticut

Conn. Gen. Stat. Ann. § 47a-21

Exemption: Excludes, among others, occupancy under a contract of sale of a dwelling unit or the property of which the unit is a part, if the occupant is the purchaser or a person who succeeds to his interest; and occupancy by a personal care assistant or other person who is employed by a person with a disability to assist and support such disabled person with daily living activities or housekeeping chores and is provided dwelling space in the personal residence of such disabled person as a benefit or condition of employment.

Limit: Two months' rent (tenant under 62 years of age); one month's rent (tenant 62 years of age or older).

Separate Account: Required.

Interest Payment: Interest payments must be made annually (or credited toward rent, at the landlord's option) and no later than 30 days after termination of tenancy. The interest rate must be equal to the average rate paid on savings deposits by insured commercial banks, rounded to the nearest 0.1%, as published by the Federal Reserve Board Bulletin.

Advance Notice of Deduction: Not required.

Deadline for Landlord to Itemize and Return Deposit: 30 days, or within 15 days of receiving tenant's forwarding address, whichever is later.

Delaware

Del. Code Ann. tit. 25, §§ 5514, 5311

Limit: One month's rent on leases for one year or more. For month to month tenancies, no limit for the first year, but after that, the limit is one month's rent (at the expiration of one year, landlord must give tenant a credit for any deposit held by the landlord that is in excess of one month's rent). No limit for furnished units. Tenant may offer to supply a surety bond in lieu of or in conjunction with a deposit, which landlord may elect to receive.

Separate Account: Required. Orally or in writing, the landlord must disclose to the tenant the location of the security deposit account.

Advance Notice of Deduction: Not required.

Deadline for Landlord to Itemize and Return Deposit: 20 days.

District of Columbia

D.C. Code Ann. § 42-3502.17; D.C. Mun. Regs. tit. 14, §§ 308 to 310

Exemption: Tenants in rent stabilized units as of July 17, 1985 cannot be asked to pay a deposit.

Limit: One month's rent.

Disclosure or Requirement: In the lease, rental agreement, or receipt, landlord must state the terms and conditions under which the security deposit was collected (to secure tenant's obligations under the lease or rental agreement).

Separate Account: Required.

Interest Payment: Required. Interest payments at the prevailing statement savings rate must be made at termination of tenancy.

Advance Notice of Deduction: Not required.

Deadline for Landlord to Itemize and Return Deposit: 45 days.

Florida

Fla. Stat. Ann. §§ 83.49, 83.43 (12)

Exemption: Occupancy under a contract of sale of a dwelling unit or the property of which it is a part in which the buyer has paid at least 12 months' rent or in which the buyer has paid at least 1 month's rent and a deposit of at least 5% of the purchase price of the property; cooperative properties, condominiums, and transient residencies.

State Security Deposit Rules (continued)

Limit: No statutory limit.

Disclosure or Requirement: Within 30 days of receiving the security deposit, the landlord must disclose in writing whether it will be held in an interest- or non-interest-bearing account; the name of the account depository; and the rate and time of interest payments. Landlord who collects a deposit must include in the lease the disclosure statement contained in Florida Statutes § 83.49.

Separate Account: Required. Landlord may post a security bond securing all tenants' deposits instead.

Interest Payment: Interest payments, if any (account need not be interest bearing) must be made annually and at termination of tenancy. However, no interest is due a tenant who wrongfully terminates the tenancy before the end of the rental term.

Advance Notice of Deduction: Required.

Deadline for Landlord to Itemize and Return Deposit: 15 to 60 days depending on whether tenant disputes deductions.

Georgia

Ga. Code Ann. §§ 44-7-30 to 44-7-37

Exemption: Landlord who owns ten or fewer rental units, unless these units are managed by an outside party, need not supply written list of preexisting damage, nor place deposit in an escrow account. Rules for returning the deposit still apply.

Limit: No statutory limit.

Disclosure or Requirement: Landlord must give tenant a written list of preexisting damage to the rental before collecting a security deposit.

Separate Account: Required. Landlord must place the deposit in an escrow account in a state or federally regulated depository, and must inform the tenant of the location of this account. Landlord may post a security bond securing all tenants' deposits instead.

Advance Notice of Deduction: Required.

Deadline for Landlord to Itemize and Return Deposit: One month.

Hawaii

Haw. Rev. Stat. § 521-44

Limit: One month's rent. (Landlord may require an additional one month's rent as security deposit for tenants who keep a pet.)

Advance Notice of Deduction: Not required.

Deadline for Landlord to Itemize and Return Deposit: 14 days.

Idaho

Idaho Code § 6-321

Limit: No statutory limit.

Advance Notice of Deduction: Not required.

Deadline for Landlord to Itemize and Return Deposit: 21 days or up to 30 days if landlord and tenant agree.

Illinois

765 Ill. Comp. Stat. 710/1, 715/2, & 715/3

Limit: No statutory limit.

Interest Payment: Landlords who rent 25 or more units in either a single building or a complex located on contiguous properties must pay interest on deposits held for more than six months. The interest rate is the rate paid for minimum deposit savings accounts by the largest commercial bank in the state, as of December 31 of the calendar year immediately preceding the start of the tenancy. Within 30 days after the end of each 12-month rental period, landlord must pay any interest that has accumulated to an amount of $5 or more, by cash or credit applied to rent due, except when the tenant is in default under the terms of the lease. Landlord must pay all interest that has accumulated and remains unpaid, regardless of the amount, upon termination of the tenancy.

Advance Notice of Deduction: Not required.

Deadline for Landlord to Itemize and Return Deposit: For properties with 5 or more units, 30 to 45 days, depending on whether tenant disputes deductions or if statement and receipts are furnished.

State Security Deposit Rules (continued)

Indiana

Ind. Code Ann. §§ 32-31-3-9 to 32-31-3-19

Exemption: Does not apply to, among others, occupancy under a contract of sale of a rental unit or the property of which the rental unit is a part if the occupant is the purchaser or a person who succeeds to the purchaser's interest; and occupancy by an employee of a landlord whose right to occupancy is conditional upon employment in or about the premises. Does apply to leases signed after July 1, 2008, that contain an option to purchase.

Limit: No statutory limit.

Advance Notice of Deduction: Not required.

Deadline for Landlord to Itemize and Return Deposit: 45 days.

Iowa

Iowa Code Ann. § 562A.12

Limit: Two months' rent.

Separate Account: Required.

Interest Payment: Interest payment, if any (account need not be interest bearing), must be made at termination of tenancy. Interest earned during first five years of tenancy belongs to landlord.

Advance Notice of Deduction: Not required.

Deadline for Landlord to Itemize and Return Deposit: 30 days.

Kansas

Kan. Stat. Ann. §§ 58-2550, 58-2548

Exemption: Excludes, among others, occupancy under a contract of sale of a dwelling unit or the property of which it is a part, if the occupant is the purchaser or a person who succeeds to the purchaser's interest; and occupancy by an employee of a landlord whose right to occupancy is conditional upon employment in and about the premises

Limit: One month's rent (unfurnished); one and one-half months' rent (furnished); for pets, add extra one-half month's rent.

Advance Notice of Deduction: Not required.

Deadline for Landlord to Itemize and Return Deposit: 30 days.

Kentucky

Ky. Rev. Stat. Ann. § 383.580

Limit: No statutory limit.

Disclosure or Requirement: Orally or in writing, landlord must disclose where the security deposit is being held and the account number.

Separate Account: Required.

Advance Notice of Deduction: Required.

Deadline for Landlord to Itemize and Return Deposit: 30 to 60 days depending on whether tenant disputes deductions.

Louisiana

La. Rev. Stat. Ann. § 9:3251

Limit: No statutory limit.

Advance Notice of Deduction: Not required.

Deadline for Landlord to Itemize and Return Deposit: One month.

Maine

Me. Rev. Stat. Ann. tit. 14, §§ 6031 to 6038

Exemption: Entire security deposit law does not apply to rental unit that is part of structure with five or fewer units, one of which is occupied by landlord

Limit: Two months' rent.

Disclosure or Requirement: Upon request by the tenant, landlord must disclose orally or in writing the account number and the name of the institution where the security deposit is being held.

Separate Account: Required.

Advance Notice of Deduction: Not required.

Deadline for Landlord to Itemize and Return Deposit: 30 days (if written rental agreement) or 21 days (if tenancy at will).

Maryland

Md. Code Ann. [Real Prop.] § 8-203, § 8-203.1

Limit: Two months' rent.

State Security Deposit Rules (continued)

Disclosure or Requirement: Landlord must provide a receipt that describes tenant's rights to move-in and move-out inspections (and to be present at each), and right to receive itemization of deposit deductions and balance, if any; and penalties for landlord's failure to comply. Landlord may include this information in the lease.

Separate Account: Required. Landlord may hold all tenants' deposits in secured certificates of deposit, or in securities issued by the federal government or the State of Maryland.

Interest Payment: For security deposits of $50 or more, when landlord has held the deposit for at least six months: Within 45 days of termination of tenancy, interest must be paid at the daily U.S. Treasury yield curve rate for 1 year, as of the first business day of each year, or 1.5% a year, whichever is greater, less any damages rightfully withheld. Interest accrues monthly but is not compounded, and no interest is due for any period less than one month. (See the Department of Housing and Community Development website for a calculator.) Deposit must be held in a Maryland banking institution.

Advance Notice of Deduction: Required.

Deadline for Landlord to Itemize and Return Deposit: 45 days.

Massachusetts

Mass. Gen. Laws Ann. ch. 186, § 15B

Limit: One month's rent.

Disclosure or Requirement: At the time of receiving a security deposit, landlord must furnish a receipt indicating the amount of the deposit; the name of the person receiving it and, if received by a property manager, the name of the lessor for whom the security deposit is received; the date on which it is received; and a description of the premises leased or rented. The receipt must be signed by the person receiving the security deposit.

Separate Account: Required. Within 30 days of receiving security deposit, landlord must disclose the name and location of the bank in which the security deposit has been deposited, and the amount and account number of the deposit.

Interest Payment: Landlord must pay tenant 5% interest per year or the amount received from the bank (which must be in Massachusetts) that holds the deposit. Interest should be paid yearly, and within 30 days of termination date. Interest will not accrue for the last month for which rent was paid in advance.

Advance Notice of Deduction: Not required.

Deadline for Landlord to Itemize and Return Deposit: 30 days.

Michigan

Mich. Comp. Laws §§ 554.602 to 554.616

Limit: One and one-half months' rent.

Disclosure or Requirement: Within 14 days of tenant's taking possession of the rental, landlord must furnish in writing the landlord's name and address for receipt of communications, the name and address of the financial institution or surety where the deposit will be held, and the tenant's obligation to provide in writing a forwarding mailing address to the landlord within 4 days after termination of occupancy. The notice shall include the following statement in 12-point boldface type that is at least 4 points larger than the body of the notice or lease agreement: "You must notify your landlord in writing within 4 days after you move of a forwarding address where you can be reached and where you will receive mail; otherwise your landlord shall be relieved of sending you an itemized list of damages and the penalties adherent to that failure."

Separate Account: Required. Landlord must place deposits in a regulated financial institution, and may use the deposits as long as the landlord deposits with the secretary of state a cash or surety bond.

Advance Notice of Deduction: Required. Tenants must dispute the landlord's stated deductions within 7 days of receiving the itemized list and balance, if any, or give up any right to dispute them.

State Security Deposit Rules (continued)

Deadline for Landlord to Itemize and Return Deposit: 30 days.

Minnesota

Minn. Stat. Ann. §§ 504B.175, 504B.178, & 504B.195

Limit: No statutory limit. If landlord collects a "prelease deposit" and subsequently rents to tenant, landlord must apply the prelease deposit to the security deposit.

Disclosure or Requirement: Before collecting rent or a security deposit, landlord must provide a copy of all outstanding inspection orders for which a citation has been issued, pertaining to a rental unit or common area, specifying code violations that threaten the health or safety of the tenant, and all outstanding condemnation orders and declarations that the premises are unfit for human habitation. Citations for violations that do not involve threats to tenant health or safety must be summarized and posted in an obvious place. With some exceptions, landlord who has received notice of a contract for deed cancellation or notice of a mortgage foreclosure sale must so disclose before entering a lease, accepting rent, or accepting a security deposit; and must furnish the date on which the contract cancellation period or the mortgagor's redemption period ends.

Interest Payment: Landlord must pay 1% simple, noncompounded interest per year. (Deposits collected before 8/1/03 earn interest at 3%, up to 8/1/03, then begin earning at 1%.) Any interest amount less than $1 is excluded.

Advance Notice of Deduction: Not required.

Deadline for Landlord to Itemize and Return Deposit: Three weeks after tenant leaves and landlord receives forwarding address; five days if tenant must leave due to building condemnation.

Mississippi

Miss. Code Ann. § 89-8-21

Limit: No statutory limit.

Advance Notice of Deduction: Not required.

Deadline for Landlord to Itemize and Return Deposit: 45 days.

Missouri

Mo. Ann. Stat. § 535.300

Limit: Two months' rent.

Advance Notice of Deduction: Not required.

Deadline for Landlord to Itemize and Return Deposit: 30 days.

Montana

Mont. Code Ann. §§ 70-25-101 to 70-25-206

Limit: No statutory limit.

Advance Notice of Deduction: Required. Tenant is entitled to advance notice of cleaning charges, but only if such cleaning is required as a result of tenant's negligence and is not part of the landlord's cyclical cleaning program.

Advance Notice of Deduction: Required.

Deadline for Landlord to Itemize and Return Deposit: 30 days; 10 days if no deductions.

Nebraska

Neb. Rev. Stat. § 76-1416

Limit: One month's rent (no pets); one and one-quarter months' rent (pets).

Advance Notice of Deduction: Not required.

Deadline for Landlord to Itemize and Return Deposit: 14 days.

Nevada

Nev. Rev. Stat. Ann. §§ 118A.240 to 118A.250

Limit: Three months' rent; if both landlord and tenant agree, tenant may use a surety bond for all or part of the deposit.

Disclosure or Requirement: Lease or rental agreement must explain the conditions under which the landlord will refund the deposit.

Deadline for Landlord to Itemize and Return Deposit: 30 days.

State Security Deposit Rules (continued)

New Hampshire

N.H. Rev. Stat. Ann. §§ 540-A:5 to 540-A:8; 540-B:10

Exemption: Entire security deposit law does not apply to landlord who leases a single-family residence and owns no other rental property, or landlord who leases rental units in an owner-occupied building of five units or fewer (exemption does not apply to any individual unit in owner-occupied building that is occupied by a person 60 years of age or older).

Limit: One month's rent or $100, whichever is greater; when landlord and tenant share facilities, no statutory limit.

Disclosure or Requirement: Unless tenant has paid the deposit by personal or bank check, or by a check issued by a government agency, landlord must provide a receipt stating the amount of the deposit and the institution where it will be held. Regardless of whether a receipt is required, landlord must inform tenant that if tenant finds any conditions in the rental in need of repair, tenant may note them on the receipt or other written instrument, and return either within five days.

Separate Account: Required. Upon request, landlord must disclose the account number, the amount on deposit, and the interest rate. Landlord may post a bond covering all deposits instead of putting deposits in a separate account.

Interest Payment: Landlord who holds a security deposit for a year or longer must pay interest at a rate equal to the rate paid on regular savings accounts in the New Hampshire bank, savings & loan, or credit union where it's deposited. If a landlord mingles security deposits in a single account, the landlord must pay the actual interest earned proportionately to each tenant. A tenant may request the interest accrued every three years, 30 days before that year's tenancy expires. The landlord must comply with the request within 15 days of the expiration of that year's tenancy.

Advance Notice of Deduction: Not required.

Deadline for Landlord to Itemize and Return Deposit: 30 days; for shared facilities, if the deposit is more than 30 days' rent, landlord must provide written agreement acknowledging receipt and specifying when deposit will be returned—if no written agreement, 20 days after tenant vacates.

New Jersey

N.J. Stat. Ann. §§ 46:8-19, 44:8-21, 44:8-26

Exemption: Security deposit law does not apply to owner-occupied buildings with three or fewer units unless tenant gives 30 days' written notice to the landlord of the tenant's wish to invoke the law.

Limit: One and one-half months' rent. Any additional security deposit, collected annually, may be no greater than 10% of the current security deposit.

Separate Account: Required. Within 30 days of receiving the deposit and every time the landlord pays the tenant interest, landlord must disclose the name and address of the banking organization where the deposit is being held, the type of account, current rate of interest, and the amount of the deposit.

Interest Payment: Landlord with 10 or more units must invest deposits as specified by statute or place deposit in an insured money market fund account, or in another account that pays quarterly interest at a rate comparable to the money market fund. Landlords with fewer than 10 units may place deposit in an interest-bearing account in any New Jersey financial institution insured by the FDIC. All landlords may pay tenants interest earned on account annually or credit toward payment of rent due.

Advance Notice of Deduction: Not required.

Deadline for Landlord to Itemize and Return Deposit: 30 days; five days in case of fire, flood, condemnation, or evacuation.

New Mexico

N.M. Stat. Ann. § 47-8-18

Limit: One month's rent (for rental agreement of less than one year); no limit for leases of one year or more.

State Security Deposit Rules (continued)

Interest Payment: Landlord who collects a deposit larger than than one month's rent on a year's lease must pay interest, on an annual basis, equal to the passbook interest.

Advance Notice of Deduction: Not required.

Deadline for Landlord to Itemize and Return Deposit: 30 days.

New York

N.Y. Gen. Oblig. Law §§ 7-103 to 7-108

Limit: No statutory limit for nonregulated units.

Disclosure or Requirement: If deposit is placed in a bank, landlord must disclose the name and address of the banking organization where the deposit is being held, and the amount of such deposit.

Separate Account: Statute requires that deposits not be commingled with landlord's personal assets, but does not explicitly require placement in a banking institution (however, deposits collected in buildings of six or more units must be placed in New York bank accounts).

Interest Payment: Landlord who rents out non-regulated units in buildings with five or fewer units need not pay interest. Interest must be paid at the prevailing rate on deposits received from tenants who rent units in buildings containing six or more units. The landlord in every rental situation may retain an administrative fee of 1% per year on the sum deposited. Interest can be subtracted from the rent, paid at the end of the year, or paid at the end of the tenancy according to the tenant's choice.

Advance Notice of Deduction: Not required.

Deadline for Landlord to Itemize and Return Deposit: A "reasonable time."

North Carolina

N.C. Gen. Stat. §§ 42-50 to 42-56

Exemption: Not applicable to single rooms rented on a weekly, monthly, or annual basis.

Limit: One and one-half months' rent for month-to-month rental agreements; two months' rent if term is longer than two months; may add an additional "reasonable" nonrefundable pet deposit.

Disclosure or Requirement: Within 30 days of the beginning of the lease term, landlord must disclose the name and address of the banking institution where the deposit is located.

Separate Account: Required. The landlord may, at his option, furnish a bond from an insurance company licensed to do business in the state.

Advance Notice of Deduction: Not required.

Deadline for Landlord to Itemize and Return Deposit: 30 days; if landlord's claim against the deposit cannot be finalized within that time, landlord may send an interim accounting and a final accounting within 60 days of the tenancy's termination.

North Dakota

N.D. Cent. Code § 47-16-07.1

Limit: One month's rent. If tenant has a pet that is not a service or companion animal that tenant keeps as a reasonable accommodation under fair housing laws, an additional pet deposit of up to $2,500 or two months' rent, whichever is greater.

Separate Account: Required.

Interest Payment: Landlord must pay interest if the period of occupancy is at least nine months. Money must be held in a federally insured interest-bearing savings or checking account for benefit of the tenant. Interest must be paid upon termination of the lease.

Advance Notice of Deduction: Not required.

Deadline for Landlord to Itemize and Return Deposit: 30 days.

Ohio

Ohio Rev. Code Ann. § 5321.16

Limit: No statutory limit.

Interest Payment: Any deposit in excess of $50 or one month's rent, whichever is greater, must bear interest on the excess at the rate of 5% per annum if the tenant stays for six months or more. Interest must be paid annually and upon termination of tenancy.

State Security Deposit Rules (continued)

Advance Notice of Deduction: Not required.

Deadline for Landlord to Itemize and Return Deposit: 30 days.

Oklahoma

Okla. Stat. Ann. tit. 41, § 115

Limit: No statutory limit.

Separate Account: Required.

Advance Notice of Deduction: Not required.

Deadline for Landlord to Itemize and Return Deposit: 45 days.

Oregon

Or. Rev. Stat. § 90.300

Limit: No statutory limit. Landlord may not impose or increase deposit within first year unless parties agree to modify the rental agreement to allow for a pet or other cause, and the imposition or increase relates to that modification.

Advance Notice of Deduction: Not required.

Deadline for Landlord to Itemize and Return Deposit: 31 days.

Pennsylvania

68 Pa. Cons. Stat. Ann. §§ 250.511a to 250.512

Limit: Two months' rent for first year of renting; one month's rent during second and subsequent years of renting.

Disclosure or Requirement: For deposits over $100, landlord must deposit them in a federally or state-regulated institution, and give tenant the name and address of the banking institution and the amount of the deposit.

Separate Account: Required. Instead of placing deposits in a separate account, landlord may purchase a bond issued by a bonding company authorized to do business in the state.

Interest Payment: Tenant who occupies rental unit for two or more years is entitled to interest beginning with the 25th month of occupancy. Landlord must pay tenant interest (minus 1% fee) at the end of the third and subsequent years of the tenancy.

Advance Notice of Deduction: Not required.

Deadline for Landlord to Itemize and Return Deposit: 30 days.

Rhode Island

R.I. Gen. Laws § 34-18-19

Limit: One month's rent.

Advance Notice of Deduction: Not required.

Deadline for Landlord to Itemize and Return Deposit: 20 days.

South Carolina

S.C. Code Ann. § 27-40-410

Limit: No statutory limit.

Advance Notice of Deduction: Not required.

Deadline for Landlord to Itemize and Return Deposit: 30 days.

South Dakota

S.D. Codified Laws Ann. § 43.32-6.1, § 43-32-24

Limit: One month's rent (higher deposit may be charged if special conditions pose a danger to maintenance of the premises).

Advance Notice of Deduction: Not required.

Deadline for Landlord to Itemize and Return Deposit: Two weeks, and must supply reasons for withholding any portion; 45 days for a written, itemized accounting, if tenant requests it.

Tennessee

Tenn. Code Ann. § 66-28-301

Exemption: Does not apply in counties having a population of less than 75,000, according to the 2010 federal census or any subsequent federal census.

Limit: No statutory limit.

Separate Account: Required. Orally or in writing, landlord must disclose the location of the separate account (but not the account number) used by landlord for the deposit.

Advance Notice of Deduction: Required.

State Security Deposit Rules (continued)

Texas

Tex. Prop. Code Ann. §§ 92.101 to 92.109

Limit: No statutory limit.

Advance Notice of Deduction: Not required.

Deadline for Landlord to Itemize and Return Deposit: 30 days. Landlord need not refund deposit if lease requires tenant to give written notice of tenant's intention to surrender the premises.

Utah

Utah Code Ann. §§ 57-17-1 to 57-17-5

Limit: No statutory limit.

Disclosure or Requirement: For written leases or rental agreements only, if part of the deposit is nonrefundable, landlord must disclose this feature.

Advance Notice of Deduction: Not required.

Deadline for Landlord to Itemize and Return Deposit: 30 days.

Vermont

Vt. Stat. Ann. tit. 9, § 4461

Limit: No statutory limit.

Advance Notice of Deduction: Not required.

Deadline for Landlord to Itemize and Return Deposit: 14 days; 60 days if the rental is seasonal and not intended as the tenant's primary residence.

Virginia

Va. Code Ann. § 55-248.15:1

Exemption: Single-family residences are exempt where the owner(s) are natural persons or their estates who own in their own name no more than two single-family residences subject to a rental agreement. Exemption applies to the entire Virginia Residential Landlord and Tenant Act.

Limit: Two months' rent.

Advance Notice of Deduction: Not required.

Deadline for Landlord to Itemize and Return Deposit: 45 days; tenant has right to be present at final inspection.

Washington

Wash. Rev. Code Ann. §§ 59.18.260 to 59.18.285

Exemption: Security deposit rules do not apply to a lease of a single-family dwelling for a year or more, or to any lease of a single-family dwelling containing a bona fide option to purchase by the tenant, provided that an attorney for the tenant has approved on the face of the agreement any lease so exempted. Rules also do not apply to occupancy by an employee of a landlord whose right to occupy is conditioned upon employment in or about the premises; or the lease of single-family rental in connection with a lease of land to be used primarily for agricultural purposes; or rental agreements for seasonal agricultural employees.

Limit: No statutory limit.

Disclosure or Requirement: In the lease, landlord must disclose the circumstances under which all or part of the deposit may be withheld, and must provide a receipt with the name and location of the banking institution where the deposit is being held. No deposit may be collected unless the rental agreement is in writing and a written checklist or statement specifically describing the condition and cleanliness of or existing damages to the premises and furnishings is provided to the tenant at the start of the tenancy.

Separate Account: Required.

Advance Notice of Deduction: Not required.

Deadline for Landlord to Itemize and Return Deposit: 21 days.

West Virginia

W.Va. Code § 37-6A-1 et seq.

Deadline for Landlord to Itemize and Return Deposit: 60 days from the date the tenancy has terminated, or within 45 days of the occupancy of a subsequent tenant, whichever is shorter. If the damage exceeds the amount of the security deposit and the landlord has to hire a contractor to fix it, the notice period is extended 15 days.

State Security Deposit Rules (continued)

Wisconsin

Wis. Admin. Code ATCP 134.06, Wis. Stat. § 704.28

Exemption: Security deposit rules do not apply to a dwelling unit occupied, under a contract of sale, by the purchaser of the dwelling unit or the purchaser's successor in interest; or to a dwelling unit that the landlord provides free to any person, or that the landlord provides as consideration to a person whom the landlord currently employs to operate or maintain the premises.

Limit: No Statutory limit.

Disclosure or Requirement: Before accepting the deposit, landlord must inform tenant of tenant's inspection rights, disclose all habitability defects and show tenant any outstanding building and housing code violations, inform tenant of the means by which shared utilities will be billed, and inform tenant if utilities are not paid for by landlord.

Advance Notice of Deduction: Not required.

Deadline for Landlord to Itemize and Return Deposit: 21 days.

Wyoming

Wyo. Stat. §§ 1-21-1207, 1-21-1208

Limit: No statutory limit.

Disclosure or Requirement: Lease or rental agreement must state whether any portion of a deposit is non-refundable, and landlord must give tenant written notice of this fact when collecting the deposit.

Advance Notice of Deduction: Not required.

Deadline for Landlord to Itemize and Return Deposit: 30 days, when applying it to unpaid rent (or within 15 days of receiving tenant's forwarding address, whichever is later); additional 30 days allowed for deductions due to damage.

Required Landlord Disclosures

Many states require landlords to inform tenants of important state laws or individual landlord policies, either in the lease or rental agreement or in another writing. Common disclosures include a landlord's imposition of nonrefundable fees (where permitted), tenants' rights to move-in checklists, and the identity of the landlord or landlord's agent or manager. Disclosures concerning the security deposit are in the chart, "State Security Deposit Rules."

Alabama

Ala. Code § 35-9A-202

Owner or agent identity: Landlord must disclose to the tenant in writing at or before the commencement of the tenancy the name and address of the person authorized to manage the premises, and an owner of the premises or a person authorized to act for and on behalf of the owner for the purpose of service of process and for the purpose of receiving notices and demands. (Exception: does not apply to resident purchaser under a contract of sale (but does apply to a resident who has an option to buy), nor to the continuation of occupancy by the seller or a member of the seller's family for a period of not more than 36 months after the sale of a dwelling unit or the property of which it is a part.)

Alaska

Alaska Stat. §§ 34.03.080, 34.03.150

Owner or agent identity: Landlord must disclose to the tenant in writing at or before the commencement of the tenancy the name and address of the person authorized to manage the premises, and an owner of the premises or a person authorized to act for and on behalf of the owner for the purpose of service of process and for the purpose of receiving notices and demands. (Alaska Stat. § 34.03.080)

Extended absence: The rental agreement must require that the tenant notify the landlord of an anticipated extended absence from the premises in excess of seven days; however, the notice maybe given as soon as reasonably possible after the tenant knows the absence will exceed seven days. (Alaska Stat. § 34.03.150)

Arizona

Ariz. Rev. Stat. §§ 33-1314, 33-1314.01, 33-1319, 33-1321, 33-1322

Nonrefundable fees permitted? Yes. The purpose of all nonrefundable fees or deposits must be stated in writing. Any fee or deposit not designated as nonrefundable is refundable.

Move-in checklist required? Yes. Tenants also have the right to be present at a move-out inspection.

Separate utility charges: If landlord charges separately for gas, water, wastewater, solid waste removal, or electricity by installing a submetering system, landlord may recover the charges imposed on the landlord by the utility provider, plus an administrative fee for the landlord for actual administrative costs only, and must disclose separate billing and fee in the rental agreement. If landlord uses a ratio utility billing system, the rental agreement must contain a specific description of the ratio utility billing method used to allocate utility costs. (Ariz. Rev. Stat. § 33-1314.01)

Owner or agent identity: Landlord must disclose to the tenant in writing at or before the commencement of the tenancy the name and address of the person authorized to manage the premises, and an owner of the premises or a person authorized to act for and on behalf of the owner for the purpose of service of process and for the purpose of receiving notices and demands. (Ariz. Rev. Stat. § 33-1322)

Business tax pass-through: If the landlord pays a local tax based on rent and that tax increases, landlord may pass through the increase by increasing the rent upon 30 days' notice (but not before the new tax is effective), but only if the landlord's right to adjust the rent is disclosed in the rental agreement. (Ariz. Rev. Stat. § 33-1314)

Availability of landlord and tenant act: Landlord must inform tenant in writing that the Residential Landlord and Tenant Act is available on the Arizona department of housing's website. (Ariz. Rev. Stat. § 33-1322)

Required Landlord Disclosures (continued)

Bedbug Information. Landlords must provide existing and new tenants with educational materials on bedbugs, including information and physical descriptions, prevention and control measures, behavioral attraction risk factors, information from federal, state, and local centers for disease control and prevention, health or housing agencies, nonprofit housing organizations, or information developed by the landlord. (Ariz. Rev. Stat. § 33-1319)

Arkansas

No disclosure statutes.

California

Cal. Civ. Code §§ 1950.5(m), 1940.6, 1940.7, 1940.8, 1940.9, 1947.5, 2079.10a
Cal. Health & Safety Code §§ 26147, 26148
Cal. Bus. & Prof. Code § 8538

Nonrefundable fees permitted? No.

Move-in checklist required? No.

Registered sexual offender database: Landlords must include the following language in their rental agreements: "Notice: Pursuant to Section 290.46 of the Penal Code, information about specified registered sex offenders is made available to the public via an Internet Web site maintained by the Department of Justice at www.meganslaw.ca.gov. Depending on an offender's criminal history, this information will include either the address at which the offender resides or the community of residence and ZIP Code in which he or she resides." (Cal. Civ. Code § 2079.10a)

Tenant paying for others' utilities: Prior to signing a rental agreement, landlord must disclose whether gas or electric service to tenant's unit also serves other areas, and must disclose the manner by which costs will be fairly allocated. (Cal. Civ. Code § 1940.9)

Ordnance locations: Prior to signing a lease, landlord must disclose known locations of former federal or state ordnance in the neighborhood (within one mile of rental). (Cal. Civ. Code § 1940.7)

Toxic mold: Prior to signing a rental agreement, landlord must provide written disclosure when landlord knows, or has reason to know, that mold exceeds permissible exposure limits or poses a health threat. Landlords must distribute a consumer handbook, developed by the State Department of Health Services, describing the potential health risks from mold. (Cal. Health & Safety Code §§ 26147, 26148)

Pest control service: When the rental agreement is signed, landlord must provide tenant with any pest control company disclosure landlord has received, which describes the pest to be controlled, pesticides used and their active ingredients, a warning that pesticides are toxic, and the frequency of treatment under any contract for periodic service. (Cal. Civ. Code § 1940.8, Cal. Bus. & Prof. Code § 8538)

Intention to demolish rental unit: Landlords or their agents who have applied for a permit to demolish a rental unit must give written notice of this fact to prospective tenants, before accepting any deposits or screening fees. (Cal. Civ. Code § 1940.6)

No-smoking policy. For leases and rental agreements signed after January 1, 2012: If the landlord prohibits or limits the smoking of tobacco products on the rental property, the lease or rental agreement must include a clause describing the areas where smoking is limited or prohibited (does not apply if the tenant has previously occupied the dwelling unit). For leases and rental agreements signed before January 1, 2012: A newly adopted policy limiting or prohibiting smoking is a change in the terms of the tenancy (will not apply to leaseholding tenants until they renew their leases; tenants renting month-to-month must be given 30 days' written notice). Does not preempt any local ordinances prohibiting smoking in effect on January 1, 2012. (Cal. Civ. Code § 1947.5)

Notice of default. Lessors of single-family homes and multifamily properties of four units or less, who have received a notice of default for the rental property that has not been rescinded, must disclose this fact to potential renters before they sign a lease. The notice must be in English or in Spanish, Chinese, Tagalog, Vietnamese, or Korean (if the lease was negotiated in one of these languages), and must follow the language specified in Cal. Civil Code § 2924.85(d).

Required Landlord Disclosures (continued)

Colorado

No disclosure statutes.

Connecticut

Conn. Gen. Stat. Ann. §§ 47a-3e, 47a-6

Common interest community: When rental is in a common interest community, landlord must give tenant written notice before signing a lease. (Conn. Gen. Stat. Ann. § 47a-3e)

Owner or agent identity: Before the beginning of the tenancy, landlord must disclose the name and address of the person authorized to manage the premises and the person who is authorized to receive all notices, demands and service of process. (Conn. Gen. Stat. Ann. § 47a-6)

Summary of Landlord-Tenant Code: A summary of the code, as prepared by the Consumer Protection Unit of the Attorney General's office, must be given to tenants at the beginning of the rental term. Failure to do so enables the tenant to plead ignorance of the law as a defense.

Delaware

Stoltz Management Co. v. Phillip, 593 A.2d 583 (1990); 25 Del. Code Ann. §§ 5105, 5118, 5311

Nonrefundable fees permitted? No, except for an optional service fee for actual services rendered, such as a pool fee or tennis court fee. Tenant may elect, subject to the landlord's acceptance, to purchase an optional surety bond instead of or in combination with a security deposit.

Owner or agent identity: On each written rental agreement, the landlord must prominently disclose the names and usual business addresses of all persons who are owners of the rental unit or the property of which the rental unit is a part, or the names and business addresses of their appointed resident agents. (25 Del. Code Ann. § 5105)

Summary of Landlord-Tenant law: A summary of the Landlord-Tenant Code, as prepared by the Consumer Protection Unit of the Attorney General's Office or its successor agency, must be given to the new tenant at the beginning of the rental term. If the landlord fails to provide the summary, the tenant may plead ignorance of the law as a defense. (25 Del. Code Ann. § 5118)

District of Columbia

14 D.C. Mun. Regs. § 300

Rental regulations: At the start of every new tenancy, landlord must give tenant a copy of the District of Columbia Municipal Regulations, CDCR Title 14, Housing, Chapter 3, Landlord and Tenant; and a copy of Title 14, Housing, Chapter 1, § 101 (Civil Enforcement Policy) and Chapter 1, § 106 (Notification of Tenants Concerning Violations).

Florida

Fla. Stat. Ann. §§ 83.50, 404.056

Nonrefundable fees permitted? Yes, allowed by custom, although there is no statute.

Landlord identity: The landlord, or a person authorized to enter into a rental agreement on the landlord's behalf, must disclose in writing to the tenant, at or before the commencement of the tenancy, the name and address of the landlord or a person authorized to receive notices and demands on the landlord's behalf. (Fla. Stat. Ann. § 83.50)

Radon: In all leases, landlord must include this warning: "RADON GAS: Radon is a naturally occurring radioactive gas that, when it has accumulated in a building in sufficient quantities, may present health risks to persons who are exposed to it over time. Levels of radon that exceed federal and state guidelines have been found in buildings in Florida. Additional information regarding radon and radon testing may be obtained from your county health department." (Fla. Stat. Ann. § 404.056)

Required Landlord Disclosures (continued)

Georgia

Ga. Code Ann. §§ 44-1-16, 44-7-20, 44-7-3, 44-7-33

Nonrefundable fees permitted? Yes, nonrefundable fees, such as pet fees, are allowed by custom, although there is no statute.

Move-in checklist required? Yes, Landlords cannot collect a security deposit until they have given tenant a list of preexisting damages. (Ga. Code Ann. § 44-7-33)

Flooding: Before signing a lease, if the living space or attachments have been damaged by flooding three or more times within the past five years, landlord must so disclose in writing. (Ga. Code Ann. § 44-7-20)

Owner or agent identity: When or before a tenancy begins, landlord must disclose in writing the names and addresses of the owner of record or a person authorized to act for the owner for purposes of service of process and receiving and receipting demands and notices; and the person authorized to manage the premises. If such information changes during the tenancy, landlord must advise tenant within 30 days in writing or by posting a notice in a conspicuous place. (Ga. Code Ann. § 44-7-3)

Former residents, crimes. If asked by a prospective tenant, landlord must answer truthfully when questioned about whether the rental was the site of a homicide or other felony, or a suicide or a death by accidental or natural causes; or whether it was occupied by a person who was infected with a virus or any other disease that has been determined by medical evidence as being highly unlikely to be transmitted through the occupancy of a dwelling place presently or previously occupied by such an infected person. (Ga. Code Ann. § 44-1-16)

Hawaii

Haw. Rev. Stat. §§ 521-42, 521-43

Nonrefundable fees permitted? No.

Other fees: The landlord may not require or receive from or on behalf of a tenant at the beginning of a rental agreement any money other than the money for the first month's rent and a security deposit as provided in this section.

Move-in checklist required? Yes.

Owner or agent identity: Landlord must disclose name of owner or agent; if owner lives in another state or on another island, landlord must disclose name of agent on the island. (Haw. Rev. Stat. § 521-43)

Tax excise number: Landlord must furnish its tax excise number so that tenant can file for a low-income tax credit. (Haw. Rev. Stat. § 521-43)

Idaho

No disclosure statutes.

Illinois

Utilities: *765 Ill. Comp. Stat. § 740/5*

Rent concessions: *765 Ill. Comp. Stat. §§ 730/0.01 to 730/6*

Radon: *420 Ill. Comp. Stat. §§ 46/15, 46/25*

Utilities: Where tenant pays a portion of a master metered utility, landlord must give tenant a copy in writing either as part of the lease or another written agreement of the formula used by the landlord for allocating the public utility payments among the tenants. (765 Ill. Comp. Stat. § 740/5)

Rent concessions: Any rent concessions must be described in the lease, in letters not less than one-half inch in height consisting of the words "Concession Granted," including a memorandum on the margin or across the face of the lease stating the amount or extent and nature of each such concession. Failure to comply is a misdemeanor. (765 Ill. Comp. Stat. §§ 730/0 to 730/6)

Radon: Landlords are not required to test for radon, but if the landlord tests and learns that a radon hazard is present in the dwelling unit, landlord must disclose this information to current and prospective tenants. If a tenant notifies a landlord that a radon test indicates the existence of a radon hazard in the rental unit, landlord must disclose that risk to any prospective tenant of that unit, unless a subsequent test by the landlord shows that a radon hazard does not exist. Requirements do not apply if the dwelling unit is on the third or higher story above ground level,

Required Landlord Disclosures (continued)

or when the landlord has undertaken mitigation work and a subsequent test shows that a radon hazard does not exist. (420 Ill. Comp. Stat. §§ 46/15, 46/25)

Indiana

Ind. Code Ann. § 32-31-3-18

Owner or agent identity: Landlord's agent must disclose in writing the name and address of a person living in Indiana who is authorized to manage the property and to act as the owner's agent.

Iowa

Iowa Code § 562A.13

Owner or agent identity: Landlord must disclose to the tenant in writing at or before the commencement of the tenancy the name and address of the person authorized to manage the premises, and an owner of the premises or a person authorized to act for and on behalf of the owner for the purpose of service of process and for the purpose of receiving notices and demands. (Iowa Code § 562A.13)

Utilities: For shared utilities, landlord must fully explain utility rates, charges, and services to the prospective tenant before the rental agreement is signed. (Iowa Code § 562A.13)

Contamination: The landlord or a person authorized to enter into a rental agreement on behalf of the landlord must disclose to each tenant, in writing before the commencement of the tenancy, whether the property is listed in the comprehensive environmental response compensation and liability information system maintained by the federal Environmental Protection Agency. (Iowa Code § 562A.13)

Kansas

Kan. Stat. Ann. §§ 58-2548, 58-2551

Move-in checklist required? Yes. Within 5 days of move-in, landlord and tenant must jointly inventory the rental.

Owner or agent identity: Landlord must disclose to the tenant in writing at or before the commencement of the tenancy the name and address of the person authorized to manage the premises, and an owner of the premises or a person authorized to act for and on behalf of the owner for the purpose of service of process and for the purpose of receiving notices and demands. (Kan. Stat. Ann. §§ 58-2548, 58-2551)

Kentucky

Ky. Rev. Stat. Ann. §§ 383.580, 383.585

Move-in checklist required? Yes. Landlord and tenant must complete a checklist before landlord can collect a security deposit.

Owner or agent identity: Landlord must disclose to the tenant in writing at or before the commencement of the tenancy the name and address of the person authorized to manage the premises, and an owner of the premises or a person authorized to act for and on behalf of the owner for the purpose of service of process and for the purpose of receiving notices and demands.

Louisiana

La. Stat. Ann. § 9:3260.1

Foreclosure: Before entering into a lease or rental agreement, landlord must disclose to potential tenants their right to receive notification of any future foreclosure action. If the premises are currently subject to a foreclosure action, landlord must also disclose this in writing. (La. Stat. Ann. § 9:3260.1)

Maine

14 Me. Rev. Stat. Ann. §§ 6021-A, 6024, 6030-C, 6030-D, 6030-E

Utilities: No landlord may lease or offer to lease a dwelling unit in a multiunit residential building where the expense of furnishing electricity to the common areas or other area not within the unit is the sole responsibility of the tenant in that unit, unless both parties to the lease have agreed in writing that the tenant will pay for such costs in return for a stated

Required Landlord Disclosures (continued)

reduction in rent or other specified fair consideration that approximates the actual cost of electricity to the common areas. (14 Me. Rev. Stat. Ann. § 6024)

Energy efficiency: Landlord must provide to potential tenants who will pay for energy costs (or upon request from others) a residential energy efficiency disclosure statement in accordance with Title 35-A, section 10006, subsection 1, that includes, but is not limited to, information about the energy efficiency of the property. Before a tenant enters into a contract or pays a deposit to rent or lease a property, the landlord must provide the statement to the tenant, obtain the tenant's signature on the statement, and sign the statement. The landlord must retain the signed statement for at least 3 years. Alternatively, the landlord may include in the application for the residential property the name of each supplier of energy that previously supplied the unit, if known, and the following statement: "You have the right to obtain a 12-month history of energy consumption and the cost of that consumption from the energy supplier." (14 Me. Rev. Stat. Ann. § 6030-C)

Radon: By 2012 and every ten years thereafter, landlord must test for radon and disclose to prospective and existing tenants the date and results of the test and the risks of of radon, using a disclosure form prepared by the Department of Health and Human Services (tenant must sign acknowledgment of receipt). (14 Me. Rev. Stat. Ann. § 6030-D)

Bedbugs: Before renting a dwelling unit, landlord must disclose to a prospective tenant if an adjacent unit or units are currently infested with or are being treated for bedbugs. Upon request from a tenant or prospective tenant, landlord must disclose the last date that the dwelling unit the landlord seeks to rent or an adjacent unit or units were inspected for a bedbug infestation and found to be free of a bedbug infestation. (Me. Rev. Stat. Ann. § 6021-A)

Smoking policy. Landlord must give tenant written disclosure stating whether smoking is prohibited on the premises, allowed on the entire premises, or allowed in limited areas of the premises. If the landlord allows smoking in limited areas on the premises, the notice must identify the areas on the premises where smoking is allowed. Disclosure must be in the lease or separate written notice, landlord must disclose before tenant signs a lease or pays a deposit, and must obtain a written acknowledgment of notification from the tenant. (14 Me. Rev. Stat. Ann. § 6030-E)

Maryland

Md. Code Ann., [Real Prop.] § 8-203.1
Habitation: *Md. Code Ann., [Real Prop.] § 8-208*
Owner disclosure: *Md. Code Ann., [Real Prop.] § 8-210*

Move-in checklist required? Yes. Before collecting a deposit, landlord must supply a receipt with details on move-in and move-out inspections, and the receipt must be part of the lease.

Habitation: A lease must include a statement that the premises will be made available in a condition permitting habitation, with reasonable safety, if that is the agreement, or if that is not the agreement, a statement of the agreement concerning the condition of the premises; and the landlord's and the tenant's specific obligations as to heat, gas, electricity, water, and repair of the premises. (Md. Code Ann. [Real Prop.] § 8-208)

Owner or agent identity: The landlord must include in a lease or post the name and address of the landlord; or the person, if any, authorized to accept notice or service of process on behalf of the landlord. (Md. Code Ann. [Real Prop.] § 8-210)

Massachusetts

186 Mass. Gen. Laws §§ 15B(2)(c), 21

Move-in checklist required? Yes, if landlord collects a security deposit.

Insurance: Upon tenant's request and within 15 days, landlord must furnish the name of the company insuring the property against loss or damage by fire and the amount of insurance provided by each such

Required Landlord Disclosures (continued)

company and the name of any person who would receive payment for a loss covered by such insurance.

Michigan

Stutelberg v. Practical Management Co., 245 N.W.2d 737 (1976); Mich. Comp. Laws §§ 554.601b, 554.608, 554.634

Nonrefundable fees permitted? Yes.

Move-in checklist required? Yes. However, the requirement does not need to be included in the rental agreement. (Mich. Comp. Laws § 554.608)

Owner or agent identity: A rental agreement must include the name and address at which notice can be given to the landlord. (Mich. Comp. Laws § 554.634)

Truth in Renting Act: A rental agreement must also state in a prominent place in type not smaller than the size of 12-point type, or in legible print with letters not smaller than 1/8 inch, a notice in substantially the following form: "NOTICE: Michigan law establishes rights and obligations for parties to rental agreements. This agreement is required to comply with the Truth in Renting Act. If you have a question about the interpretation or legality of a provision of this agreement, you may want to seek assistance from a lawyer or other qualified person." (Mich. Comp. Laws § 554.634)

Rights of domestic violence victims: A rental agreement or lease may contain a provision stating, "A tenant who has a reasonable apprehension of present danger to him or her or his or her child from domestic violence, sexual assault, or stalking may have special statutory rights to seek a release of rental obligation under MCL 554.601b." If the rental agreement or lease does not contain such a provision, the landlord must post an identical written notice visible to a reasonable person in the landlord's property management office, or deliver written notice to the tenant when the lease or rental agreement is signed. (Mich. Comp. Laws §§ 554.601b)

Minnesota

Minn. Stat. Ann. §§ 504B.181, 504B.195, 504B.171

Owner or agent identity: Landlord must disclose to the tenant in writing at or before the commencement of the tenancy the name and address of the person authorized to manage the premises, and an owner of the premises or a person authorized to act for and on behalf of the owner for the purpose of service of process and for the purpose of receiving notices and demands. (Minn. Stat. Ann. § 504B.181)

Outstanding inspection orders, condemnation orders, or declarations that the property is unfit: The landlord must disclose the existence of any such orders or declarations before the tenant signs a lease or pays a security deposit. (Minn. Stat. Ann. § 504B.195)

Buildings in financial distress: Once a landlord has received notice of a deed cancellation or notice of foreclosure, landlord may not enter into a periodic tenancy where the tenancy term is more than two months, or a lease where the lease extends beyond the redemption period (other restrictions may apply). (Minn. Stat. Ann. § 504B.151)

Landlord and tenant mutual promises: This mutual promise must appear in every lease or rental agreement: "Landlord and tenant promise that neither will unlawfully allow within the premises, common areas, or curtilage of the premises (property boundaries): controlled substances, prostitution or prostitution-related activity; stolen property or property obtained by robbery; or an act of domestic violence, as defined by MN Statute Section 504B.206 (1)(e), against a tenant, licensee, or any authorized occupant. They further promise that the aforementioned areas will not be used by themselves or anyone acting under their control to manufacture, sell, give away, barter, deliver, exchange, distribute, purchase, or possess a controlled substance in violation of any criminal provision of chapter 152."

Mississippi

No disclosure statutes.

Missouri

Mo. Rev. Stat. §§ 441.236, 535.185

Required Landlord Disclosures (continued)

Meth Labs: Landlord who knows that the premises were used to produce methamphetamine must disclose this fact to prospective tenants, irrespective of whether the people involved in the production were convicted for such production. (Mo. Rev. Stat. § 441.236)

Owner or agent identity: Landlord must disclose to the tenant in writing at or before the commencement of the tenancy the name and address of the person authorized to manage the premises, and an owner of the premises or a person authorized to act for and on behalf of the owner for the purpose of service of process and for the purpose of receiving notices and demands. (Mo. Rev. Stat. § 535.185)

Montana

Mont. Code Ann. §§ 70-24-301, 70-25-101(4), 70-25-206

Nonrefundable fees permitted? No. A fee or charge for cleaning and damages, no matter how designated, is presumed to be a security deposit. (Not a clear statement that such a fee isn't nonrefundable, but by implication it must be.)

Move-in checklists required? Yes, checklists are required when landlords collect a security deposit.

Owner or agent identity: A landlord or a person authorized to enter into a rental agreement on his behalf must disclose to the tenant in writing at or before the commencement of the tenancy the name and address of the person authorized to manage the premises; and the owner of the premises or a person authorized to act for the owner for the purpose of service of process and receiving notices and demands.

Nebraska

Neb. Rev. Stat. §§ 76-1417

Owner or agent identity: The landlord or any person authorized to enter into a rental agreement on his or her behalf must disclose to the tenant in writing at or before the commencement of the tenancy the name and address of the person authorized to manage the premises, and an owner of the premises or a person authorized to act for and on behalf of the owner

for the purpose of service of process and receiving notices and demands.

Nevada

Nev. Rev. Stat. Ann. §§ 118A.200, 118A.275

Nonrefundable fees permitted? Yes. Lease must explain fees that are required and the purposes for which they are required.

Move-in checklist required? Yes. Lease must include tenants' rights to a checklist and a signed record of the inventory and condition of the premises under the exclusive custody and control of the tenant.

Nuisance and flying the flag: Lease must include a summary of the provisions of NRS 202.470 (penalties for permitting or maintaining a nuisance); information regarding the procedure a tenant may use to report to the appropriate authorities a nuisance, a violation of a building, safety, or health code or regulation; and information regarding the right of the tenant to engage in the display of the flag of the United States, as set forth in NRS 118A.325. (Nev. Rev. Stat. Ann. § 118A.200)

Foreclosure proceedings: Landlord must disclose to any prospective tenant, in writing, whether the premises to be rented is the subject of a foreclosure proceeding (disclosure need not be in the lease). (Nev. Rev. Stat. Ann. § 118A.275)

New Hampshire

N.H. Rev. Stat. Ann. § 540-A:6

Move-in checklist required? Yes. Landlord must inform tenant that if tenant finds any conditions in the rental in need of repair, tenant may note them on the security deposit receipt or other writing. Not a true checklist.

New Jersey

N.J. Stat. Ann. §§ 46:8-44, 46:8-45, 46:8-46, 46:8-50, N.J. Admin. Code § 5:10-27.1

Flood zone: Prior to move-in, landlord must inform tenant if rental is in a flood zone or area (does not apply to properties containing two or fewer dwelling

Required Landlord Disclosures (continued)

units, or to owner-occupied properties of three or fewer units). (N.J. Stat. Ann. § 46:8-50)

Truth in Renting Act: Except in buildings of 2 or fewer units, and owner-occupied premises of 3 or fewer units, landlord must distribute to new tenants at or prior to move-in the Department of Community Affairs' statement of legal rights and responsibilities of tenants and landlords of rental dwelling units (Spanish also). (N.J.S.A. §§ 46:8-44, 46:8-45, 46:8-46)

Child protection windowguards: Landlords of multi-family properties must include information in the lease about tenants' rights to request windowguards. The Legislature's Model Lease and Notice clause reads as follows: "The owner (landlord) is required by law to provide, install and maintain window guards in the apartment if a child or children 10 years of age or younger is, or will be, living in the apartment or is, or will be, regularly present there for a substantial period of time if the tenant gives the owner (landlord) a written request that the window guards be installed. The owner (landlord) is also required, upon the written request of the tenant, to provide, install and maintain window guards in the hallways to which persons in the tenant's unit have access without having to go out of the building. If the building is a condominium, cooperative or mutual housing building, the owner (landlord) of the apartment is responsible for installing and maintaining window guards in the apartment and the association is responsible for installing and maintaining window guards in hallway windows. Window guards are only required to be provided in first floor windows where the window sill is more than six feet above grade or there are other hazardous conditions that make installation of window guards necessary to protect the safety of children." The notice must be conspicuous and in boldface type. (N.J. Admin. Code § 5:10-27.1)

New Mexico

N.M. Stat. Ann. § 47-8-19

Owner or agent identity: Landlord must disclose to the tenant in writing at or before the commence-

ment of the tenancy the name and address of the person authorized to manage the premises, and an owner of the premises or a person authorized to act for and on behalf of the owner for the purpose of service of process and for the purpose of receiving notices and demands.

New York

N.Y. ECL § 27-2405

Air contamination: Landlord who receives a government report showing that air in the building has, or may have, concentrations of volatile organic compounds (VOCs) that exceed governmental guidelines must give written notice to prospective and current tenants. The notice must appear in at least 12-point boldface type on the first page of the lease or rental agreement. It must read as follows: "NOTIFICATION OF TEST RESULTS: The property has been tested, for contamination of indoor air: test results and additional information are available upon request."

North Carolina

N.C. Stat. Ann. § 42-46

Nonrefundable fees permitted? Yes. Fee policy must be stated in the rental agreement. Landlord may collect only one of the following, when specific conditions are met: Complaint filing fee, court appearance fee, and second trial fee. Failure to pay the fees cannot support a termination notice. (N.C. Stat. Ann § 42-46)

North Dakota

N.D. Cent. Code § 47-16-07.2

Move-in checklist required? Yes. Landlord must give tenant a statement describing the condition of the premises when tenant signs the rental agreement. Both parties must sign the statement. (N.D. Cent. Code § 47-16-07.2)

Ohio

Ohio Rev. Code Ann. § 5321.18

Owner or agent identity: Every written rental agreement must contain the name and address of

Required Landlord Disclosures (continued)

the owner and the name and address of the owner's agent, if any. If the owner or the owner's agent is a corporation, partnership, limited partnership, association, trust, or other entity, the address must be the principal place of business in the county in which the residential property is situated. If there is no place of business in such county, then its principal place of business in this state must be disclosed, including the name of the person in charge thereof.

Oklahoma

41 Okla. Stat. Ann. §§ 113a, 116

Flooding: If the premises to be rented has been flooded within the past five (5) years and such fact is known to the landlord, the landlord shall include such information prominently and in writing as part of any written rental agreements. (41 Okla. Stat. Ann. § 113a)

Owner information: As a part of any rental agreement the lessor shall prominently and in writing identify what person at what address is entitled to accept service or notice under this act. Landlord must disclose to the tenant in writing at or before the commencement of the tenancy the name and address of the person authorized to manage the premises, and an owner of the premises or a person authorized to act for and on behalf of the owner for the purpose of service of process and receiving notices and demands. (41 Okla. Stat. Ann. § 116)

Oregon

Or. Rev. Stat. §§ 30.701(5), 90.228, 90.302, 90.305, 90.310, 90.315, 90.316, 90.317, 90.318, 90.220, 90.367

Nonrefundable fees permitted? Landlords' written rules may not provide for tenant fees, except for specified events as they arise, including a late rent payment; tenant's late payment of a utility or service charge; a dishonored check, pursuant to Ore. Rev. Stat. § 30.701(5); failure to clean up pet waste in areas other than tenant's unit; failure to clean up garbage and rubbish (outside tenant's dwelling unit); failure to clean pet waste of a service or companion animal from areas other than the dwelling unit; parking violations and improper use of vehicles within the

premises; smoking in a designated nonsmoking area; keeping an unauthorized pet capable of inflicting damage on persons or property; and tampering or disabling a smoke detector.

Owner or agent identity: Landlord must disclose to the tenant in writing at or before the commencement of the tenancy the name and address of the person authorized to manage the premises, and an owner of the premises or a person authorized to act for and on behalf of the owner for the purpose of service of process and for the purpose of receiving notices and demands. (Ore. Rev. Stat. § 90.305)

Legal proceedings: If at the time of the execution of a rental agreement for a dwelling unit in premises containing no more than four dwelling units the premises are subject to any of the following circumstances, the landlord must disclose that circumstance to the tenant in writing before the execution of the rental agreement: (a) Any outstanding notice of default under a trust deed, mortgage, or contract of sale, or notice of trustee's sale under a trust deed; (b) Any pending suit to foreclose a mortgage, trust deed, or vendor's lien under a contract of sale; (c) Any pending declaration of forfeiture or suit for specific performance of a contract of sale; or (d) Any pending proceeding to foreclose a tax lien. (Ore. Rev. Stat. § 90.310)

Utilities: The landlord must disclose to the tenant in writing at or before the commencement of the tenancy any utility or service that the tenant pays directly to a utility or service provider that directly benefits the landlord or other tenants. A tenant's payment for a given utility or service benefits the landlord or other tenants if the utility or service is delivered to any area other than the tenant's dwelling unit. A landlord may require a tenant to pay to the landlord a utility or service charge that has been billed by a utility or service provider to the landlord for utility or service provided directly to the tenant's dwelling unit or to a common area available to the tenant as part of the tenancy. A utility or service charge that shall be assessed to a tenant for a common area must be described in the

Required Landlord Disclosures (continued)

written rental agreement separately and distinctly from such a charge for the tenant's dwelling unit. Unless the method of allocating the charges to the tenant is described in the tenant's written rental agreement, the tenant may require that the landlord give the tenant a copy of the provider's bill as a condition of paying the charges. (Ore. Rev. Stat. § 90.315)

Recycling: In a city or the county within the urban growth boundary of a city that has implemented multifamily recycling service, a landlord who has five or more residential dwelling units on a single premises must notify new tenants at the time of entering into a rental agreement of the opportunity to recycle. (Ore. Rev. Stat. § 90.318)

Smoking policy. Landlord must disclose the smoking policy for the premises, by stating whether smoking is prohibited on the premises, allowed on the entire premises, or allowed in limited areas. If landlord allows smoking in limited areas, the disclosure must identify those areas. (Ore. Rev. Stat. § 90.220)

Carbon monoxide alarm instructions: If rental contains a CO source (a heater, fireplace, appliance, or cooking source that uses coal, kerosene, petroleum products, wood, or other fuels that emit carbon monoxide as a byproduct of combustion; or an attached garage with an opening that communicates directly with a living space), landlord must install one or more CO monitors and give tenant written instructions for testing the alarm(s), before tenant takes possession. (Ore. Rev. Stat. §§ 90.316, 90.317)

Flood zone: If a dwelling unit is located in a 100-year flood plain, the landlord must provide notice in the dwelling unit rental agreement that the dwelling unit is located within the flood plain. If a landlord fails to provide a notice as required under this section, and the tenant of the dwelling unit suffers an uninsured loss due to flooding, the tenant may recover from the landlord the lesser of the actual damages for the uninsured loss or two months' rent. (Ore. Rev. Stat. § 90.228)

Renters' insurance: Landlord may require tenants to maintain liability insurance (certain low-income and subsidized tenancies excepted), but only if the landlord obtains and maintains comparable liability insurance and provides documentation to any tenant who requests the documentation, orally or in writing. The landlord may provide documentation to a tenant in person, by mail, or by posting in a common area or office. The documentation may consist of a current certificate of coverage. Any landlord who requires tenants to obtain renters' insurance must disclose the requirement and amount in writing prior to entering into a new tenancy, and may require the tenant to provide documentation before the tenancy begins. (Ore. Rev. Stat. § 90.367)

Homeowner Assessments: If landlord wants to pass on homeowners' association assessments that are imposed on anyone moving into or out of the unit, the written rental agreement must include this requirement. Landlord must give tenants a copy of each assessment before charging the tenant. (Ore. Rev. Stat. § 90.302)

Pennsylvania

No disclosure statutes.

Rhode Island

R.I. Gen. Laws §§ 34-18-20, 34-18-22.1

Owner disclosure: Landlord must disclose to the tenant in writing at or before the commencement of the tenancy the name and address of the person authorized to manage the premises, and an owner of the premises or a person authorized to act for and on behalf of the owner for the purpose of service of process and for the purpose of receiving notices and demands. (R.I. Gen. Laws § 34-18-20)

Code violations: Before entering into any residential rental agreement, landlord must inform a prospective tenant of any outstanding minimum housing code violations that exist on the building that is the subject of the rental agreement. (R.I. Gen. Laws § 34-18-22.1)

Notice of Foreclosure: A landlord who becomes delinquent on a mortgage securing real estate upon which the rental is located for a period of 120 days must notify the tenant that the property may be

Required Landlord Disclosures (continued)

subject to foreclosure; and until the foreclosure occurs, the tenant must continue to pay rent to the landlord as provided under the rental agreement.

South Carolina

S.C. Code Ann. §§ 27-40-410, 27-40-420

Owner or agent identity: Landlord must disclose to the tenant in writing at or before the commencement of the tenancy the name and address of the person authorized to manage the premises, and an owner of the premises or a person authorized to act for and on behalf of the owner for the purpose of service of process and for the purpose of receiving notices and demands. (S.C. Code Ann. § 27-40-420)

Unequal security deposits: If landlord rents five or more adjoining units on the premises, and imposes different standards for calculating deposits required of tenants, landlord must, before a tenancy begins, post in a conspicuous place a statement explaining the standards by which the various deposits are calculated (or, landlord may give the tenant the written statement). (S.C. Code Ann. § 27-40-410)

South Dakota

S.D. Codified Laws Ann. § 43-32-30

Meth labs: Landlord who has actual knowledge of the existence of any prior manufacturing of methamphetamines on the premises must disclose that information to any lessee or any person who may become a lessee. If the residential premises consists of two or more housing units, the disclosure requirements apply only to the unit where there is knowledge of the existence of any prior manufacturing of methamphetamines.

Tennessee

Tenn. Code Ann. § 66-28-302, 66-28-403

Owner or agent identity: The landlord or any person authorized to enter into a rental agreement on the landlord's behalf must disclose to the tenant in writing at or before the commencement of the tenancy the name and address of the agent authorized to manage the premises, and an owner of the premises or a person or agent authorized to act for and on behalf of the owner for the acceptance of service of process and for receipt of notices and demands. (Tenn. Code Ann. § 66-28-302)

Showing rental to prospective tenants: Landlord may enter to show the premises to prospective renters during the final 30 days of a tenancy (with 24 hours' notice), but only if this right of access is set forth in the rental agreement or lease. (Tenn. Code Ann. § 66-28-403)

Texas

Tex. Prop. Code Ann. §§ 92.201, 92.159, 92.056, 92.0161, 92.103, 92.0131, 92.008

Nonrefundable fees permitted? Yes. (*Holmes v. Canlen Management Corp.*, 542 S.W.2d 199 (1976))

Owner or agent identity: In the lease, other writing, or posted on the property, landlord must disclose the name and address of the property's owner and, if an entity located off-site from the dwelling is primarily responsible for managing the dwelling, the name and street address of the management company. (Tex. Prop. Code Ann. § 92.201)

Security device requests: If landlord wants tenant requests concerning security devices to be in writing, this requirement must be in the lease in boldface type or underlined. (Tex. Prop. Code Ann. § 92.159)

Return of security deposit: A requirement that a tenant give advance notice of moving out as a condition for refunding the security deposit is effective only if the requirement is in the lease, underlined or printed in conspicuous bold print. (Tex. Prop. Code Ann. § 92.103)

Domestic violence victims' rights: Victims of sexual abuse or assault on the premises may break a lease, after complying with specified procedures, without responsibility for future rent. Tenants will be responsible for any unpaid back rent, but only if the lease includes the following statement, or one substantially like it: "Tenants may have special statutory rights to terminate the lease early in certain situations

Required Landlord Disclosures (continued)

involving family violence or a military deployment or transfer." (Tex. Prop. Code Ann. § 92.016)

Tenant's rights when landlord fails to repair: A lease must contain language in underlined or bold print that informs the tenant of the remedies available when the landlord fails to repair a problem that materially affects the physical health or safety of an ordinary tenant. These rights include the right to repair and deduct; terminate the lease; and obtain a judicial order that the landlord make the repair, reduce the rent, pay the tenant damages (including a civil penalty), and pay the tenant's court and attorneys' fees. (Tex. Prop. Code Ann. § 92.056)

Landlord's towing or parking rules and policies: For tenants in multiunit properties, if the landlord has vehicle towing or parking rules or policies that apply to the tenant, the landlord must give the tenant a copy of the rules or policies before the lease agreement is signed. The copy must be signed by the tenant, included in the lease or rental agreement, or be made an attachment to either. If included, the clause must be titled "Parking" or "Parking Rules" and be capitalized, underlined, or printed in bold print. (Tex. Prop. Code Ann. § 92.0131)

Electric service interruption. Landlord who submeters electric service, or who allocates master metered electricity according to a prorated system, may interrupt tenant's electricity service if tenant fails to pay the bill, but only after specific notice and according to a complex procedure. Exceptions for ill tenants and during extreme weather. (Tex. Prop. Code Ann. § 92.008(h))

Utah

Utah Code § 57-22-4

Move-in checklists required? Yes. Landlords must give prospective renters a written inventory of the condition of the residential rental unit, excluding ordinary wear and tear; give the renter a form to document the condition of the residential rental and allow the resident a reasonable time after the renter's occupancy of the unit to complete and return the form; or provide the prospective renter an opportunity to conduct a walkthrough inspection of the rental. (Utah Code Ann. § 57-22-4)

Nonrefundable fees permitted? Yes. By custom, if there is a written agreement and if any part of the deposit is nonrefundable, it must be so stated in writing to the renter at the time the deposit is taken.

Vermont

No disclosure statutes.

Virginia

Va. Code Ann. §§ 55-226.2, 55-248.11:1, 55-248.11:2, 55-248.12, 55-248.12:1, 55-248.12:2, 55-248.16

Move-in checklist required? Yes. Within 5 days of move-in, landlord or tenant or both together must prepare a written report detailing the condition of the premises. Landlord must disclose within this report the known presence of mold.

Owner or agent identity: Landlord must disclose to the tenant in writing at or before the commencement of the tenancy the name and address of the person authorized to manage the premises, and an owner of the premises or a person authorized to act for and on behalf of the owner for the purpose of service of process and for the purpose of receiving notices and demands. (Va. Code Ann. § 55-248.12)

Military zone: The landlord of property in any locality in which a military air installation is located, or any person authorized to enter into a rental agreement on his behalf, must provide to a prospective tenant a written disclosure that the property is located in a noise zone or accident potential zone, or both, as designated by the locality on its official zoning map. (Va. Code Ann. § 55-248.12:1)

Mold: Move-in inspection report must include whether there is any visible evidence of mold (deemed correct unless tenant objects within five days); if evidence is present, tenant may terminate or not move in. If tenant stays, landlord must remediate the mold condition within five business

Required Landlord Disclosures (continued)

days, reinspect, and issue a new report indicating that there is no evidence of mold. (Va. Code Ann. § 55-248.11:2) If evidence of mold appears during the tenancy, landlord must promptly remediate, reinspect, and make available to the tenant copies of any available written information on how to get rid of mold. (Va. Code Ann. § 55-248.16)

Ratio utility billing: Landlord who uses a ratio utility billing service, who intends to collect monthly billing and other administrative and late fees, must disclose these fees in a written rental agreement. (Va. Code Ann. § 55-226.2)

Condominium plans: If an application for registration as a condominium or cooperative has been filed with the Real Estate Board, or if there is within six months an existing plan for tenant displacement resulting from demolition or substantial rehabilitation of the property, or conversion of the rental property to office, hotel, or motel use or planned unit development, the landlord or any person authorized to enter into a rental agreement on his behalf must disclose that information in writing to any prospective tenant. (Va. Code Ann. § 55-248.12(C))

Defective drywall: Landlords who know of the presence of unrepaired defective drywall in the rental must disclose this before the tenant signs a lease or rental agreement. (Va. Code Ann. § 55-248.12:2.)

Washington

Wash. Rev. Code Ann. §§ 59.18.060, 59.18.257, 59.18.260, 59.18.285

Move-in checklists required? Yes, checklists are required when landlords collect a security deposit. If landlord fails to provide checklist, landlord is liable to the tenant for the amount of the deposit.

Nonrefundable fees permitted? Yes. If landlord collects a nonrefundable fee, the rental document must clearly specify that it is nonrefundable.

Fire protection: At the time the lease is signed, landlord must provide fire protection and safety information, including whether the building has a smoking policy, an emergency notification plan, or an evacuation plan. (Wash. Rev. Code Ann. § 59.18.060)

Owner or agent identity: In the rental document or posted conspicuously on the premises, landlord must designate to the tenant the name and address of the person who is the landlord by a statement on the rental agreement or by a notice conspicuously posted on the premises. If the person designated does not reside in Washington, landlord must also designate a person who resides in the county to act as an agent for the purposes of service of notices and process. (Wash. Rev. Code Ann. § 59.18.060)

Mold: At the time the lease is signed, landlord must provide tenant with information provided or approved by the department of health about the health hazards associated with exposure to indoor mold. (Wash. Rev. Code Ann. § 59.18.060)

Screening criteria. Before obtaining any information about an applicant, landlord must provide (in writing or by posting) the type of information to be accessed, criteria to be used to evaluate the application, and (for consumer reports) the name and address of the consumer reporting agency to be used, including the applicant's rights to obtain a free copy of the report and dispute its accuracy. Landlord must advise tenants whether landlord will accept a comprehensive reusable tenant screening report done by a consumer reporting agency (in which case the landlord may not charge the tenant a fee for a screening report). If landlord maintains a website that advertises residential rentals, the home page must include this information. (Wash. Rev. Code Ann. § 59.18.257)

Tenant screening fee: Landlords who do their own screening may charge a fee for time and costs to obtain background information, but only if they provide the information explained in "Screening Criteria," above. (Wash. Rev. Code Ann. § 59.18.257)

West Virginia

W.Va. Code § 37-6A-1(14)

Nonrefundable fees permitted? Nonrefundable fee must be expressly agreed to in writing.

Required Landlord Disclosures (continued)

Wisconsin

Wis. Admin. Code §§ 134.04, 134.06, 134.09

Wis. Stat. Ann. § 704.07(2)(bm), 704.05, 704.05 (5), 704.08

Move-in checklist required? Yes. Tenant has a right to inspect the rental and give landlord a list of defects, and to receive a list of damages charged to the prior tenant. Tenant has 7 days after start of the tenancy to return the list to the landlord.

Owner or agent identity: Landlord must disclose to the tenant in writing, at or before the time a rental agreement is signed, the name and address of: the person or persons authorized to collect or receive rent and manage and maintain the premises, and who can readily be contacted by the tenant; and the owner of the premises or other person authorized to accept service of legal process and other notices and demands on behalf of the owner. The address must be an address within the state at which service of process can be made in person. (Wis. Admin. Code § 134.04)

Nonstandard rental provisions: If landlord wants to enter premises for reasons not specified by law, landlord must disclose the provision in a separate written document entitled "NONSTANDARD RENTAL PROVISIONS" before the rental agreement is signed. (Wis. Admin. Code § 134.09)

Uncorrected code violations: Before signing a rental contract or accepting a security deposit, the landlord must disclose to the tenant any uncorrected code violation of which the landlord is actually aware, which affects the dwelling unit or a common area and poses a significant threat to the tenant's health or safety. "Disclosure" consists of showing prospective tenants the portions of the building affected, as well as the notices themselves. (Wis. Stat. §§ 704.07(2) (bm), 134.04)

Habitability deficiencies: Landlord must disclose serious problems that affect the rental unit's habitability. (Wis. Admin. Code § 134.04)

Utility charges: If charges for water, heat or electricity are not included in the rent, the landlord must disclose this fact to the tenant before entering into a rental agreement or accepting any earnest money or security deposit from the prospective tenant. If individual dwelling units and common areas are not separately metered, and if the charges are not included in the rent, the landlord must disclose the basis on which charges for utility services will be allocated among individual dwelling units. (Wis. Admin. Code § 134.04)

Disposing of abandoned property: If landlord intends to immediately dispose of any tenant property left behind after move-out, landlord must notify tenant at the time lease is signed. (But landlord must hold prescription medications and medical equipment for seven days, and must give notice before disposing of vehicles or manufactured homes to owner and any known secured party.) (Wis. Stat. § 704.05 (5))

Wyoming

Wyo. Stat. § 1-21-1207

Nonrefundable fees permitted? Yes. If any portion of the deposit is not refundable, rental agreement must include this information and tenant must be told before paying a deposit.

State Laws on Landlord's Access to Rental Property

This is a synopsis of state laws that specify circumstances when a landlord may enter rental premises and the amount of notice required for such entry.

State	State Law Citation	Amount of Notice Required in Nonemergency Situations	To Deal With an Emergency	To Inspect the Premises	To Make Repairs, Alterations, or Improvements	To Show Property to Prospective Tenants or Purchasers	During Tenant's Extended Absence
			Reasons Landlord May Enter				
Alabama	Ala. Code §§ 35-9A-303, 35-9A-423	Two days	✓	✓	✓	✓	✓
Alaska	Alaska Stat. §§ 34.03.140, 34.03.230	24 hours	✓	✓	✓	✓	✓
Arizona	Ariz. Rev. Stat. Ann. § 33-1343	Two days (written or oral notice); notice period does not apply, and tenant's consent is assumed, if entry is pursuant to tenant's request for maintenance as prescribed in Ariz. Rev. Stat. § 33-1341, paragraph 8	✓	✓	✓	✓	
Arkansas	Ark. Code Ann. § 18-17-602	No notice specified		✓	✓	✓	
California	Cal. Civ. Code § 1954	24 hours (48 hours for initial move-out inspection)	✓	✓	✓	✓	
Colorado	No statute						
Connecticut	Conn. Gen. Stat. Ann. §§ 47a-16 to 47a-16a	Reasonable notice	✓	✓	✓	✓	
Delaware	Del. Code Ann. tit. 25, §§ 5509, 5510	Two days	✓	✓	✓	✓	
Dist. of Columbia	D.C. Code Ann. § 42-3505.31	48 hours	✓	✓	✓	✓	✓
Florida	Fla. Stat. Ann. § 83.53	12 hours	✓	✓	✓	✓	✓
Georgia	No statute						
Hawaii	Haw. Rev. Stat. §§ 521-53, 521-70(b)	Two days	✓	✓	✓	✓	✓
Idaho	No statute						
Illinois	No statute						
Indiana	Ind. Code Ann. § 32-31-5-6	Reasonable notice	✓	✓	✓	✓	
Iowa	Iowa Code Ann. §§ 562A.19, 562A.28, 562A.29	24 hours	✓	✓	✓	✓	✓
Kansas	Kan. Stat. Ann. §§ 58-2557, 58-2565	Reasonable notice	✓	✓	✓	✓	✓
Kentucky	Ky. Rev. Stat. Ann. §§ 383.615, 383.670	Two days	✓	✓	✓	✓	✓
Louisiana	La. Civ. Code art. 2693	No notice specified			✓		

State Laws on Landlord's Access to Rental Property (continued)

State	State Law Citation	Amount of Notice Required in Nonemergency Situations	Reasons Landlord May Enter				
			To Deal With an Emergency	To Inspect the Premises	To Make Repairs, Alterations, or Improvements	To Show Property to Prospective Tenants or Purchasers	During Tenant's Extended Absence
Maine	Me. Rev. Stat. Ann. tit. 14, § 6025	24 hours	✓	✓	✓	✓	
Maryland	No statute						
Massachusetts	Mass. Gen. Laws Ann. ch. 186, § 15B(1)(a)	No notice specified	✓	✓	✓	✓	
Michigan	No statute						
Minnesota	Minn. Stat. Ann. § 504B.211	Reasonable notice	✓	✓	✓	✓	
Mississippi	No statute						
Missouri	No statute						
Montana	Mont. Code Ann. §§ 70-24-312, 70-24-426	24 hours	✓	✓	✓	✓	✓
Nebraska	Neb. Rev. Stat. §§ 76-1423, 76-1432	One day	✓	✓	✓	✓	✓
Nevada	Nev. Rev. Stat. Ann. § 118A.330	24 hours	✓	✓	✓	✓	
New Hampshire	N.H. Rev. Stat. Ann. § 540-A:3	Notice that is adequate under the circumstances	✓	✓	✓	✓	
New Jersey	N.J.A.C. 5:10-5.1	One day, by custom; in buildings with three or more units, one day (by regulation)	✓	✓	✓	✓	
New Mexico	N.M. Stat. Ann. §§ 47-8-24, 47-8-34	24 hours	✓	✓	✓	✓	✓
New York	No statute						
North Carolina	No statute						
North Dakota	N.D. Cent. Code § 47-16-07.3	Reasonable notice	✓	✓	✓	✓	
Ohio	Ohio Rev. Code Ann. §§ 5321.04(A)(8), 5321.05(B)	24 hours	✓	✓	✓	✓	
Oklahoma	Okla. Stat. Ann. tit. 41, § 128	One day	✓	✓	✓	✓	
Oregon	Or. Rev. Stat. §§ 90.322, 90.410	24 hours	✓	✓	✓	✓	✓
Pennsylvania	No statute						
Rhode Island	R.I. Gen. Laws § 34-18-26	Two days	✓	✓	✓	✓	✓
South Carolina	S.C. Code Ann. §§ 27-40-530, 27-40-730	24 hours	✓	✓	✓	✓	
South Dakota	No statute						

	State Laws on Landlord's Access to Rental Property (continued)						
			Reasons Landlord May Enter				
State	**State Law Citation**	**Amount of Notice Required in Nonemergency Situations**	**To Deal With an Emergency**	**To Inspect the Premises**	**To Make Repairs, Alterations, or Improvements**	**To Show Property to Prospective Tenants or Purchasers**	**During Tenant's Extended Absence**
Tennessee	Tenn. Code Ann. §§ 66-28-403, 66-28-507	24 hours (applies only within the final thirty days of the rental agreement term, when landlord intends to show the premises to prospective renters and this right of access is set forth in the rental agreement)	✓	✓	✓	✓	✓
Texas	No statute						
Utah	Utah Code Ann. §§ 57-22-4, 57-22-5(2)(c)	24 hours, unless rental agreement specifies otherwise	✓		✓		
Vermont	Vt. Stat. Ann. tit. 9, § 4460	48 hours	✓	✓	✓	✓	
Virginia	Va. Code Ann. §§ 55-248.18, 55-248.33	For routine maintenance only: 24 hours, but no notice needed if entry follows tenant's request for maintenance	✓	✓	✓	✓	✓
Washington	Wash. Rev. Code Ann. § 59.18.150	Two days; one day to show property to actual or prospective tenants or buyers	✓	✓	✓	✓	
West Virginia	No statute						
Wisconsin	Wis. Stat. Ann. § 704.05(2)	Advance notice	✓	✓	✓	✓	✓
Wyoming	No statute						

How to Use the Downloadable Forms on the Nolo Website

This book comes with e-forms that you can access online at:

www.nolo.com/back-of-book/LEAR.html

To use the files, your computer must have specific software programs installed. Here is a list of types of files provided by this book, as well as the software programs you'll need to access them.

- **RTF.** You can open, edit, save, and print these form files with most word processing programs such as Microsoft *Word*, Windows *WordPad*, and recent versions of *WordPerfect*.
- **PDF.** You can view these files with Adobe *Reader*, free software from www.adobe.com. Government PDFs are sometimes fillable using your computer, but most PDFs are designed to be printed out and completed by hand.

Editing RTFs

Here are some general instructions about editing RTF forms in your word processing program. Refer to the book's instructions and sample agreements for help about what should go in each blank.

- **Underlines.** Underlines indicate where to enter information. After filling in the needed text, delete the underline. In most word processing programs you can do this by highlighting the underlined portion and typing CTRL-U.

- **Bracketed and italicized text.** Bracketed and italicized text indicates instructions. Be sure to remove all instructional text before you finalize your document.
- **Optional text.** Optional text gives you the choice to include or exclude text. Delete any optional text you don't want to use. Renumber numbered items, if necessary.
- **Alternative text.** Alternative text gives you the choice between two or more text options. Delete those options you don't want to use. Renumber numbered items, if necessary.
- **Signature lines.** Signature lines should appear on a page with at least some text from the document itself.

Every word processing program uses different commands to open, format, save, and print documents, so refer to your software's help documents for help using your program. Nolo cannot provide technical support for questions about how to use your computer or your software.

CAUTION

In accordance with U.S. copyright laws, the forms provided by this book are for your personal use only.

List of Forms Available on the Nolo Website

Use the tables below to find the file name for each form. All forms listed are available for download at: **www.nolo.com/back-of-book/LEAR.html**

Forms in RTF Format	
Form Title	**File Name**
Notice of Conditional Acceptance Based on Credit Report or Other Information	Acceptance.rtf
Rental Application	Application.rtf
Consent to Contact References and Perform Credit Check	CheckConsent.rtf
Landlord/Tenant Checklist	Checklist.rtf
Notice of Denial Based on Credit Report or Other Information	Denial.rtf
Fixed-Term Residential Lease	FixedLease.rtf
Fixed-Term Residential Lease (Spanish Version)	PlazoFijo.rtf
Month-to-Month Residential Rental Agreement	MonthToMonth.rtf
Month-to-Month Residential Rental Agreement (Spanish Version)	Mensual.rtf
Move-In Letter	MoveIn.rtf
Move-Out Letter	MoveOut.rtf
Tenant's Notice of Intent to Move Out	MoveNotice.rtf
Tenant References	References.rtf

The following files are in PDF:

Forms in PDF Format	
Form Title	**File Name**
Rental Application	Application.pdf
Tenant's Notice of Intent to Move Out	MoveNotice.pdf
Protect Your Family From Lead in Your Home Pamphlet	leadpdfe.pdf
Protect Your Family From Lead in Your Home Pamphlet (Spanish Version)	leadpdfs.pdf
Disclosure of Information on Lead-Based Paint or Lead-Based Paint Hazards	lesr_eng.pdf
Disclosure of Information on Lead-Based Paint or Lead-Based Paint Hazards (Spanish Version)	spanless.pdf

Forms

Month-to-Month Residential Rental Agreement

Clause 1. Identification of Landlord and Tenant

This Agreement is entered into between _____

_____ [Tenant] and

_____ [Landlord].

Each Tenant is jointly and severally liable for the payment of rent and performance of all other terms of this Agreement.

Clause 2. Identification of Premises

Subject to the terms and conditions in this Agreement, Landlord rents to Tenant, and Tenant rents from Landlord, for residential purposes only, the premises located at _____

_____ [the premises],

together with the following furnishings and appliances: _____

_____ .

Rental of the premises also includes _____

_____

_____ .

Clause 3. Limits on Use and Occupancy

The premises are to be used only as a private residence for Tenant(s) listed in Clause 1 of this Agreement, and their minor children. Occupancy by guests for more than _____ is prohibited without Landlord's written consent and will be considered a breach of this Agreement.

Clause 4. Term of the Tenancy

The rental will begin on _____ , and continue on a month-to-month basis. Landlord may terminate the tenancy or modify the terms of this Agreement by giving the Tenant _____ days' written notice. Tenant may terminate the tenancy by giving the Landlord _____ days' written notice.

Clause 5. Payment of Rent

Regular monthly rent

Tenant will pay to Landlord a monthly rent of $_____ , payable in advance on the first day of each month, except when that day falls on a weekend or legal holiday, in which case rent is due on the next business day. Rent will be paid in the following manner unless Landlord designates otherwise:

Delivery of payment

Rent will be paid:

☐ by mail, to _____

☐ in person, at _____

Form of payment

Landlord will accept payment in these forms:

☐ personal check made payable to _____

☐ cashier's check made payable to _____

☐ credit card

☐ money order

☐ automatic credit card debit

☐ electronic funds transfer

☐ cash

Prorated first month's rent

For the period from Tenant's move-in date, _____ , through the end of the

month, Tenant will pay to Landlord the prorated monthly rent of $_____ . This amount will be

paid on or before the date the Tenant moves in.

Clause 6. Late Charges

If Tenant fails to pay the rent in full before the end of the _____ day after it's due, Tenant will pay

Landlord a late charge as follows: _____

_____ .

Landlord does not waive the right to insist on payment of the rent in full on the date it is due.

Clause 7. Returned Check and Other Bank Charges

If any check offered by Tenant to Landlord in payment of rent or any other amount due under this Agreement is

returned for lack of sufficient funds, a "stop payment," or any other reason, Tenant will pay Landlord a returned

check charge of $_____ .

Clause 8. Security Deposit

On signing this Agreement, Tenant will pay to Landlord the sum of $_____ as a security

deposit. Tenant may not, without Landlord's prior written consent, apply this security deposit to the last

month's rent or to any other sum due under this Agreement. Within _____

after Tenant has vacated the premises, returned keys, and provided Landlord with a forwarding address,

Landlord will return the deposit in full or give Tenant an itemized written statement of the reasons for, and the

dollar amount of, any of the security deposit retained by Landlord, along with a check for any deposit balance.

Clause 9. Utilities

Tenant will pay all utility charges, except for the following, which will be paid by Landlord:

_____

_____ .

Clause 10. Prohibition of Assignment and Subletting

Tenants will not sublet any part of the premises or assign this Agreement without the prior written consent of Landlord.

☐ a. Tenants shall not sublet or rent any part of the Premises for short-term stays of any duration, including but not limited to vacation rentals.

☐ b. Short-stay rentals are prohibited except as authorized by law. Any short-stay rental is expressly conditioned upon the tenants' following all regulations, laws, and other requirements as a condition to offering a short-stay rental. Failure to follow all laws, ordinances, regulations, and other requirements, including any registration requirement, will be deemed a material, noncurable breach of this Agreement and will furnish cause for termination.

Clause 11. Tenant's Maintenance Responsibilities

Tenant will: (1) keep the premises clean, sanitary, and in good condition and, upon termination of the tenancy, return the premises to Landlord in a condition identical to that which existed when Tenant took occupancy, except for ordinary wear and tear; (2) immediately notify Landlord of any defects or dangerous conditions in and about the premises of which Tenant becomes aware; and (3) reimburse Landlord, on demand by Landlord, for the cost of any repairs to the premises damaged by Tenant or Tenant's guests or business invitees through misuse or neglect.

Tenant has examined the premises, including appliances, fixtures, carpets, drapes, and paint, and has found them to be in good, safe, and clean condition and repair, except as noted in the Landlord-Tenant Checklist.

Clause 12. Repairs and Alterations by Tenant

a. Except as provided by law, or as authorized by the prior written consent of Landlord, Tenant will not make any repairs or alterations to the premises, including nailing holes in the walls or painting the rental unit.

b. Tenant will not, without Landlord's prior written consent, alter, rekey, or install any locks to the premises or install or alter any security alarm system. Tenant will provide Landlord with a key or keys capable of unlocking all such rekeyed or new locks as well as instructions on how to disarm any altered or new security alarm system.

Clause 13. Prohibition Against Violating Laws and Causing Disturbances

Tenant is entitled to quiet enjoyment of the premises. Tenant and guests or invitees will not use the premises or adjacent areas in such a way as to: (1) violate any law or ordinance, including laws prohibiting the use, possession, or sale of illegal drugs; (2) commit waste (severe property damage); or (3) create a nuisance by annoying, disturbing, inconveniencing, or interfering with the quiet enjoyment and peace and quiet of any other tenant or nearby resident.

Clause 14. Pets

No animal may be kept on the premises without Landlord's prior written consent, except animals needed by tenants who have a disability, as that term is understood by law, except for the following: _____

_____

under the following conditions: _____

_____ .

Clause 15. Landlord's Right to Access

Landlord or Landlord's agents may enter the premises in the event of an emergency, to make repairs or improvements, or to show the premises to prospective buyers or tenants. Landlord may also enter the premises to conduct an annual inspection to check for safety or maintenance problems. Except in cases of emergency, Tenant's abandonment of the premises, court order, or where it is impractical to do so, Landlord will give Tenant _____ notice before entering.

Clause 16. Extended Absences by Tenant

Tenant will notify Landlord in advance if Tenant will be away from the premises for _____ or more consecutive days. During such absence, Landlord may enter the premises at times reasonably necessary to maintain the property and inspect for damage and needed repairs.

Clause 17. Possession of the Premises

   a. *Tenant's failure to take possession.*

   If, after signing this Agreement, Tenant fails to take possession of the premises, Tenant will still be responsible for paying rent and complying with all other terms of this Agreement.

   b. *Landlord's failure to deliver possession.*

   If Landlord is unable to deliver possession of the premises to Tenant for any reason not within Landlord's control, including, but not limited to, partial or complete destruction of the premises, Tenant will have the right to terminate this Agreement upon proper notice as required by law. In such event, Landlord's liability to Tenant will be limited to the return of all sums previously paid by Tenant to Landlord.

Clause 18. Tenant Rules and Regulations

   ☐ Tenant acknowledges receipt of, and has read a copy of, tenant rules and regulations, which are labeled Attachment A and attached to and incorporated into this Agreement by this reference. Tenant understands that serious or repeated violations of the rules may be grounds for termination. Landlord may change the rules and regulations without notice.

Clause 19. Payment of Court Costs and Attorneys' Fees in a Lawsuit

   In any action or legal proceeding to enforce any part of this Agreement, the prevailing party ☐ shall not / ☐ shall recover reasonable attorneys' fees and court costs.

Clause 20. Disclosures

   Tenant acknowledges that Landlord has made the following disclosures regarding the premises:

   ☐ *Disclosure of Information on Lead-Based Paint and/or Lead-Based Paint Hazards*

   ☐ Other disclosures: _____

   _____

   _____

   _____ .

Clause 21. Authority to Receive Legal Papers

   The Landlord, any person managing the premises, and anyone designated by the Landlord are authorized to accept service of process and receive other notices and demands, which may be delivered to:

   ☐ The Landlord, at the following address: _____

   _____ .

   ☐ The manager, at the following address: _____

   _____ .

   ☐ The following person, at the following address: _____

   _____ .

Clause 22. Additional Provisions

Additional provisions are as follows: _____

_____

_____

_____

_____ .

Clause 23. Validity of Each Part

If any portion of this Agreement is held to be invalid, its invalidity will not affect the validity or enforceability of any other provision of this Agreement.

Clause 24. Grounds for Termination of Tenancy

The failure of Tenant or Tenant's guests or invitees to comply with any term of this Agreement, or the misrepresentation of any material fact on Tenant's rental application, is grounds for termination of the tenancy, with appropriate notice to Tenant and procedures as required by law.

Clause 25. Entire Agreement

This document constitutes the entire Agreement between the parties, and no promises or representations, other than those contained here and those implied by law, have been made by Landlord or Tenant. Any modifications to this Agreement must be in writing, signed by Landlord and Tenant.

_____ _____ _____
Date   Landlord or Landlord's Agent Title

_____
Street Address

_____ _____ _____ _____
City   State   Zip Code Phone

_____
Email

_____ _____ _____
Date   Tenant   Phone

_____ _____ _____
Date   Tenant   Phone

_____ _____ _____
Date   Tenant   Phone

Contrato Mensual de Arrendamiento

Cláusula 1. Identificación del Arrendador y de los Inquilinos.

Este Contrato se hace entre _____

_____ [Inquilinos] y

_____ [Arrendador]. Cada

Inquilino es conjuntamente e individualmente responsable del pago de renta y del cumplimiento de todos los

demás términos de este Contrato.

Cláusula 2. Identificación de la Propiedad.

De acuerdo con los términos y condiciones referidas en este Contrato, el Arrendador renta al Inquilino, y éste

renta del Arrendador, sólamente para residir, la propiedad ubicada en _____

_____ , [la propiedad],

junto con el mobiliario y los aparatos electrodomésticos siguientes: _____

_____

La renta de la propiedad también incluye _____

_____ .

Cláusula 3. Límitaciones en el Uso y Ocupación.

La propiedad se utilizará sólo como residencia privada por el Inquilino designado en la Cláusula 1 de este

Contrato y sus hijos menores. Está prohibido que invitados habiten la propiedad por más de _____

_____ , excepto con previo consentimiento por escrito del Arrendador. De lo contrario,

será considerado como una violación a este Contrato.

Cláusula 4. Período de Arrendamiento.

La renta comenzará el día _____ de _____ de _____ , y podrá continuarse el

arrendamiento, mediante la renovación por cada mes. El Arrendador puede terminar este Contrato o modificar

sus términos, siempre que notifique por escrito, al Inquilino, con _____

días de anticipación. El Inquilino puede terminar este Contrato, notificándoselo al Arrendador por escrito y con

_____ días de anticipación.

Cláusula 5. Renta y Fechas de Pago.

Renta Regular Mensual.

El Inquilino pagará por adelantado, una renta mensual de $ _____ , el primer día del mes; excepto

cuando éste sea en un fin de semana o en un día feriado oficial, en cuyo caso deberá ser pagada el próximo día

laboral. Si no existe otra decisión por parte del Arrendador, la renta deberá ser pagada de la manera siguiente:

Entrega de pago.

El arriendo será pagado:

☐ Por correo, dirigido a _____

☐ Personalmente, en _____

Forma de Pago.

El Arrendador recibirá los pagos en:

☐ Cheque Personal escrito en favor de _____

☐ Cheque de Caja escrito en favor de _____

☐ Tarjeta de Crédito

☐ Giro Postal

☐ Débito Automático de su Tarjeta de Crédito

☐ Efectivo

☐ Transferencia Electrónica de Fondos

Prorrateo del primer mes de renta.

Para el período comenzando con la fecha en que se mudará el Inquilino, el día _____ de _____

de _____ , hasta el fin del mes en curso, el Inquilino pagará al Arrendador la renta mensual prorratada de

$ _____ . Esta suma se pagará antes o en la fecha en que se mude el Inquilino a la propiedad.

Cláusula 6. Cobros por Mora.

Si el Inquilino falla en el pago total de la renta, antes del final del día _____ después de la fecha de

pago, tendrá que pagar costos por atrasos como se explica a continuación: _____

_____ .

El Arrendador no descartará el derecho de insistir en el pago total de la renta en la fecha debida.

Cláusula 7. Pagos por Cheques Sin Fondo y Recargos Bancarios.

En el caso de cualquier cheque, ofrecido por el Inquilino al Arrendador como pago de renta o cualquier otra

suma debida bajo este Contrato, sea regresado por insuficiencia de fondos, un "paro de pago," o cualquier otra

razón, el Inquilino deberá pagar un recargo por la cantidad de $_____ .

Cláusula 8. Depósito de Garantía.

Al firmar el presente Contrato, el Inquilino pagará al Arrendador, la cantidad de $_____ como

depósito de seguridad. Este depósito no puede aplicarse al último mes de renta o a cualquier cantidad

debida bajo este Contrato; excepto con previo consentimiento por escrito del Arrendador. Dentro de

_____ , después de que el Inquilino haya desocupado la propiedad, haya

entregado las llaves y proporcionado la dirección donde contactarse, el Arrendador le entregará el depósito

en su totalidad o le detallará de manera escrita, las razones y la cantidad que es retenida por él, junto con un

cheque por la cantidad de su diferencia.

[Si quiere incluir alguna claúsula opcional, escríbalo aquí]

Cláusula 9. Servicios Públicos.

El Inquilino pagará todos los servicios públicos, exceptuando los siguientes, los cuales serán pagados por el

Arrendador: _____

_____ .

Cláusula 10. Prohibición de Traspasar el Arrendamiento o Subarrendar la Propiedad.

Los Inquilinos no sub-arrendarán cualquier parte de la Propiedad o traspasar este Contrato, sin previo consentimiento por escrito del Arrendador.

☐ a. Los Inquilinos no deberían subarrendar o alquilar de cualquier parte de la Propiedad para estancias cortas de cualquier duración, incluyendo pero no limitado a alquileres de vacaciones.

☐ b. Alquileres a corto plazo son prohibidos, excepto los que son autorizado por ley. Los Inquilinos deben seguir todas las regulaciones, leyes, y otros requistos como condición para poder ofrecer un alquiler a corto plazo. El incumplimiento de las leyes, ordenanzas, regulaciones, y otros requerimientos, incluso cualquier requisito de registro, se considerará un violación material e incurable de este Contratoy puede ser motivo de su terminación.

Cláusula 11. Responsabilidad del Inquilino de Mantenimiento de la Propiedad.

El Inquilino acepta: (1) mantener la propiedad limpia e higiénica, en buena condición, y cuando el arrendamiento termine, regresar la propiedad al Arrendador en idéntica condición a la que existía cuando la habitaron, exceptuando el deterioro causado por el uso; (2) Notificar de inmediato al Arrendador, sobre cualquier defecto o condición peligrosa que note en o alrededor de la propiedad; y (3) reembolsar al Arrendador, bajo demanda de éste, los costos de cualquier reparación de daños a la propiedad, ocasionados por uso indebido o negligencia del Inquilino o sus invitados.

El Inquilino ha revisado la propiedad, incluyendo los aparatos electrodomésticos, accesorios, alfombras, cortinas, y pintura, y los ha encontrado en buenas condiciones, seguras, y limpias, exceptuando las que están en la Lista Arrendador-Inquilino.

Cláusula 12. Reparaciones y Modificaciones Hechas por el Inquilino.

a. Exceptuando lo provisto por la ley o con la autorización previa y por escrito del Arrendador, el Inquilino no debe hacer modificaciones o reparaciones en la propiedad, incluído el hacer hoyos en las paredes o pintar el lugar.

b. El Inquilino no debe alterar las cerraduras, ni cambiarlas, ni instalar o modificar el sistema de alarma de seguridad; excepto que haya recibido del Arrendador, una autorización previa y por escrito. El Inquilino deberá proveer al Arrendador una copia de llave o llaves para abrir cada cerradura modificada o nueva, así como instrucciones de cómo desarmar un sistema de alarma de seguridad modificado o nuevo.

Cláusula 13. Prohibición de Causar Disturbios y Violar Leyes.

El Inquilino tiene derecho al goce pacífico de la propiedad. Este y sus invitados no deben usar la propiedad o áreas aledañas, de manera que: (1) Viole cualquier ley o reglamento, incluyendo leyes que prohiben el uso, posesión o venta ilegal de drogas; (2) Permite el uso abusivo de la propiedad (daño serio a la propiedad); o (3) Cree un estorbo al molestar, provocar disturbios, provocar inconvenientes, o interferir en el disfrute de paz y tranquilidad de otros inquilinos o vecinos.

Cláusula 14. Mascotas.

Ningún animal puede ser mantenida en la propiedad, sin previa autorización escrita del Arrendador, excepto los animales necesitados para los Inquilinos que tienen una discapacidad, como ese término se entiende por la ley, con excepción de los siguente: _____

_____, de acuerdo

con las condiciones siguientes:_____ .

Cláusula 15. Derecho del Arrendador al Acceso a la Propiedad.

El Arrendador o agentes de éste pueden entrar a la propiedad, en caso de emergencia, para hacer reparaciones o mejoras, o para mostrar la propiedad a potenciales nuevos inquilinos o compradores en perspectiva. También podrá entrar para la inspección anual para revisar la seguridad o chequear problemas de mantenimiento. Excepto en caso de emergencia, por el abandono de la propiedad por parte del Inquilino, orden de la corte, o cuando no sea práctico, el Arrendador deberá notificarle al Inquilino de su intención de entrar a la propiedad con _____ de anticipación.

Cláusula 16. Ausencias Prolongadas del Inquilino.

El Inquilino deberá previamente notificar al Arrendador, si estará ausente de la propiedad por _____ días consecutivos o más. Durante este tiempo, el Arrendador podrá entrar, cuando sea necesario, a la propiedad para mantenimiento y inspeccionar en busca de daños y reparaciones necesarias.

Cláusula 17. Tomar Posesión de la Propiedad.

a. *Falla del Inquilino en tomar posesión de la propiedad.*

Si después de haber firmado este Contrato, el Inquilino no toma posesión de la propiedad, aún será responsable por pago de la renta y cumplimiento de todos los demás términos de este Contrato.

b. *Falla del Arrendador en entregar la propiedad.*

Si el Arrendador no puede entregar la posesión de la propiedad al Inquilino, por cualquier razón fuera de su control, incluyendo, pero no limitado a, destrucción parcial o completa de la propiedad, el Inquilino tendrá el derecho de terminar este Contrato, mediante aviso previo y apropiado como lo señala la ley. En tal situación, la responsabilidad del Arrendador hacia el Inquilino, estará limitada a la devolución de todas las cantidades previamente pagadas por el Inquilino al Arrendador.

Cláusula 18. Normas y Regulaciones del Inquilino.

☐ El Inquilino reconoce lo recibido y que ha leído una copia de las Normas y Regulaciones del Inquilino; que están marcados con "Accesorio A" y están adjuntas e incorporadas al presente Contrato. Inquilino entiende que violaciones graves o repetidas de las reglas pueden ser motivos de la terminación. El Arrendador puede cambiar las reglas y regulaciones sin previo aviso.

Cláusula 19. Pago del Abogado y Costos de la Corte en Caso de un Juicio.

☐ En cualquier acción jurídico-legal para hacer cumplir total o parcialmente este Contrato, la parte prevaleciente ☐ No deberá / ☐ Deberá recuperar honorarios justos del abogado y costos de la corte.

Cláusula 20. Divulgaciones.

El Inquilino reconoce que el Arrendador le ha hecho las siguientes divulgaciones con respecto a la propiedad:

☐ *Declaración de Información sobre Pintura a Base de Plomo y/o Peligros de la Pintura a Base de Plomo.*

☐ Otras divulgaciones: _____

_____

_____.

Cláusula 21. Personal Autorizado para Recibir Documentos Legales.

El Arrendador, la persona que administre la propiedad, o a quien haya designado el Arrendador, están autorizados para aceptar servicio de proceso, y recibir otras noticias y demandas, las cuales pueden ser entregadas a:

☐ El Arrendador, a la siguiente dirección: _____

_____

☐ El Administrador, a la siguiente dirección: _____

_____

☐ A la persona designada, a la siguiente dirección: _____

_____

Cláusula 22. Disposiciones Adicionales.

Disposiciones adicionales son las siguientes: _____

_____

_____

_____

_____

_____

_____ .

Cláusula 23. Validez de las Cláusulas de este Contrato.

Si cualquier cláusula de este Contrato es invalidado, ésto no afectará la validez o cumplimiento de las partes restantes de este Contrato.

Cláusula 24. Razones para Cancelar el Contrato de Arrendamiento.

El incumplimiento de cualesquiera de los términos de este Contrato, por parte del Inquilino o sus invitados o la relación falsa de un hecho esencial en la solicitud del Inquilino, será razón para dar por cancelado el Contrato de arrendamiento, seguido con la debida notificación al Inquilino, de acuerdo con lo requerido por la ley.

Cláusula 25. Contrato Completo.

Este documento constituye el Contrato completo entre las partes, y el Arrendador y el Inquilino no han hecho otro compromiso, a no ser los contenidos en este Contrato o los señalados por la ley. Cualquier modificación al presente documento, debe ser por escrito y firmado por ambas partes.

_____   _____   _____
Fecha   Arrendador o su representante   Título

_____
Número y Nombre de la Calle

_____   _____   _____   _____
Ciudad   Estado   Código Postal   Teléfono

_____
Email

_____   _____   _____
Fecha   Nombre del Inquilino   Teléfono

_____   _____   _____
Fecha   Nombre del Inquilino   Teléfono

_____   _____   _____
Fecha   Nombre del Inquilino   Teléfono

Fixed-Term Residential Lease

Clause 1. Identification of Landlord and Tenant

This Agreement is entered into between _____

_____ [Tenant] and

_____ [Landlord].

Each Tenant is jointly and severally liable for the payment of rent and performance of all other terms of this Agreement.

Clause 2. Identification of Premises

Subject to the terms and conditions in this Agreement, Landlord rents to Tenant, and Tenant rents from Landlord, for residential purposes only, the premises located at _____

_____ [the premises],

together with the following furnishings and appliances: _____

_____

_____ .

Rental of the premises also includes _____

_____

_____ .

Clause 3. Limits on Use and Occupancy

The premises are to be used only as a private residence for Tenant(s) listed in Clause 1 of this Agreement, and their minor children. Occupancy by guests for more than _____

is prohibited without Landlord's written consent and will be considered a breach of this Agreement.

Clause 4. Term of the Tenancy

The term of the rental will begin on _____ , and end on _____

_____ . If Tenant vacates before the term ends, Tenant will be liable for the balance of the rent for the remainder of the term.

Clause 5. Payment of Rent

Regular monthly rent

Tenant will pay to Landlord a monthly rent of $_____ , payable in advance on the first day of each month, except when that day falls on a weekend or legal holiday, in which case rent is due on the next business day. Rent will be paid in the following manner unless Landlord designates otherwise:

Delivery of payment

Rent will be paid:

☐ by mail, to _____

☐ in person, at _____

Form of payment

Landlord will accept payment in these forms:

☐ personal check made payable to _____

☐ cashier's check made payable to _____

☐ credit card

☐ money order

☐ automatic credit card debit

☐ electronic funds transfer

☐ cash

Prorated first month's rent

For the period from Tenant's move-in date, _____, through the end of the

month, Tenant will pay to Landlord the prorated monthly rent of $_____. This amount will be

paid on or before the date the Tenant moves in.

Clause 6. Late Charges

If Tenant fails to pay the rent in full before the end of the _____ day after it's due, Tenant will pay

Landlord a late charge as follows: _____

_____ .

Landlord does not waive the right to insist on payment of the rent in full on the date it is due.

Clause 7. Returned Check and Other Bank Charges

If any check offered by Tenant to Landlord in payment of rent or any other amount due under this Agreement is

returned for lack of sufficient funds, a "stop payment," or any other reason, Tenant will pay Landlord a returned

check charge of $_____ .

Clause 8. Security Deposit

On signing this Agreement, Tenant will pay to Landlord the sum of $_____ as a security

deposit. Tenant may not, without Landlord's prior written consent, apply this security deposit to the last

month's rent or to any other sum due under this Agreement. Within _____

after Tenant has vacated the premises, returned keys, and provided Landlord with a forwarding address,

Landlord will return the deposit in full or give Tenant an itemized written statement of the reasons for, and the

dollar amount of, any of the security deposit retained by Landlord, along with a check for any deposit balance.

Clause 9. Utilities

Tenant will pay all utility charges, except for the following, which will be paid by Landlord:

_____

_____ .

Clause 10. Prohibition of Assignment and Subletting

Tenants will not sublet any part of the premises or assign this Agreement without the prior written consent of Landlord.

☐ a. Tenants shall not sublet or rent any part of the Premises for short-term stays of any duration, including but not limited to vacation rentals.

☐ b. Short-stay rentals are prohibited except as authorized by law. Any short-stay rental is expressly conditioned upon the tenants' following all regulations, laws, and other requirements as a condition to offering a short-stay rental. Failure to follow all laws, ordinances, regulations, and other requirements, including any registration requirement, will be deemed a material, noncurable breach of this Agreement and will furnish cause for termination.

Clause 11. Tenant's Maintenance Responsibilities

Tenant will: (1) keep the premises clean, sanitary, and in good condition and, upon termination of the tenancy, return the premises to Landlord in a condition identical to that which existed when Tenant took occupancy, except for ordinary wear and tear; (2) immediately notify Landlord of any defects or dangerous conditions in and about the premises of which Tenant becomes aware; and (3) reimburse Landlord, on demand by Landlord, for the cost of any repairs to the premises damaged by Tenant or Tenant's guests or business invitees through misuse or neglect.

Tenant has examined the premises, including appliances, fixtures, carpets, drapes, and paint, and has found them to be in good, safe, and clean condition and repair, except as noted in the Landlord-Tenant Checklist.

Clause 12. Repairs and Alterations by Tenant

a. Except as provided by law, or as authorized by the prior written consent of Landlord, Tenant will not make any repairs or alterations to the premises, including nailing holes in the walls or painting the rental unit.

b. Tenant will not, without Landlord's prior written consent, alter, rekey, or install any locks to the premises or install or alter any security alarm system. Tenant will provide Landlord with a key or keys capable of unlocking all such rekeyed or new locks as well as instructions on how to disarm any altered or new security alarm system.

Clause 13. Prohibition Against Violating Laws and Causing Disturbances

Tenant is entitled to quiet enjoyment of the premises. Tenant and guests or invitees will not use the premises or adjacent areas in such a way as to: (1) violate any law or ordinance, including laws prohibiting the use, possession, or sale of illegal drugs; (2) commit waste (severe property damage); or (3) create a nuisance by annoying, disturbing, inconveniencing, or interfering with the quiet enjoyment and peace and quiet of any other tenant or nearby resident.

Clause 14. Pets

No animal may be kept on the premises without Landlord's prior written consent, except animals needed by tenants who have a disability, as that term is understood by law, except for the following: _____

_____

under the following conditions: _____

_____ .

Clause 15. Landlord's Right to Access

Landlord or Landlord's agents may enter the premises in the event of an emergency, to make repairs or improvements, or to show the premises to prospective buyers or tenants. Landlord may also enter the premises to conduct an annual inspection to check for safety or maintenance problems. Except in cases of emergency, Tenant's abandonment of the premises, court order, or where it is impractical to do so, Landlord will give Tenant _____ notice before entering.

Clause 16. Extended Absences by Tenant

Tenant will notify Landlord in advance if Tenant will be away from the premises for _____ or more consecutive days. During such absence, Landlord may enter the premises at times reasonably necessary to maintain the property and inspect for damage and needed repairs.

Clause 17. Possession of the Premises

a. Tenant's failure to take possession.

If, after signing this Agreement, Tenant fails to take possession of the premises, Tenant will still be responsible for paying rent and complying with all other terms of this Agreement.

b. Landlord's failure to deliver possession.

If Landlord is unable to deliver possession of the premises to Tenant for any reason not within Landlord's control, including, but not limited to, partial or complete destruction of the premises, Tenant will have the right to terminate this Agreement upon proper notice as required by law. In such event, Landlord's liability to Tenant will be limited to the return of all sums previously paid by Tenant to Landlord.

Clause 18. Tenant Rules and Regulations

☐ Tenant acknowledges receipt of, and has read a copy of, tenant rules and regulations, which are labeled Attachment A and attached to and incorporated into this Agreement by this reference. Tenant understands that serious or repeated violations of the rules may be grounds for termination. Landlord may change the rules and regulations without notice.

Clause 19. Payment of Court Costs and Attorneys' Fees in a Lawsuit

In any action or legal proceeding to enforce any part of this Agreement, the prevailing party ☐ shall not / ☐ shall recover reasonable attorneys' fees and court costs.

Clause 20. Disclosures

Tenant acknowledges that Landlord has made the following disclosures regarding the premises:

☐ *Disclosure of Information on Lead-Based Paint and/or Lead-Based Paint Hazards*

☐ Other disclosures: _____

_____

_____

_____

_____

Clause 21. Authority to Receive Legal Papers

The Landlord, any person managing the premises, and anyone designated by the Landlord are authorized to accept service of process and receive other notices and demands, which may be delivered to:

☐ The Landlord, at the following address: _____

_____

☐ The manager, at the following address: _____

_____

☐ The following person, at the following address: _____

_____

Clause 22. Additional Provisions

Additional provisions are as follows: _____

_____

_____

_____

_____

_____

_____

_____

_____

Clause 23. Validity of Each Part

If any portion of this Agreement is held to be invalid, its invalidity will not affect the validity or enforceability of any other provision of this Agreement.

Clause 24. Grounds for Termination of Tenancy

The failure of Tenant or Tenant's guests or invitees to comply with any term of this Agreement, or the misrepresentation of any material fact on Tenant's rental application, is grounds for termination of the tenancy, with appropriate notice to Tenant and procedures as required by law.

Clause 25. Entire Agreement

This document constitutes the entire Agreement between the parties, and no promises or representations, other than those contained here and those implied by law, have been made by Landlord or Tenant. Any modifications to this Agreement must be in writing, signed by Landlord and Tenant.

_____   _____   _____
Date   Landlord or Landlord's Agent   Title

_____
Street Address

_____   _____   _____ _____
City   State   Zip Code   Phone

_____
Email

_____   _____   _____
Date   Tenant   Phone

_____   _____   _____
Date   Tenant   Phone

_____   _____   _____
Date   Tenant   Phone

Contrato de Arrendamiento Residencial a Plazo Fijo

Cláusula 1. Identificación del Arrendador y de los Inquilinos.

Este Contrato se hace entre _____

_____ [Inquilinos] y

_____ [Arrendador]. Cada

Inquilino es conjuntamente e individualmente responsable del pago de renta y del cumplimiento de todos los

demás términos de este Contrato.

Cláusula 2. Identificación de la Propiedad.

De acuerdo con los términos y condiciones referidas en este Contrato, el Arrendador renta al Inquilino, y éste

renta del Arrendador, sólamente para residir, la propiedad ubicada en _____

_____ , [la propiedad],

junto con el mobiliario y los aparatos electrodomésticos siguientes: _____

_____

_____ .

La renta de la propiedad también incluye _____

_____

_____ .

Cláusula 3. Límitaciones en el Uso y Ocupación.

La propiedad se utilizará sólo como residencia privada por el Inquilino designado en la Cláusula 1 de este

Contrato y sus hijos menores. Está prohibido que invitados habiten la propiedad por más de

_____, excepto con previo consentimiento por escrito del Arrendador. De lo contrario,

será considerado como una violación a este Contrato.

Cláusula 4. Período de Arrendamiento.

La renta comenzará el día _____ de _____ de _____ , y concluirá el día

_____ de _____ de _____ . Si el Inquilino desocupa antes del vencimiento

del período de renta, el Inquilino será responsable por la diferencia de la renta que falta por el resto del término.

Cláusula 5. Renta y Fechas de Pago.

Renta Regular Mensual.

El Inquilino pagará por adelantado, una renta mensual de $ _____ , el primer día del mes; excepto

cuando éste sea en un fin de semana o en un día feriado oficial, en cuyo caso deberá ser pagada el próximo día

laboral. Si no existe otra decisión por parte del Arrendador, la renta deberá ser pagada de la manera siguiente:

Entrega de Pago.

El arriendo será pagado:

☐ Por correo, dirigido a _____

☐ Personalmente, en _____

Forma de Pago.

El Arrendador recibirá los pagos en:

☐ Cheque Personal escrito en favor de _____

☐ Cheque de Caja escrito en favor de _____

☐ Tarjeta de Crédito

☐ Giro Postal

☐ Débito Automático de su Tarjeta de Crédito

☐ Efectivo

☐ Transferencia Electrónica de Fondos

Prorrateo del primer mes de renta.

Para el período comenzando con la fecha en que se mudará el Inquilino, el día _____ de _____

de _____ , hasta el fin del mes en curso, el Inquilino pagará al Arrendador la renta mensual prorratada de

$ _____ . Esta suma se pagará antes o en la fecha en que se mude el Inquilino a la propiedad.

Cláusula 6. Cobros por Mora.

Si el Inquilino falla en el pago total de la renta, antes del final del día _____ después de la fecha de

pago, tendrá que pagar costos por atrasos como se explica a continuación: _____

_____ .

El Arrendador no descartará el derecho de insistir en el pago total de la renta en la fecha debida.

Cláusula 7. Pagos por Cheques Sin Fondo y Recargos Bancarios.

En el caso de cualquier cheque, ofrecido por el Inquilino al Arrendador como pago de renta o cualquier otra

suma debida bajo este Contrato, sea regresado por insuficiencia de fondos, un "paro de pago," o cualquier otra

razón, el Inquilino deberá pagar un recargo por la cantidad de $_____ .

Cláusula 8. Depósito de Garantía.

Al firmar el presente Contrato, el Inquilino pagará al Arrendador, la cantidad de $_____ como

depósito de seguridad. Este depósito no puede aplicarse al último mes de renta o a cualquier cantidad

debida bajo este Contrato; excepto con previo consentimiento por escrito del Arrendador. Dentro de

_____ , después de que el Inquilino haya desocupado la propiedad, haya

entregado las llaves y proporcionado la dirección donde contactarse, el Arrendador le entregará el depósito

en su totalidad o le detallará de manera escrita, las razones y la cantidad que es retenida por él, junto con un

cheque por la cantidad de su diferencia.

[Si quiere incluir alguna cláusula opcional, escríbalo aquí]

Cláusula 9. Servicios Públicos.

El Inquilino pagará todos los servicios públicos, exceptuando los siguientes, los cuales serán pagados por el

Arrendador: _____

_____ .

Cláusula 10. Prohibición de Traspasar el Arrendamiento o Subarrendar la Propiedad.

Los Inquilinos no sub-arrendarán cualquier parte de la Propiedad o traspasar este Contrato, sin previo
consentimiento por escrito del Arrendador.

☐ a. Los Inquilinos no deberían subarrendar o alquilar de cualquier parte de la Propiedad para estancias
cortas de cualquier duración, incluyendo pero no limitado a alquileres de vacaciones.

☐ b. Alquileres a corto plazo son prohibidos, excepto los que son autorizado por ley. Los Inquilinos deben
seguir todas las regulaciones, leyes, y otros requistos como condición para poder ofrecer un alquiler a
corto plazo. El incumplimiento de las leyes, ordenanzas, regulaciones, y otros requerimientos, incluso
cualquier requisito de registro, se considerará un violación material e incurable de este Contratoy puede
ser motivo de su terminación.

Cláusula 11. Responsabilidad del Inquilino de Mantenimiento de la Propiedad.

El Inquilino acepta: (1) mantener la propiedad limpia e higiénica, en buena condición, y cuando el arrendamiento
termine, regresar la propiedad al Arrendador en idéntica condición a la que existía cuando la habitaron,
exceptuando el deterioro causado por el uso; (2) Notificar de inmediato al Arrendador, sobre cualquier defecto
o condición peligrosa que note en o alrededor de la propiedad; y (3) reembolsar al Arrendador, bajo demanda de
éste, los costos de cualquier reparación de daños a la propiedad, ocasionados por uso indebido o negligencia del
Inquilino o sus invitados.

El Inquilino ha revisado la propiedad, incluyendo los aparatos electrodomésticos, accesorios, alfombras, cortinas, y pintura, y los ha encontrado en buenas condiciones, seguras, y limpias, exceptuando las que están en la Lista Arrendador-Inquilino.

Cláusula 12. Reparaciones y Modificaciones Hechas por el Inquilino.

a. Exceptuando lo provisto por la ley o con la autorización previa y por escrito del Arrendador, el Inquilino no debe hacer modificaciones o reparaciones en la propiedad, incluído el hacer hoyos en las paredes o pintar el lugar.

b. El Inquilino no debe alterar las cerraduras, ni cambiarlas, ni instalar o modificar el sistema de alarma de seguridad; excepto que haya recibido del Arrendador, una autorización previa y por escrito. El Inquilino deberá proveer al Arrendador una copia de llave o llaves para abrir cada cerradura modificada o nueva, así como instrucciones de cómo desarmar un sistema de alarma de seguridad modificado o nuevo.

Cláusula 13. Prohibición de Causar Disturbios y Violar Leyes.

El Inquilino tiene derecho al goce pacífico de la propiedad. Este y sus invitados no deben usar la propiedad o áreas aledañas, de manera que: (1) Viole cualquier ley o reglamento, incluyendo leyes que prohiben el uso, posesión o venta ilegal de drogas; (2) Permite el uso abusivo de la propiedad (daño serio a la propiedad); o (3) Cree un estorbo al molestar, provocar disturbios, provocar inconvenientes, o interferir en el disfrute de paz y tranquilidad de otros inquilinos o vecinos.

Cláusula 14. Mascotas.

Ningún animal puede ser mantenida en la propiedad, sin previa autorización escrita del Arrendador, excepto los animales necesitados para los Inquilinos que tienen una discapacidad, como ese término se entiende por la ley, con excepción de los siguente: _____

_____, de acuerdo

con las condiciones siguientes:_____ .

Cláusula 15. Derecho del Arrendador al Acceso a la Propiedad.

El Arrendador o agentes de éste pueden entrar a la propiedad, en caso de emergencia, para hacer reparaciones o mejoras, o para mostrar la propiedad a potenciales nuevos inquilinos o compradores en perspectiva. También podrá entrar para la inspección anual para revisar la seguridad o chequear problemas de mantenimiento. Excepto en caso de emergencia, por el abandono de la propiedad por parte del Inquilino, orden de la corte, o cuando no sea práctico, el Arrendador deberá notificarle al Inquilino de su intención de entrar a la propiedad con _____ de anticipación.

Cláusula 16. Ausencias Prolongadas del Inquilino.

El Inquilino deberá previamente notificar al Arrendador, si estará ausente de la propiedad por _____ días consecutivos o más. Durante este tiempo, el Arrendador podrá entrar, cuando sea necesario, a la propiedad para mantenimiento y inspeccionar en busca de daños y reparaciones necesarias.

Cláusula 17. Tomar Posesión de la Propiedad.

  a. *Falla del Inquilino en tomar posesión de la propiedad.*

   Si después de haber firmado este Contrato, el Inquilino no toma posesión de la propiedad, aún será responsable por pago de la renta y cumplimiento de todos los demás términos de este Contrato.

  b. *Falla del Arrendador en entregar la propiedad.*

   Si el Arrendador no puede entregar la posesión de la propiedad al Inquilino, por cualquier razón fuera de su control, incluyendo, pero no limitado a, destrucción parcial o completa de la propiedad, el Inquilino tendrá el derecho de terminar este Contrato, mediante aviso previo y apropiado como lo señala la ley. En tal situación, la responsabilidad del Arrendador hacia el Inquilino, estará limitada a la devolución de todas las cantidades previamente pagadas por el Inquilino al Arrendador.

Cláusula 18. Normas y Regulaciones del Inquilino.

  ☐ El Inquilino reconoce lo recibido y que ha leído una copia de las Normas y Regulaciones del Inquilino; que están marcados con "Accesorio A" y están adjuntas e incorporadas al presente Contrato. Inquilino entiende que violaciones graves o repetidas de las reglas pueden ser motivos de la terminación. El Arrendador puede cambiar las reglas y regulaciones sin previo aviso.

Cláusula 19. Pago del Abogado y Costos de la Corte en Caso de un Juicio.

En cualquier acción jurídico-legal para hacer cumplir total o parcialmente este Contrato, la parte prevaleciente

☐ No deberá / ☐ Deberá recuperar honorarios justos del abogado y costos de la corte.

Cláusula 20. Divulgaciones.

El Inquilino reconoce que el Arrendador le ha hecho las siguientes divulgaciones con respecto a la propiedad:

☐ *Declaración de Información sobre Pintura a Base de Plomo y/o Peligros de la Pintura a Base de Plomo.*

☐ Otras divulgaciones: _____

_____

_____ .

Cláusula 21. Personal Autorizado para Recibir Documentos Legales.

El Arrendador, la persona que administre la propiedad, o a quien haya designado el Arrendador, están autorizados para aceptar servicio de proceso, y recibir otras noticias y demandas, las cuales pueden ser entregadas a:

☐ El Arrendador, a la siguiente dirección: _____

_____

☐ El Administrador, a la siguiente dirección: _____

_____

☐ A la persona designada, a la siguiente dirección: _____

_____

Cláusula 22. Disposiciones Adicionales.

Disposiciones adicionales son las siguientes: _____

_____

_____

_____

_____

_____

_____

_____ .

Cláusula 23. Validez de las Cláusulas de este Contrato.

Si cualquier cláusula de este Contrato es invalidado, ésto no afectará la validez o cumplimiento de las partes restantes de este Contrato.

Cláusula 24. Razones para Cancelar el Contrato de Arrendamiento.

El incumplimiento de cualesquiera de los términos de este Contrato, por parte del Inquilino o sus invitados o la relación falsa de un hecho esencial en la solicitud del Inquilino, será razón para dar por cancelado el Contrato de arrendamiento, seguido con la debida notificación al Inquilino, de acuerdo con lo requerido por la ley.

Cláusula 25. Contrato Completo.

Este documento constituye el Contrato completo entre las partes, y el Arrendador y el Inquilino no han hecho otro compromiso, a no ser los contenidos en este Contrato o los señalados por la ley. Cualquier modificación al presente documento, debe ser por escrito y firmado por ambas partes.

_____	_____	_____
Fecha	Arrendador o su representante	Título

_____
Número y Nombre de la Calle

_____	_____	_____	_____
Ciudad	Estado	Código Postal	Teléfono

_____
Email

_____	_____	_____
Fecha	Nombre del Inquilino	Teléfono
_____	_____	_____
Fecha	Nombre del Inquilino	Teléfono
_____	_____	_____
Fecha	Nombre del Inquilino	Teléfono

Disclosure of Information on Lead-Based Paint and/or Lead-Based Paint Hazards

Lead Warning Statement

Housing built before 1978 may contain lead-based paint. Lead from paint, paint chips, and dust can pose health hazards if not managed properly. Lead exposure is especially harmful to young children and pregnant women. Before renting pre-1978 housing, lessors must disclose the presence of known lead-based paint and/or lead-based paint hazards in the dwelling. Lessees must also receive a federally approved pamphlet on lead poisoning prevention.

Lessor's Disclosure

(a) Presence of lead-based paint and/or lead-based paint hazards (check (i) or (ii) below):

(i) _____ Known lead-based paint and/or lead-based paint hazards are present in the housing (explain).

_____

_____

(ii) _____ Lessor has no knowledge of lead-based paint and/or lead-based paint hazards in the housing.

(b) Records and reports available to the lessor (check (i) or (ii) below):

(i) _____ Lessor has provided the lessee with all available records and reports pertaining to lead-based paint and/or lead-based paint hazards in the housing (list documents below).

_____

_____

(ii) _____ Lessor has no reports or records pertaining to lead-based paint and/or lead-based paint hazards in the housing.

Lessee's Acknowledgment (initial)

(c) _____ Lessee has received copies of all information listed above.

(d) _____ Lessee has received the pamphlet *Protect Your Family from Lead in Your Home.*

Agent's Acknowledgment (initial)

(e) _____ Agent has informed the lessor of the lessor's obligations under 42 U.S.C. 4852d and is aware of his/her responsibility to ensure compliance.

Certification of Accuracy

The following parties have reviewed the information above and certify, to the best of their knowledge, that the information they have provided is true and accurate.

Lessor	Date	Lessor	Date
Lessee	Date	Lessee	Date
Agent	Date	Agent	Date

Declaración de Información sobre Pintura a Base de Plomo y/o Peligros de la Pintura a Base de Plomo

Declaración sobre los Peligros del Plomo

Las viviendas construidas antes del año 1978 pueden contener pintura a base de plomo. El plomo de pintura, pedazos de pintura y polvo puede representar peligros para la salud si no se maneja apropiadamente. La exposición al plomo es especialmente dañino para los niños jóvenes y las mujeres embarazadas. Antes de alquilar (rentar) una vivienda construida antes del año 1978, los arrendadores tienen la obligación de informar sobre la presencia de pintura a base de plomo o peligros de pintura a base de plomo conocidos en la vivienda. Los arrendatarios (inquilinos) también deben recibir un folleto aprobado por el Gobierno Federal sobre la prevención del envenenamiento de plomo.

Declaración del Arrendador

(a) Presencia de pintura a base de plomo y/o peligros de pintura a base de plomo (marque (i) ó (ii) abajo):

(i) _____ Confirmado que hay pintura a base de plomo y/o peligro de pintura a base de plomo en la vivienda (explique).

_____

(ii) _____ El arrendador no tiene ningún conocimiento de que haya pintura a base de plomo y/o peligro de pintura a base de plomo en la vivienda.

(b) Archivos e informes disponibles para el vendedor (marque (i) ó (ii) abajo):

(i) _____ El arrendador le ha proporcionado al comprador todos los archivos e informes disponibles relacionados con pintura a base de plomo y/o peligro de pintura a base de plomo en la vivienda (anote los documentos abajo).

_____

(ii) _____ El arrendador no tiene archivos ni informes relacionados con pintura a base de plomo y/o peligro de pintura a base de plomo en la vivienda.

Acuse de Recibo del Arrendatario o Inquilino (inicial)

(c) _____ El arrendatario ha recibido copias de toda la información indicada arriba.

(d) _____ El arrendatario ha recibido el folleto titulado *Proteja a Su Familia del Plomo en Su Casa.*

Acuse de Recibo del Agente (inicial)

(e) _____ El agente le ha informado al arrendador de las obligaciones del arrendador de acuerdo con 42 U.S.C. 4852d y está consciente de su responsabilidad de asegurar su cumplimiento.

Certificación de Exactitud

Las partes siguientes han revisado la información que aparece arriba y certifican que, según su entender, toda la información que han proporcionado es verdadera y exacta.

Arrendador	Fecha	Arrendador	Fecha
Arrendatario	Fecha	Arrendatario	Fecha
Agente	Fecha	Agente	Fecha

Are You Planning to Buy or Rent a Home Built Before 1978?

Did you know that many homes built before 1978 have **lead-based paint**? Lead from paint, chips, and dust can pose serious health hazards.

Read this entire brochure to learn:

- How lead gets into the body
- About health effects of lead
- What you can do to protect your family
- Where to go for more information

Before renting or buying a pre-1978 home or apartment, federal law requires:

- Sellers must disclose known information on lead-based paint or lead-based paint hazards before selling a house.
- Real estate sales contracts must include a specific warning statement about lead-based paint. Buyers have up to 10 days to check for lead.
- Landlords must disclose known information on lead-based paint and lead-based paint hazards before leases take effect. Leases must include a specific warning statement about lead-based paint.

If undertaking renovations, repairs, or painting (RRP) projects in your pre-1978 home or apartment:

- Read EPA's pamphlet, *The Lead-Safe Certified Guide to Renovate Right*, to learn about the lead-safe work practices that contractors are required to follow when working in your home (see page 12).

Protect
Your
Family
From
Lead in
Your
Home

 EPA United States
Environmental
Protection Agency

 United States
Consumer Product
Safety Commission

 United States
Department of Housing
and Urban Development

Lead Gets into the Body in Many Ways

Adults and children can get lead into their bodies if they:

- Breathe in lead dust (especially during activities such as renovations, repairs, or painting that disturb painted surfaces).

- Swallow lead dust that has settled on food, food preparation surfaces, and other places.

- Eat paint chips or soil that contains lead.

Lead is especially dangerous to children under the age of 6.

- At this age, children's brains and nervous systems are more sensitive to the damaging effects of lead.

- Children's growing bodies absorb more lead.

- Babies and young children often put their hands and other objects in their mouths. These objects can have lead dust on them.

Women of childbearing age should know that lead is dangerous to a developing fetus.

- Women with a high lead level in their system before or during pregnancy risk exposing the fetus to lead through the placenta during fetal development.

Simple Steps to Protect Your Family from Lead Hazards

If you think your home has lead-based paint:

- Don't try to remove lead-based paint yourself.

- Always keep painted surfaces in good condition to minimize deterioration.

- Get your home checked for lead hazards. Find a certified inspector or risk assessor at epa.gov/lead.

- Talk to your landlord about fixing surfaces with peeling or chipping paint.

- Regularly clean floors, window sills, and other surfaces.

- Take precautions to avoid exposure to lead dust when remodeling.

- When renovating, repairing, or painting, hire only EPA- or state-approved Lead-Safe certified renovation firms.

- Before buying, renting, or renovating your home, have it checked for lead-based paint.

- Consult your health care provider about testing your children for lead. Your pediatrician can check for lead with a simple blood test.

- Wash children's hands, bottles, pacifiers, and toys often.

- Make sure children avoid fatty (or high fat) foods and eat nutritious meals high in iron and calcium.

- Remove shoes or wipe soil off shoes before entering your house.

Health Effects of Lead

Lead affects the body in many ways. It is important to know that even exposure to low levels of lead can severely harm children.

In children, exposure to lead can cause:

- Nervous system and kidney damage

- Learning disabilities, attention deficit disorder, and decreased intelligence

- Speech, language, and behavior problems

- Poor muscle coordination

- Decreased muscle and bone growth

- Hearing damage

While low-lead exposure is most common, exposure to high amounts of lead can have devastating effects on children, including seizures, unconsciousness, and, in some cases, death.

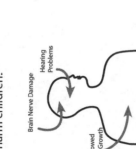

Brain Nerve Damage
Hearing Problems
Slowed Growth
Digestive Problems
Reproductive Problems (Adults)

Although children are especially susceptible to lead exposure, lead can be dangerous for adults, too.

In adults, exposure to lead can cause:

- Harm to a developing fetus

- Increased chance of high blood pressure during pregnancy

- Fertility problems (in men and women)

- High blood pressure

- Digestive problems

- Nerve disorders

- Memory and concentration problems

- Muscle and joint pain

Check Your Family for Lead

Get your children and home tested if you think your home has lead.

Children's blood lead levels tend to increase rapidly from 6 to 12 months of age, and tend to peak at 18 to 24 months of age.

Consult your doctor for advice on testing your children. A simple blood test can detect lead. Blood lead tests are usually recommended for:

- Children at ages 1 and 2

- Children or other family members who have been exposed to high levels of lead

- Children who should be tested under your state or local health screening plan

Your doctor can explain what the test results mean and if more testing will be needed.

Where Lead-Based Paint Is Found

In general, the older your home or childcare facility, the more likely it has lead-based paint.[1]

Many homes, including private, federally-assisted, federally-owned housing, and childcare facilities built before 1978 have lead-based paint. In 1978, the federal government banned consumer uses of lead-containing paint.[2]

Learn how to determine if paint is lead-based paint on page 7.

Lead can be found:

- In homes and childcare facilities in the city, country, or suburbs,
- In private and public single-family homes and apartments,
- On surfaces inside and outside of the house, and
- In soil around a home. (Soil can pick up lead from exterior paint or other sources, such as past use of leaded gas in cars.)

Learn more about where lead is found at epa.gov/lead.

---

[1] "Lead-based paint" is currently defined by the federal government as paint with lead levels greater than or equal to 1.0 milligram per square centimeter (mg/cm), or more than 0.5% by weight.

[2] "Lead-containing paint" is currently defined by the federal government as lead in new dried paint in excess of 90 parts per million (ppm) by weight.

Identifying Lead-Based Paint and Lead-Based Paint Hazards

Deteriorating lead-based paint (peeling, chipping, chalking, cracking, or damaged paint) is a hazard and needs immediate attention. **Lead-based paint** may also be a hazard when found on surfaces that children can chew or that get a lot of wear and tear, such as:

- On windows and window sills
- Doors and door frames
- Stairs, railings, banisters, and porches

Lead-based paint is usually not a hazard if it is in good condition and if it is not on an impact or friction surface like a window.

Lead dust can form when lead-based paint is scraped, sanded, or heated. Lead dust also forms when painted surfaces containing lead bump or rub together. Lead paint chips and dust can get on surfaces and objects that people touch. Settled lead dust can reenter the air when the home is vacuumed or swept, or when people walk through it. EPA currently defines the following levels of lead in dust as hazardous:

- 40 micrograms per square foot ($\mu g/ft^2$) and higher for floors, including carpeted floors
- 250 $\mu g/ft^2$ and higher for interior window sills

Lead in soil can be a hazard when children play in bare soil or when people bring soil into the house on their shoes. EPA currently defines the following levels of lead in soil as hazardous:

- 400 parts per million (ppm) and higher in play areas of bare soil
- 1,200 ppm (average) and higher in bare soil in the remainder of the yard

Remember, lead from paint chips—which you can see—and lead dust—which you may not be able to see—both can be hazards.

The only way to find out if paint, dust, or soil lead hazards exist is to test for them. The next page describes how to do this.

Checking Your Home for Lead, continued

In preparing for renovation, repair, or painting work in a pre-1978 home, Lead-Safe Certified renovators (see page 12) may:

- Take paint chip samples to determine if lead-based paint is present in the area planned for renovation and send them to an EPA-recognized lead lab for analysis. In housing receiving federal assistance, the person collecting these samples must be a certified lead-based paint inspector or risk assessor

- Use EPA-recognized tests kits to determine if lead-based paint is absent (but not in housing receiving federal assistance)

- Presume that lead-based paint is present and use lead-safe work practices

There are state and federal programs in place to ensure that testing is done safely, reliably, and effectively. Contact your state or local agency for more information, visit epa.gov/lead, or call **1-800-424-LEAD (5323)** for a list of contacts in your area.[3]

_____

[3] Hearing- or speech-challenged individuals may access this number through TTY by calling the Federal Relay Service at 1-800-877-8399.

Checking Your Home for Lead

You can get your home tested for lead in several different ways:

- A lead-based paint **inspection** tells you if your home has lead-based paint and where it is located. It won't tell you whether your home currently has lead hazards. A trained and certified testing professional, called a lead-based paint inspector, will conduct a paint inspection using methods, such as:

  - Portable x-ray fluorescence (XRF) machine

  - Lab tests of paint samples

- A **risk assessment** tells you if your home currently has any lead hazards from lead in paint, dust, or soil. It also tells you what actions to take to address any hazards. A trained and certified testing professional, called a risk assessor, will:

  - Sample paint that is deteriorated on doors, windows, floors, stairs, and walls

  - Sample dust near painted surfaces and sample bare soil in the yard

  - Get lab tests of paint, dust, and soil samples

- A combination inspection and risk assessment tells you if your home has any lead-based paint and if your home has any lead hazards, and where both are located.

Be sure to read the report provided to you after your inspection or risk assessment is completed, and ask questions about anything you do not understand.

What You Can Do Now to Protect Your Family

If you suspect that your house has lead-based paint hazards, you can take some immediate steps to reduce your family's risk:

- If you rent, notify your landlord of peeling or chipping paint.

- Keep painted surfaces clean and free of dust. Clean floors, window frames, window sills, and other surfaces weekly. Use a mop or sponge with warm water and a general all-purpose cleaner. (Remember: never mix ammonia and bleach products together because they can form a dangerous gas.)

- Carefully clean up paint chips immediately without creating dust.

- Thoroughly rinse sponges and mop heads often during cleaning of dirty or dusty areas, and again afterward.

- Wash your hands and your children's hands often, especially before they eat and before nap time and bed time.

- Keep play areas clean. Wash bottles, pacifiers, toys, and stuffed animals regularly.

- Keep children from chewing window sills or other painted surfaces, or eating soil.

- When renovating, repairing, or painting, hire only EPA- or state-approved Lead-Safe Certified renovation firms (see page 12).

- Clean or remove shoes before entering your home to avoid tracking in lead from soil.

- Make sure children avoid fatty (or high fat) foods and eat nutritious meals high in iron and calcium. Children with good diets absorb less lead.

Reducing Lead Hazards

Disturbing lead-based paint or removing lead improperly can increase the hazard to your family by spreading even more lead dust around the house.

- In addition to day-to-day cleaning and good nutrition, you can **temporarily** reduce lead-based paint hazards by taking actions, such as repairing damaged painted surfaces and planting grass to cover lead-contaminated soil. These actions are not permanent solutions and will need ongoing attention.

- You can minimize exposure to lead when renovating, repairing, or painting by hiring an EPA- or state-certified renovator who is trained in the use of lead-safe work practices. If you are a do-it-yourselfer, learn how to use lead-safe work practices in your home.

- To remove lead hazards permanently, you should hire a certified lead abatement contractor. Abatement (or permanent hazard elimination) methods include removing, sealing, or enclosing lead-based paint with special materials. Just painting over the hazard with regular paint is not permanent control.

Always use a certified contractor who is trained to address lead hazards safely.

- Hire a Lead-Safe Certified firm (see page 12) to perform renovation, repair, or painting (RRP) projects that disturb painted surfaces.

- To correct lead hazards permanently, hire a certified lead abatement professional. This will ensure your contractor knows how to work safely and has the proper equipment to clean up thoroughly.

Certified contractors will employ qualified workers and follow strict safety rules as set by their state or by the federal government.

Reducing Lead Hazards, continued

If your home has had lead abatement work done or if the housing is receiving federal assistance, once the work is completed, dust cleanup activities must be conducted until clearance testing indicates that lead dust levels are below the following levels:

- 40 micrograms per square foot (μg/ft²) for floors, including carpeted floors

- 250 μg/ft² for interior windows sills

- 400 μg/ft² for window troughs

For help in locating certified lead abatement professionals in your area, call your state or local agency (see pages 14 and 15), or visit epa.gov/lead, or call 1-800-424-LEAD.

Renovating, Remodeling, or Repairing (RRP) a Home with Lead-Based Paint

If you hire a contractor to conduct renovation, repair, or painting (RRP) projects in your pre-1978 home or childcare facility (such as pre-school and kindergarten), your contractor must:

- Be a Lead-Safe Certified firm approved by EPA or an EPA-authorized state program

- Use qualified trained individuals (Lead-Safe Certified renovators) who follow specific lead-safe work practices to prevent lead contamination

- Provide a copy of EPA's lead hazard information document, *The Lead-Safe Certified Guide to Renovate Right*

RRP contractors working in pre-1978 homes and childcare facilities must follow lead-safe work practices that:

- **Contain the work area.** The area must be contained so that dust and debris do not escape from the work area. Warning signs must be put up, and plastic or other impermeable material and tape must be used.

- **Avoid renovation methods that generate large amounts of lead-contaminated dust.** Some methods generate so much lead-contaminated dust that their use is prohibited. They are:

  - Open-flame burning or torching

  - Sanding, grinding, planing, needle gunning, or blasting with power tools and equipment not equipped with a shroud and HEPA vacuum attachment and

  - Using a heat gun at temperatures greater than 1100°F

- **Clean up thoroughly.** The work area should be cleaned up daily. When all the work is done, the area must be cleaned up using special cleaning methods.

- **Dispose of waste properly.** Collect and seal waste in a heavy duty bag or sheeting. When transported, ensure that waste is contained to prevent release of dust and debris.

To learn more about EPA's requirements for RRP projects visit epa.gov/getleadsafe, or read *The Lead-Safe Certified Guide to Renovate Right*.

Other Sources of Lead

While paint, dust, and soil are the most common sources of lead, other lead sources also exist:

- **Drinking water.** Your home might have plumbing with lead or lead solder. You cannot see, smell, or taste lead, and boiling your water will not get rid of lead. If you think your plumbing might contain lead:

  - Use only cold water for drinking and cooking.

  - Run water for 15 to 30 seconds before drinking it, especially if you have not used your water for a few hours.

  Call your local health department or water supplier to find out about testing your water, or visit epa.gov/lead for EPA's lead in drinking water information.

- **Lead smelters** or other industries that release lead into the air.

- **Your job.** If you work with lead, you could bring it home on your body or clothes. Shower and change clothes before coming home. Launder your work clothes separately from the rest of your family's clothes.

- **Hobbies** that use lead, such as making pottery or stained glass, or refinishing furniture. Call your local health department for information about hobbies that may use lead.

- Old **toys** and **furniture** may have been painted with lead-containing paint. Older toys and other children's products may have parts that contain lead.[4]

- Food and liquids cooked or stored in **lead crystal** or **lead-glazed pottery or porcelain** may contain lead.

- Folk remedies, such as **"greta"** and **"azarcon,"** used to treat an upset stomach.

---

[4] In 1978, the federal government banned toys, other children's products, and furniture with lead-containing paint (16 CFR 1303). In 2008, the federal government banned lead in most children's products. The federal government currently bans lead in excess of 100 ppm by weight in most children's products (76 FR 44463).

For More Information

The National Lead Information Center
Learn how to protect children from lead poisoning and get other information about lead hazards on the Web at epa.gov/lead and hud.gov/lead, or call **1-800-424-LEAD (5323)**.

EPA's Safe Drinking Water Hotline
For information about lead in drinking water, call **1-800-426-4791**, or visit epa.gov/lead for information about lead in drinking water.

Consumer Product Safety Commission (CPSC) Hotline
For information on lead in toys and other consumer products, or to report an unsafe consumer product or a product-related injury, call **1-800-638-2772**, or visit CPSC's website at cpsc.gov or saferproducts.gov.

State and Local Health and Environmental Agencies
Some states, tribes, and cities have their own rules related to lead-based paint. Check with your local agency to see which laws apply to you. Most agencies can also provide information on finding a lead abatement firm in your area, and on possible sources of financial aid for reducing lead hazards. Receive up-to-date address and phone information for your state or local contacts on the Web at epa.gov/lead, or contact the National Lead Information Center at **1-800-424-LEAD**.

Hearing- or speech-challenged individuals may access any of the phone numbers in this brochure through TTY by calling the toll-free Federal Relay Service at **1-800-877-8339**.

15

U. S. Environmental Protection Agency (EPA) Regional Offices

The mission of EPA is to protect human health and the environment. Your Regional EPA Office can provide further information regarding regulations and lead protection programs.

Region 1 (Connecticut, Massachusetts, Maine, New Hampshire, Rhode Island, Vermont)

Regional Lead Contact
U.S. EPA Region 1
5 Post Office Square, Suite 100, OES 05-4
Boston, MA 02109-3912
(888) 372-7341

Region 2 (New Jersey, New York, Puerto Rico, Virgin Islands)

Regional Lead Contact
U.S. EPA Region 2
2890 Woodbridge Avenue
Building 205, Mail Stop 225
Edison, NJ 08837-3679
(732) 321-6671

Region 3 (Delaware, Maryland, Pennsylvania, Virginia, DC, West Virginia)

Regional Lead Contact
U.S. EPA Region 3
1650 Arch Street
Philadelphia, PA 19103
(215) 814-2088

Region 4 (Alabama, Florida, Georgia, Kentucky, Mississippi, North Carolina, South Carolina, Tennessee)

Regional Lead Contact
U.S. EPA Region 4
AFC Tower, 12th Floor, Air, Pesticides & Toxics
61 Forsyth Street, SW
Atlanta, GA 30303
(404) 562-8998

Region 5 (Illinois, Indiana, Michigan, Minnesota, Ohio, Wisconsin)

Regional Lead Contact
U.S. EPA Region 5 (DT-8J)
77 West Jackson Boulevard
Chicago, IL 60604-3666
(312) 886-7836

Region 6 (Arkansas, Louisiana, New Mexico, Oklahoma, Texas, and 66 Tribes)

Regional Lead Contact
U.S. EPA Region 6
1445 Ross Avenue, 12th Floor
Dallas, TX 75202-2733
(214) 665-2704

Region 7 (Iowa, Kansas, Missouri, Nebraska)

Regional Lead Contact
U.S. EPA Region 7
11201 Renner Blvd.
WWPD/TOPE
Lenexa, KS 66219
(800) 223-0425

Region 8 (Colorado, Montana, North Dakota, South Dakota, Utah, Wyoming)

Regional Lead Contact
U.S. EPA Region 8
1595 Wynkoop St.
Denver, CO 80202
(303) 312-6966

Region 9 (Arizona, California, Hawaii, Nevada)

Regional Lead Contact
U.S. EPA Region 9 (CMD-4-2)
75 Hawthorne Street
San Francisco, CA 94105
(415) 947-4280

Region 10 (Alaska, Idaho, Oregon, Washington)

Regional Lead Contact
U.S. EPA Region 10
Solid Waste & Toxics Unit (WCM-128)
1200 Sixth Avenue, Suite 900
Seattle, WA 98101
(206) 553-1200

16

Consumer Product Safety Commission (CPSC)

The CPSC protects the public against unreasonable risk of injury from consumer products through education, safety standards activities, and enforcement. Contact CPSC for further information regarding consumer product safety and regulations.

CPSC

4330 East West Highway
Bethesda, MD 20814-4421
1-800-638-2772
cpsc.gov or saferproducts.gov

U. S. Department of Housing and Urban Development (HUD)

HUD's mission is to create strong, sustainable, inclusive communities and quality affordable homes for all. Contact HUD's Office of Healthy Homes and Lead Hazard Control for further information regarding the Lead Safe Housing Rule, which protects families in pre-1978 assisted housing, and for the lead hazard control and research grant programs.

HUD

451 Seventh Street, SW, Room 8236
Washington, DC 20410-3000
(202) 402-7698
hud.gov/offices/lead/

U. S. EPA Washington DC 20460
U. S. CPSC Bethesda MD 20814
U. S. HUD Washington DC 20410

EPA-747-K-12-001
September 2013

IMPORTANT!

Lead From Paint, Dust, and Soil in and Around Your Home Can Be Dangerous if Not Managed Properly

- Children under 6 years old are most at risk for lead poisoning in your home.

- Lead exposure can harm young children and babies even before they are born.

- Homes, schools, and child care facilities built before 1978 are likely to contain lead-based paint.

- Even children who seem healthy may have dangerous levels of lead in their bodies.

- Disturbing surfaces with lead-based paint or removing lead-based paint improperly can increase the danger to your family.

- People can get lead into their bodies by breathing or swallowing lead dust, or by eating soil or paint chips containing lead.

- People have many options for reducing lead hazards. Generally, lead-based paint that is in good condition is not a hazard (see page 10).

¿Está planeando comprar o alquilar una casa construida antes de 1978?

¿Sabía que muchas casas construidas antes de 1978 tienen **pintura con base de plomo**? El plomo en la pintura, las partículas y el polvo puede ser un peligro grave para la salud.

Lea todo este folleto para saber:

- Cómo entra el plomo en el cuerpo.
- Acerca de los efectos del plomo en la salud.
- Qué puede hacer para proteger a su familia.
- Adónde recurrir para obtener más información.

Antes de alquilar o comprar una casa o un apartamento construidos antes de 1978, la ley federal requiere lo siguiente:

- Los vendedores tienen que dar la información que posean acerca de la pintura con base de plomo o los peligros relacionados con dicha pintura antes de vender una casa.
- Los contratos de venta de inmuebles deben incluir una declaración de advertencia específica sobre la pintura con base de plomo. Los compradores tienen hasta 10 días para verificar la existencia de plomo.
- Los propietarios tienen que dar la información que posean acerca de la pintura con base de plomo y los peligros relacionados con dicha pintura antes de que el alquiler entre en vigencia. Los contratos de alquiler deben incluir una declaración de advertencia específica sobre la pintura con base de plomo.

Si emprenderá algún proyecto de renovación, reparación o pintura (RRP, por sus siglas en inglés) en su casa o apartamento construido antes de 1978:

- Lea el folleto de la EPA *Guía de prácticas acreditas seguras para trabajar con el plomo para remodeler correctamente.*

Proteja a su familia contra el plomo en el hogar

 **EPA** Agencia de Protección Ambiental de los Estados Unidos (EPA)

 Comisión de Seguridad de Productos del Consumidor de Estados Unidos (CPSC)

 Departamento de la Vivienda y de Desarrollo Urbano de los Estados Unidos (HUD)

Septiembre de 2013

El plomo entra al cuerpo de muchas maneras

El plomo puede entrar en el cuerpo de adultos y niños si:

- Respiran el polvo de plomo (especialmente durante las actividades de renovación, reparación y pintura que alteran las superficies pintadas).

- Tragan polvo de plomo que se ha acumulado en alimentos, superficies donde se preparan alimentos y otros lugares.

- Comen partículas de pintura o tierra que contengan plomo.

El plomo es especialmente peligroso para los niños menores de 6 años.

- A esta edad, el cerebro y el sistema nervioso de los niños son más sensibles a los efectos dañinos del plomo.

- El cuerpo en crecimiento de los niños absorbe más plomo.

- Los bebés y los niños pequeños se llevan las manos y otros objetos a la boca con frecuencia. Dichos objetos pueden estar cubiertos de polvo de plomo.

Las mujeres en edad de concebir deben saber que el plomo es peligroso para el feto en desarrollo.

- Las mujeres que tienen un nivel alto de plomo en su cuerpo antes del embarazo o mientras están embarazadas podrían exponer al feto al plomo a través de la placenta durante su desarrollo.

Medidas sencillas para proteger a su familia contra los peligros relacionados con el plomo

Si cree que su casa tiene pintura con base de plomo:

- No trate de remover usted mismo la pintura con base de plomo.

- Mantenga siempre las superficies pintadas en buenas condiciones para minimizar el deterioro.

- Haga que examinen su casa para identificar peligros relacionados con el plomo. Encuentre un inspector certificado o un asesor de riesgos en epa.gov/lead.

- Hable con el propietario para que arregle las superficies con pintura descascarada o picada.

- Limpie con regularidad los pisos, los antepechos de las ventanas y las demás superficies.

- Tome precauciones para evitar la exposición al polvo de plomo al remodelar.

- Al realizar renovaciones, reparaciones o pintura, contrate solamente a empresas de renovación certificadas en prácticas seguras con el plomo aprobadas por el estado o la EPA.

- Antes de comprar, alquilar o renovar su casa, hágala examinar para ver si tiene pintura con base de plomo.

- Consulte con su profesional de la salud sobre pruebas para detectar la presencia de plomo en sus hijos. El pediatra puede comprobar la presencia de plomo con un simple análisis de sangre.

- Lave con frecuencia las manos, los biberones, los chupones y los juguetes de los niños.

- Asegúrese de que los niños eviten los alimentos grasos (o ricos en grasas) y coman alimentos nutritivos ricos en hierro y calcio.

- Quítese los zapatos o lave la tierra de los zapatos antes de entrar a su casa.

Verifique el nivel de plomo en su familia

Haga que examinen a sus niños y a su casa si cree que esta tiene plomo.

El nivel de plomo en la sangre de los niños tiende a aumentar con rapidez entre los 6 y 12 meses de edad, y tiende a llegar al nivel más alto entre los 18 y 24 meses de edad.

Consulte a su médico en cuanto a la necesidad de examinar a sus niños. Un sencillo análisis de sangre puede detectar la presencia de plomo. Los análisis de sangre para detectar plomo se recomiendan generalmente para:

- Niños de 1 a 2 años de edad.
- Niños u otros miembros de la familia que hayan estado expuestos a niveles altos de plomo.
- Niños que deben examinarse en virtud del plan local o estatal de exámenes médicos.

Su médico puede explicarle los resultados de las pruebas y decirle si es necesario realizar más análisis.

Efectos del plomo en la salud

El plomo afecta el cuerpo de muchas maneras. Es importante saber que aun una exposición a niveles bajos de plomo puede afectar al niño gravemente.

En los niños, la exposición al plomo puede causar:

Daño nervioso en el cerebro

Problemas auditivos

Crecimiento más lento

Problemas digestivos

Problemas en la reproducción (adultos)

- Daño al sistema nervioso y los riñones.
- Problemas de aprendizaje, desorden de deficiencia de atención y disminución de la capacidad intelectual.
- Problemas del habla, del lenguaje y de comportamiento.
- Pobre coordinación muscular.
- Disminución en el crecimiento muscular y de los huesos.
- Daño en la audición.

Mientras que la exposición a niveles bajos de plomo es más común, la exposición a niveles altos de plomo puede causar efectos devastadores en los niños, incluso convulsiones, pérdida del conocimiento y, en algunos casos, la muerte.

Aunque los niños son especialmente susceptibles a la exposición al plomo, también puede ser peligroso para los adultos.

En los adultos, la exposición al plomo puede causar:

- Daño a un feto en desarrollo.
- Mayor probabilidad de tener tensión arterial alta durante el embarazo.
- Problemas de fertilidad (en hombres y mujeres).
- Tensión arterial alta.
- Problemas digestivos.
- Trastornos nerviosos.
- Problemas de memoria y concentración.
- Dolores musculares y articulares.

Dónde se encuentra la pintura con base de plomo

Generalmente, cuanto más vieja sea su casa o centro de cuidado infantil, mayor será la posibilidad de que tenga pintura con base de plomo.[1]

Muchas viviendas —incluidas las viviendas privadas, las de propiedad federal y las que reciben ayuda federal— y centros de cuidado infantil construidos antes de 1978 tienen pintura con base de plomo. En 1978, el gobierno federal prohibió el uso por parte del consumidor de pintura que contenga plomo.[2]

En la página 7, encontrará cómo establecer si la pintura tiene plomo.

El plomo puede encontrarse en:

- Casas y centros de cuidado infantil en la ciudad, el campo o los suburbios;

- Casas y apartamentos unifamiliares privados y públicos;

- Superficies dentro y fuera de la casa; y

- La tierra alrededor de la casa (la tierra puede acumular plomo de la pintura exterior u otras fuentes, tales como la gasolina con plomo que se usaba en el pasado en los automóviles).

Obtenga más información sobre dónde se encuentra plomo en epa.gov/lead.

---

[1] En la actualidad, el gobierno federal define la "pintura con base de plomo" como pintura con niveles de plomo superiores o iguales a 1.0 miligramo por centímetro cuadrado (mg/cm) o con más de 0.5 % por peso.

[2] En la actualidad, el gobierno federal define la "pintura que contiene plomo" como plomo en pintura nueva seca que supere las 90 partes por millón (ppm) por peso.

Identificando la pintura con base de plomo y los peligros de la pintura con base de plomo

La pintura con base de plomo deteriorada (descascarada, picada, pulverizada, agrietada o dañada) es un peligro y requiere atención inmediata. **La pintura con base de plomo** también puede ser un peligro si se encuentra en superficies que los niños puedan morder o que se desgasten mucho, tales como:

- Ventanas y antepechos de ventanas.

- Puertas y marcos de puertas.

- Escaleras, pasamanos, barandas y porches.

La pintura con base de plomo generalmente no es peligrosa si está en buenas condiciones y no está en una superficie de impacto o de fricción, como en una ventana.

El polvo de plomo puede formarse al raspar, lijar o calentar la pintura con base de plomo. También se forma cuando las superficies pintadas que contienen polvo se golpean o frotan entre sí. Las partículas y el polvo de la pintura que contiene plomo pueden acumularse en superficies y objetos que las personas tocan. El polvo de plomo que se ha acumulado puede volver a mezclarse con el aire cuando se aspira o barre la casa, o cuando las personas caminan sobre el mismo. Actualmente, la EPA define como peligrosos los siguientes niveles de plomo en el polvo:

- 40 microgramos por pie cuadrado (μg/pie^2) o más en pisos, incluidos pisos alfombrados.

- 250 μg/pie^2 o más en los antepechos de ventanas interiores.

El plomo en la tierra puede ser peligroso cuando los niños juegan en tierra descubierta o cuando las personas meten tierra en la casa con los zapatos. Actualmente, la EPA define como peligrosos los siguientes niveles de plomo en la tierra:

- 400 partes por millón (ppm) o más en áreas de juego de tierra descubierta.

- 1,200 ppm (promedio) o más en la tierra descubierta del resto del jardín.

Recuerde que el plomo de las partículas de pintura —que puede ver— y el polvo de plomo —que tal vez no pueda ver— pueden ser peligrosos.

La única forma de saber si existe peligro debido a la presencia de plomo en pintura, polvo o tierra es realizando pruebas. En la página siguiente se describe cómo hacer esto.

Verificando si su casa tiene plomo

Puede evaluar su casa de diferentes maneras para determinar si tiene plomo:

- Una **inspección** de la pintura con base de plomo le dirá si su casa tiene pintura con base de plomo y dónde se localiza. Sin embargo, esta inspección no le dirá si en su casa existen actualmente peligros relacionados con el plomo. Un profesional experto en pruebas capacitado y certificado, que se llama inspector de pintura con base de plomo, realizará la inspección de la pintura utilizando métodos como:

  - Máquina portátil de fluorescencia por rayos X (XRF, por sus siglas en inglés).
  - Pruebas de laboratorio de muestras de pintura.

- Una **evaluación de riesgo** le dirá si en su casa existe actualmente algún peligro relacionado con el plomo debido a la presencia de plomo en la pintura, el polvo o la tierra. También le dirá qué acciones debe llevar a cabo para eliminar estos peligros. Un profesional experto en pruebas capacitado y certificado, que se llama asesor de riesgo, hará lo siguiente:

  - Tomará muestras de la pintura deteriorada de puertas, ventanas, pisos, escaleras y paredes.
  - Tomará muestras del polvo cerca de las superficies pintadas y muestras de tierra descubierta del patio.
  - Hará pruebas de laboratorio con las muestras de pintura, polvo y tierra.

- Una combinación de evaluación de riesgo e inspección le dirá si en su casa hay pintura con base de plomo, si existe algún peligro relacionado con el plomo y dónde se localizan ambos.

Asegúrese de leer el informe que le entreguen una vez finalizada la inspección o la evaluación de riesgo, y pregunte todo lo que no entienda.

Verificando si su casa tiene plomo (continuación)

Al preparar un trabajo de renovación, reparación o pintura en una casa construida antes de 1978, los renovadores certificados para prácticas seguras con el plomo (vea la página 12) pueden:

- Tomar muestras de partículas de pintura para determinar si hay pintura con base de plomo en el área que se prevé renovar y enviarlas para analizar a un laboratorio especializado en plomo reconocido por la EPA. En viviendas que reciben ayuda federal, la persona que recolecte estas muestras debe ser un evaluador de riesgo o inspector certificado de pintura con base de plomo.

- Utilizar juegos de pruebas reconocidos por la EPA para determinar si no hay pintura con base de plomo (no se deben usar en viviendas que reciban ayuda federal).

- Suponer que hay pintura con base de plomo y utilizar prácticas de trabajo seguras con el plomo.

Existen programas estatales y federales para garantizar que las pruebas se realicen de modo seguro, confiable y con eficacia. Comuníquese con la agencia estatal o local para obtener más información, visite epa.gov/lead o llame al **1-800-424-LEAD (5323)** para obtener una lista de contactos en su área.[3]

---

[3] Las personas con impedimentos auditivos o del habla pueden acceder a este número a través del sistema TTY llamando al Federal Relay Service (Servicio Federal de Retransmisión) al 1-800-877-8399.

Lo que usted puede hacer en estos momentos para proteger a su familia

Si sospecha que su casa tiene algún peligro relacionado con pintura con base de plomo, puede tomar algunas medidas inmediatas para reducir el riesgo de su familia:

- Si alquila, infórmele al propietario si hay pintura descascarándose o picándose.

- Mantenga las superficies pintadas limpias y sin polvo. Limpie semanalmente los pisos, los marcos y antepechos de las ventanas y las demás superficies. Use un trapeador o una esponja con agua tibia y un limpiador para usos múltiples. (Recuerde: nunca mezcle productos de amoníaco con blanqueadores, ya que pueden formar gases peligrosos.)

- Limpie inmediatamente y con cuidado las partículas de pintura sin generar polvo.

- Enjuague bien y con frecuencia las esponjas y las cabezas de los trapeadores mientras limpia las áreas sucias o con polvo, y vuelva a hacerlo cuando termine de limpiar.

- Lávese con frecuencia las manos y también las de sus hijos, especialmente antes de comer, antes de la siesta y antes de irse a dormir.

- Mantenga limpias las áreas de juego. Lave con regularidad los biberones, los chupones, los juguetes y los animales de peluche.

- No permita que los niños muerdan los antepechos de las ventanas ni las demás superficies pintadas, ni tampoco que coman tierra.

- Al realizar renovaciones, reparaciones o pintura, contrate a empresas de renovación certificadas en prácticas seguras con el plomo aprobadas por el estado o la EPA (vea la página 12).

- Límpiese o quítese los zapatos antes de entrar a la casa para evitar meter el plomo de la tierra.

- Asegúrese de que los niños eviten los alimentos grasos (o ricos en grasas) y coman alimentos nutritivos ricos en hierro y calcio. Los niños con buenas dietas absorben menos plomo.

Reduciendo los peligros del plomo

Alterar la pintura con base de plomo o remover incorrectamente el plomo puede aumentar el peligro para su familia, ya que esparce aún más el polvo de plomo en la casa.

- Además de la limpieza diaria y la buena nutrición, usted puede reducir **temporariamente** los riesgos relacionados con la pintura con base de plomo tomando medidas, como la reparación de las superficies pintadas que estén dañadas y plantar césped para cubrir la tierra contaminada con plomo. Estas medidas no son soluciones permanentes y necesitarán atención continua.

- Para minimizar la exposición al plomo cuando renueve, repare o pinte su casa, contrate a un renovador certificado por el estado o la EPA que esté capacitado en el uso de prácticas de trabajo seguras con el plomo. Si es una persona que suele hacer los trabajos por su cuenta, aprenda a utilizar prácticas de trabajo seguras con el plomo en su casa.

- Para remover permanentemente los peligros relacionados con el plomo, debe contratar a un contratista certificado para que "remueva" el plomo. Los métodos para remover (o eliminar permanentemente el peligro) incluyen la eliminación, el sellado o el revestimiento de la pintura con base de plomo con materiales especiales. Simplemente pintar sobre la pintura que presenta riesgos con una pintura común no es un control permanente.

Siempre recurra a un contratista certificado que esté capacitado para corregir los peligros relacionados con el plomo de manera segura.

- Contrate a una empresa certificada en prácticas seguras con el plomo (vea la página 12) para realizar proyectos de renovación, reparación o pintura (RRP) a fin de no alterar las superficies pintadas.

- Para corregir permanentemente los peligros relacionados con el plomo, contrate a un profesional certificado para que "remueva" el plomo. Esto asegurará que el contratista sepa cómo trabajar en forma segura y tenga el equipo apropiado para limpiar minuciosamente.

Los contratistas certificados contratarán a trabajadores cualificados y seguirán reglas estrictas de seguridad según lo dicta el estado o el gobierno federal.

Reduciendo los peligros del plomo (continuación)

Si en su casa se realizó un trabajo para remover el plomo o si se trata de una vivienda que recibe ayuda federal, una vez que se termine el trabajo, deben realizarse las actividades de limpieza del polvo hasta que las pruebas de aprobación indiquen que los niveles de polvo de plomo están por debajo de los siguientes niveles:

- 40 microgramos por pie cuadrado (μg/pie²) en pisos, incluidos pisos alfombrados.

- 250 μg/pie² en los antepechos de ventanas interiores.

- 400 μg/pie² en los canales de ventanas.

Para obtener ayuda para localizar en su área profesionales certificados que remuevan el plomo, llame a la agencia estatal o local (vea las páginas 14 y 15), visite epa.gov/lead o llame al 1-800-424-LEAD.

Renovación, remodelación o reparación (RRP) de una casa que tiene pintura con base de plomo

Si contrata a un contratista para que realice proyectos de renovación, reparación o pintura (RRP) en una casa o centro de cuidado infantil construidos antes de 1978 (como centros preescolares y jardines de infancia), el contratista debe:

- Ser una empresa certificada en prácticas seguras con el plomo, aprobada por la EPA o por un programa estatal autorizado por la EPA.

- Utilizar personas cualificadas y capacitadas (renovadores certificados en prácticas seguras con el plomo) que empleen prácticas de trabajo seguras con el plomo específicas, a fin de evitar la contaminación con plomo.

- Darle una copia del documento informativo de la EPA sobre peligros relacionados con el plomo que se titula *Guía de prácticas acreditas seguras para trabajar con el plomo para remodeler correctamente.*

Los contratistas de RRP que trabajen en casas o centros de cuidado infantil construidos antes de 1978 deben seguir prácticas de trabajo seguras con el plomo que:

- **Contengan el área de trabajo.** Debe contenerse el área para que el polvo y los escombros no se escapen cel área de trabajo. Deben colocarse letreros de advertencia, y debe usarse cinta y material plástico u otro tipo de material impermeable.

- **Eviten los métodos de renovación que generan grandes cantidades de polvo contaminado con plomo.** Algunos métodos producen tanto polvo contaminado con plomo que su uso está prohibido. Entre estos métodos se incluyen:

  · Quema o flameado a llama abierta.

  · Lijado, esmerilado, cepillado, uso de pistolas de aguja o limpieza a chorro con herramientas eléctricas y equipos sin cubierta y accesorio de aspiradora HEPA.

  · Pistola de aire caliente a temperaturas superiores a 1100 °F.

- **Limpien minuciosamente.** El área de trabajo debe limpiarse diariamente. Una vez terminado todo el trabajo, debe limpiarse el área con métodos de limpieza especiales.

- **Eliminen los desechos adecuadamente.** Recoja los residuos en una bolsa o lámina de alta resistencia y séllela. Cuando transporte los residuos, asegúrese de que la bolsa o lámina esté bien cerrada para que el polvo y los escombros no se escapen.

Para obtener más información sobre los requisitos de la EPA para los proyectos de RRP, visite epa.gov/getleadsafe o lea *Guía de prácticas acreditas seguras para trabajar con el plomo para remodeler correctamente.*

Otras fuentes de plomo

Aunque la pintura, el polvo y la tierra son las fuentes más comunes de plomo, existen también otras fuentes de plomo:

- **El agua potable.** Su casa podría tener tuberías de plomo o con soldaduras de plomo. El plomo no puede verse, olerse ni tiene sabor, y al hervir el agua no eliminará el plomo. Si cree que sus tuberías podrían tener plomo:

  - Use solamente agua fría para beber y cocinar.

  - Deje correr el agua durante 15 a 30 segundos antes de beberla, especialmente si no se ha usado el agua durante algunas horas.

  Llame al departamento de salud o proveedor de agua local para averiguar sobre las pruebas para el agua de su casa, o visite epa.gov/lead para obtener información de la EPA sobre el plomo en el agua potable.

- **Los hornos de fundición de plomo** u otras industrias que emiten plomo al aire.

- **Su trabajo.** Si trabaja con plomo, podría traerlo a su casa en el cuerpo o la ropa. Báñese y cámbiese la ropa antes de volver a su casa. Lave la ropa de trabajo por separado del resto de la ropa de la familia.

- **Los pasatiempos** que usan plomo, tales como hacer trabajos en cerámica, pintar en vidrio o restaurar muebles. Llame al departamento de salud local para obtener información sobre los pasatiempos en los que se puede usarse plomo.

- Los **juguetes y muebles** viejos que pueden haberse pintado con pintura que contenga plomo. Los juguetes viejos y otros productos para niños pueden contener partes con plomo.[4]

- Los alimentos y líquidos cocinados o almacenados en **cristal de plomo**, o en **cerámica o porcelana con esmalte de plomo** pueden contener plomo.

- Los remedios caseros, tales como **"greta" y "azarcón"**, que se usan para tratar padecimientos estomacales.

---

[4] En 1978, el gobierno federal prohibió los juguetes, otros productos para niños y los muebles con pintura que contenga plomo (16 CFR 1303). En 2008, el gobierno federal también prohibió el plomo en la mayoría de los productos para niños, y actualmente prohíbe el plomo en cantidades superiores a 100 ppm por peso en la mayoría de los productos para niños (76 FR 44463).

Para obtener más información

The National Lead Information Center (Centro Nacional de Información sobre el Plomo)
Averigüe cómo proteger a los niños del envenenamiento por plomo y obtenga otra información sobre los peligros relacionados con el plomo por Internet en epa.gov/lead y hud.gov/lead, o llame al **1-800-424-LEAD (5323)**.

Línea directa de agua potable segura de la EPA
Para obtener información sobre el plomo en el agua potable, llame al **1-800-426-4791** o visite epa.gov/lead para obtener información sobre el plomo en el agua potable.

Línea directa de la Comisión de Seguridad de Productos del Consumidor de Estados Unidos (CPSC)
Para pedir información relacionada con el plomo en los juguetes y en otros productos del consumidor, o para denunciar un producto del consumidor inseguro o una lesión relacionada con un producto, llame al **1-800-638-2772**, o visite el sitio web de la CPSC en cpsc.gov o saferproducts.gov.

Agencias del medio ambiente y de salud estatales y locales
Algunos estados, tribus y ciudades tienen sus propias reglas relacionadas con la pintura con base de plomo. Consulte con su agencia local para ver cuáles leyes se le aplican. La mayoría de las agencias también pueden proporcionarle información para encontrar en su área una empresa para remover el plomo, y para conseguir posibles fuentes de ayuda económica para la reducción de los peligros relacionados con el plomo. Obtenga direcciones e información telefónica actualizadas de contactos locales o estatales por Internet en epa.gov/lead, o comuníquese con el Centro Nacional de Información sobre el Plomo llamando al **1-800-424-LEAD.**

Las personas con impedimentos auditivos o del habla pueden acceder a cualquiera de los números de teléfono que se indican en este folleto a través del sistema TTY llamando en forma gratuita al Federal Relay Service (Servicio Federal de Retransmisión) al **1-800-877-8339.**

Oficinas regionales de la Agencia de Protección Ambiental de los Estados Unidos (EPA)

La misión de la EPA es proteger la salud de los seres humanos y el medio ambiente. La Oficina Regional de la EPA puede darle más información sobre la normativa y los programas de protección contra el plomo.

Región 1 (Connecticut, Massachusetts, Maine, New Hampshire, Rhode Island, Vermont)

Regional Lead Contact
(Contacto regional para el plomo)
U.S. EPA Region 1
Suite 1100 (CPT) One Congress Street
Boston, MA 02114-2023
(617) 918-1524

Región 2 (New Jersey, New York, Puerto Rico, Virgin Islands)

Regional Lead Contact
(Contacto regional para el plomo)
U.S. EPA Region 2
2890 Woodbridge Avenue
Building 205, Mail Stop 225
Edison, NJ 08837-3679
(732) 321-6671

Región 3 (Delaware, Maryland, Pennsylvania, Virginia, DC, West Virginia)

Regional Lead Contact
(Contacto regional para el plomo)
U.S. EPA Region 3
1650 Arch Street
Philadelphia, PA 19103
(215) 814-2088

Región 4 (Alabama, Florida, Georgia, Kentucky, Mississippi, North Carolina, South Carolina, Tennessee)

Regional Lead Contact
(Contacto regional para el plomo)
U.S. EPA Region 4
AFC Tower, 12th Floor, Air, Pesticides & Toxics
61 Forsyth Street, SW
Atlanta, GA 30303
(404) 562-8998

Región 5 (Illinois, Indiana, Michigan, Minnesota, Ohio, Wisconsin)

Regional Lead Contact
(Contacto regional para el plomo)
U.S. EPA Region 5 (DT-8J)
77 West Jackson Boulevard
Chicago, IL 60604-3666
(312) 886-7836

Región 6 (Arkansas, Louisiana, New Mexico, Oklahoma, Texas y 66 tribus)

Regional Lead Contact
(Contacto regional para el plomo)
U.S. EPA Region 6
1445 Ross Avenue, 12th Floor
Dallas, TX 75202-2733
(214) 665-2704

Región 7 (Iowa, Kansas, Missouri, Nebraska)

Regional Lead Contact
(Contacto regional para el plomo)
U.S. EPA Region 7
11201 Renner Blvd.
WWPD/TOPE
Lenexa, KS 66219
(800) 223-0425

Región 8 (Colorado, Montana, North Dakota, South Dakota, Utah, Wyoming)

Regional Lead Contact
(Contacto regional para el plomo)
U.S. EPA Region 8
1595 Wynkoop St.
Denver, CO 80202
(303) 312-6966

Región 9 (Arizona, California, Hawaii, Nevada)

Regional Lead Contact
(Contacto regional para el plomo)
U.S. EPA Region 9 (CMD-4-2)
75 Hawthorne Street
San Francisco, CA 94105
(415) 947-4280

Región 10 (Alaska, Idaho, Oregon, Washington)

Regional Lead Contact
(Contacto regional para el plomo)
U.S. EPA Region 10
Solid Waste & Toxics Unit (WCM-128)
1200 Sixth Avenue, Suite 900
Seattle, WA 98101
(206) 553-1200

Comisión de Seguridad de Productos del Consumidor de Estados Unidos (CPSC)

La CPSC protege al público contra el riesgo irrazonable de daños causados por productos del consumidor a través de educación, actividades relacionadas con normas de seguridad y aplicación de la ley. Comuníquese con la CPSC para obtener más información sobre los reglamentos y la seguridad de los productos del consumidor.

CPSC

4330 East West Highway
Bethesda, MD 20814-4421
1-800-638-2772
cpsc.gov o saferproducts.gov

Departamento de la Vivienda y de Desarrollo Urbano de los Estados Unidos (HUD)

La misión del HUD es crear comunidades fuertes, sustentables e inclusivas, así como hogares de calidad asequibles para todos. Comuníquese con la Oficina de Hogares Saludables y Control de Peligros Relacionados con el Plomo del HUD para obtener más información acerca de la Regla sobre Viviendas Seguras en relación con el Plomo, que protege a las familias que residen en viviendas construidas antes de 1978 que reciben ayuda económica, y acerca de los programas de control de los peligros relacionados con el plomo y de subvenciones para investigación.

HUD

451 Seventh Street, SW, Room 8236
Washington, DC 20410-3000
(202) 402-7698
hud.gov/offices/lead/

EPA-747-K-13-001
Septiembre de 2013

U. S. EPA Washington DC 20460
U. S. CPSC Bethesda MD 20814
U. S. HUD Washington DC 20410

¡IMPORTANTE!

El plomo de la pintura, del polvo y de la tierra en la casa y alrededor de esta puede ser peligroso si no se maneja adecuadamente

- Los niños menores de 6 años son los que corren mayor riesgo de envenenamiento por plomo en la casa.

- La exposición al plomo puede hacerle daño a los niños pequeños y aun a los bebés antes del nacimiento.

- Es probable que las casas, las escuelas y los centros de cuidado infantil construidos antes de 1978 contengan pintura con base de plomo.

- Aun los niños que aparentan estar saludables pueden tener niveles peligrosos de plomo en el cuerpo.

- Alterar las superficies con pintura con base de plomo o remover incorrectamente la pintura con base de plomo puede aumentar los peligros para su familia.

- El plomo puede entrar en el cuerpo de las personas al respirar o tragar polvo de plomo, o al comer tierra o partículas de pintura que contengan plomo.

- Las personas tienen muchas opciones para reducir los peligros relacionados con el plomo. Generalmente, la pintura con base de plomo que está en buenas condiciones no es peligrosa (vea la página 10).

Rental Application

Separate application required from each applicant age 18 or older.

Date and time received by landlord _____

THIS SECTION TO BE COMPLETED BY LANDLORD

Address of Property to Be Rented: _____

Rental Term: ☐ month-to-month   ☐ lease from _____ to _____

Amounts Due Prior to Occupancy

First month's rent: .... $_____

Security deposit: .... $_____

Credit-check fee: .... $_____

Other (specify): _____ $_____

TOTAL $_____

Applicant

Full Name—include all names you use(d): _____

Home Phone: _____ Work Phone: _____ Cell Phone: _____

Email: _____ Fax:* _____

Social Security Number: _____ Driver's License Number/State: _____

Other Identifying Information: _____

Vehicle Make: _____ Model: _____ Color: _____ Year: _____

License Plate Number/State: _____

Additional Occupants

List everyone, including minor children, who will live with you:

Full Name	**Relationship to Applicant**
_____	_____
_____	_____
_____	_____
_____	_____
_____	_____

Rental History

FIRST-TIME RENTERS: ATTACH A DESCRIPTION OF YOUR HOUSING SITUATION FOR THE PAST FIVE YEARS.

Current Address: _____

Dates Lived at Address: _____ Rent $ _____ Security Deposit $ _____

Landlord/Manager: _____ Landlord/Manager's Phone: _____

Reason for Leaving: _____

* By providing this fax number I agree to receive facsimile advertisements from the Landlord or management company.

Previous Address: _____

Dates Lived at Address: _____ Rent $ _____ Security Deposit $ _____

Landlord/Manager: _____ Landlord/Manager's Phone: _____

Reason for Leaving: _____

Previous Address: _____

Dates Lived at Address: _____ Rent $ _____ Security Deposit $ _____

Landlord/Manager: _____ Landlord/Manager's Phone: _____

Reason for Leaving: _____

Employment History

SELF-EMPLOYED APPLICANTS: ATTACH TAX RETURNS FOR THE PAST TWO YEARS.

Name and Address of Current Employer: _____

_____ Phone: ( ) _____

Name of Supervisor: _____ Supervisor's Phone: ( ) _____

Dates Employed at This Job: _____ Position or Title: _____

Name and Address of Previous Employer: _____

_____ Phone: ( ) _____

Name of Supervisor: _____ Supervisor's Phone: ( ) _____

Dates Employed at This Job: _____ Position or Title: _____

ATTACH PAY STUBS FOR THE PAST TWO YEARS, FROM THIS EMPLOYER OR PRIOR EMPLOYERS.

Income

1. Your gross monthly employment income (before deductions): $_____

2. Average monthly amounts of other income (specify sources): $_____

_____ $_____

_____ $_____

                                    TOTAL: $_____

Bank/Financial Accounts

	Account Number	Bank/Institution	Branch	

Savings Account: _____

Checking Account: _____

Money Market or Similar Account: _____

_____

_____

_____

_____

Credit Card Accounts

Major Credit Card: ☐ VISA ☐ MC ☐ Discover Card ☐ Am Ex ☐ Other: _____

Issuer: _____ Account No. _____

Balance $ _____ Average Monthly Payment $ _____

Major Credit Card: ☐ VISA ☐ MC ☐ Discover Card ☐ Am Ex ☐ Other: _____

Issuer: _____ Account No. _____

Balance $ _____ Average Monthly Payment $ _____

Loans

Type of Loan (mortgage, car, student loan, etc.)	Name of Creditor	Account Number	Amount Owed	Monthly Payment

Other Major Obligations

Type	Payee		Amount Owed	Monthly Payment

Miscellaneous

Describe the number and type of pets you want to have in the rental property: _____

_____ .

Describe water-filled furniture you want to have in the rental property: _____

_____ .

Do you smoke?　　☐ yes ☐ no

Have you ever:

Filed for bankruptcy?	☐ yes ☐ no	How many times _____
Been sued?	☐ yes ☐ no	How many times _____
Sued someone else?	☐ yes ☐ no	How many times _____
Been evicted?	☐ yes ☐ no	How many times _____
Been convicted of a crime?	☐ yes ☐ no	How many times _____

Explain any "yes" listed above: _____

_____

_____

_____

References and Emergency Contact

Personal Reference: _____ Relationship: _____

Address: _____

_____ Phone: (____) _____

Personal Reference: _____ Relationship: _____

Address: _____

_____ Phone: (____) _____

Contact in Emergency: _____ Relationship: _____

Address: _____

_____ Phone: (____) _____

Source

Where did you learn of this vacancy? _____

_____

I certify that all the information given above is true and correct and understand that my lease or rental agreement may be terminated if I have made any material false or incomplete statements in this application. I authorize verification of the information provided in this application from my credit sources, credit bureaus, current and previous landlords and employers, and personal references. This permission will survive the expiration of my tenancy.

_____ _____

Applicant   Date

Notes (Landlord/Manager): _____

_____

_____

_____

_____

_____

_____

_____

_____

_____

_____

_____

_____

Consent to Contact References and Perform Credit Check

I authorize _____

to obtain information about me from my credit sources, current and previous landlords, employers, and personal

references, to enable _____ to

evaluate my rental application.

I give permission for the landlord or its agent to obtain a consumer report about me for the purpose of this

application, to ensure that I continue to meet the terms of the tenancy, for the collection and recovery of any

financial obligations relating to my tenancy, or for any other permissible purpose.

_____

Applicant Signature

_____

Printed Name

_____

Address

_____

Phone Number

_____

Date

Tenant References

Name of Applicant: _____

Address of Rental Unit: _____

Previous Landlord or Manager

Contact (name, property owner or manager, address of rental unit): _____

_____

Date: _____

Questions

When did tenant rent from you (move-in and move-out dates)? _____

What was the monthly rent? _____ Did tenant pay rent on time? ☐ Yes ☐ No

If rent was not paid on time, did you have to give tenant a legal notice demanding the rent? ☐ Yes ☐ No

If rent was not paid on time, provide details _____

_____

Did you give tenant notice of any lease violation for other than nonpayment of rent? ☐ Yes ☐ No

If you gave a lease violation notice, what was the outcome? _____

Was tenant considerate of neighbors—that is, no loud parties and fair, careful use of common areas?

_____

_____

Did tenant have any pets? ☐ Yes ☐ No   If so, were there any problems? _____

_____

Did tenant make any unreasonable demands or complaints? ☐ Yes ☐ No   If so, explain: _____

_____

Why did tenant leave? _____

_____

Did tenant give the proper amount of notice before leaving? ☐ Yes ☐ No

Did tenant leave the place in good condition? Did you need to use the security deposit to cover damage?

_____

Any particular problems you'd like to mention? _____

_____

Would you rent to this person again? _____

_____

Other comments: _____

_____

_____

Previous Landlord or Manager

Contact (name, property owner or manager, address of rental unit): _____

_____

Date: _____

Questions

When did tenant rent from you (move-in and move-out dates)? _____

What was the monthly rent? _____ Did tenant pay rent on time? ☐ Yes ☐ No

If rent was not paid on time, did you have to give tenant a legal notice demanding the rent? ☐ Yes ☐ No

If rent was not paid on time, provide details _____

_____

Did you give tenant notice of any lease violation for other than nonpayment of rent? ☐ Yes ☐ No

If you gave a lease violation notice, what was the outcome? _____

Was tenant considerate of neighbors—that is, no loud parties and fair, careful use of common areas?

_____

_____

Did tenant have any pets? ☐ Yes ☐ No   If so, were there any problems? _____

_____

Did tenant make any unreasonable demands or complaints? ☐ Yes ☐ No   If so, explain: _____

_____

Why did tenant leave? _____

_____

Did tenant give the proper amount of notice before leaving? ☐ Yes ☐ No

Did tenant leave the place in good condition? Did you need to use the security deposit to cover damage?

_____

Any particular problems you'd like to mention? _____

_____

Would you rent to this person again? _____

_____

Other comments: _____

_____

_____

_____

_____

_____

Employment Verification

Contact (name, company, position): _____

Date: _____ Salary $ _____

Dates of Employment: _____

Comments: _____

_____

_____

_____

_____

_____

_____

Personal Reference

Contact (name and relationship to applicant): _____

Date: _____ How long have you known the applicant? _____

Would you recommend this person as a prospective tenant? _____

Comments: _____

_____

_____

_____

_____

_____

_____

Credit and Financial Information

_____

_____

_____

_____

Notes, Including Reasons for Rejecting Applicant

_____

_____

_____

_____

_____

_____

Notice of Denial Based on Credit Report or Other Information

To: _____
Applicant

_____
Street Address

_____
City, State, and Zip Code

Your rights under the Fair Credit Reporting Act and Fair and Accurate Credit Transactions (FACT) Act of 2003. (15 U.S.C. §§ 1681 and following.)

THIS NOTICE is to inform you that your application to rent the property at _____

_____

[rental property address] has been denied because of [*check all that apply*]:

☐ Insufficient information in the credit report provided by:

Credit reporting agency: _____

Address, phone number, URL: _____

_____

☐ Negative information in the credit report provided by:

Credit reporting agency: _____

Address, phone number, URL: _____

_____

☐ The credit score supplied on the credit report, _____ , was used in whole or in part when making the selection.

☐ The consumer credit reporting agency noted above did not make the decision not to offer you this rental. It only provided information about your credit history. You have the right to obtain a free copy of your credit report from the consumer credit reporting agency named above, if your request is made within 60 days of this notice or if you have not requested a free copy within the past year. You also have the right to dispute the accuracy or completeness of your credit report. The agency must reinvestigate within a reasonable time, free of charge, and remove or modify inaccurate information. If the reinvestigation does not resolve the dispute to your satisfaction, you may add your own "consumer statement" (up to 100 words) to the report, which must be included (or a clear summary) in future reports.

☐ Information supplied by a third party other than a credit reporting agency or you and gathered by someone other than myself or any employee. You have the right to learn of the nature of the information if you ask me in writing within 60 days of the date of this notice.

_____   _____
Landlord/Manager   Date

Notice of Conditional Acceptance Based on Credit Report or Other Information

To: _____
Applicant

_____
Street Address

_____
City, State, and Zip Code

Your application to rent the property at _____

_____ [rental property address] has been accepted, conditioned on your

willingness and ability to: _____

_____

Your rights under the Fair Credit Reporting Act and Fair and Accurate Credit Transactions (FACT) Act of 2003. (15 U.S.C. §§ 1681 and following.)

Source of information prompting conditional acceptance

My decision to conditionally accept your application was prompted in whole or in part by:

☐ Insufficient information in the credit report provided by

   Credit reporting agency: _____

   Address, phone number, URL: _____

   _____

☐ Negative information in the credit report provided by:

   Credit reporting agency: _____

   Address, phone number, URL: _____

   _____

☐ The consumer credit reporting agency noted above did not make the decision to offer you this conditional

   acceptance. It only provided information about your credit history. You have the right to obtain a free copy

   of your credit report from the consumer credit reporting agency named above, if your request is made

   within 60 days of this notice or if you have not requested a free copy within the past year. You also have the

   right to dispute the accuracy or completeness of your credit report. The agency must reinvestigate within a

   reasonable time, free of charge, and remove or modify inaccurate information. If the reinvestigation does not

   resolve the dispute to your satisfaction, you may add your own "consumer statement" (up to 100 words) to

   the report, which must be included (or a clear summary) in future reports.

☐ Information supplied by a third party other than a credit reporting agency or you and gathered by someone

   other than myself or any employee. You have the right to learn of the nature of the information if you ask me

   in writing within 60 days of the date of this notice.

_____   _____
Landlord/Manager   Date

Landlord-Tenant Checklist

GENERAL CONDITION OF RENTAL UNIT AND PREMISES

Street Address   Unit No.   City

	Condition on Arrival	Condition on Departure	Estimated Cost of Repair/ Replacement
Living Room			
Floors & Floor Coverings			
Drapes & Window Coverings			
Walls & Ceilings			
Light Fixtures			
Windows, Screens, & Doors			
Front Door & Locks			
Fireplace			
Other			
Other			
Kitchen			
Floors & Floor Coverings			
Walls & Ceilings			
Light Fixtures			
Cabinets			
Counters			
Stove/Oven			
Refrigerator			
Dishwasher			
Garbage Disposal			
Sink & Plumbing			
Windows, Screens, & Doors			
Other			
Other			
Dining Room			
Floors & Floor Covering			
Walls & Ceilings			
Light Fixtures			
Windows, Screens, & Doors			
Other			

	Condition on Arrival			Condition on Departure			Estimated Cost of Repair/ Replacement
Bathroom(s)	Bath #1		Bath #2	Bath #1		Bath #2	
Floors & Floor Coverings							
Walls & Ceilings							
Windows, Screens, & Doors							
Light Fixtures							
Bathtub/Shower							
Sink & Counters							
Toilet							
Other							
Other							
Bedroom(s)	Bdrm #1	Bdrm #2	Bdrm #3	Bdrm #1	Bdrm #2	Bdrm #3	
Floors & Floor Coverings							
Windows, Screens, & Doors							
Walls & Ceilings							
Light Fixtures							
Other							
Other							
Other							
Other							
Other Areas							
Heating System							
Air Conditioning							
Lawn/Garden							
Stairs and Hallway							
Patio, Terrace, Deck, etc.							
Basement							
Parking Area							
Other							
Other							
Other							
Other							
Other							

☐ Tenants acknowledge that all smoke detectors were tested in their presence and found to be in working order, and that the testing procedure was explained to them. Tenants agree to promptly notify Landlord in writing should any smoke detector appear to be malfunctioning or inoperable. Tenants will not refuse Landlord access for the purpose of inspecting, maintaining, repairing, or installing legally-required smoke detectors.

	Condition on Arrival		Condition on Departure		Estimated Cost of Repair/ Replacement
Living Room					
Coffee Table					
End Tables					
Lamps					
Chairs					
Sofa					
Other					
Other					
Kitchen					
Broiler Pan					
Ice Trays					
Other					
Other					
Dining Room					
Chairs					
Stools					
Table					
Other					
Other					
Bathroom(s)	Bath #1	Bath #2	Bath #1	Bath #2	
Mirrors					
Shower Curtain					
Hamper					
Other					

Bedroom(s)	Bdrm #1	Bdrm #2	Bdrm #3	Bdrm #1	Bdrm #2	Bdrm #3	
Beds (single)							
Beds (double)							
Chairs							
Chests							
Dressing Tables							
Lamps							
Mirrors							
Night Tables							

	Condition on Arrival			Condition on Departure			Estimated Cost of Repair/ Replacement
Other							
Other							
Other Areas							
Bookcases							
Desks							
Pictures							
Other							
Other							

Use this space to provide any additional explanation:

_____

_____

_____

_____

_____

_____

_____

_____

_____

Landlord-Tenant Checklist completed on moving in on _____ and approved by:

_____ and _____
Landlord/Manager   Tenant

_____
Tenant

_____
Tenant

Landlord-Tenant Checklist completed on moving out on _____ and approved by:

_____ and _____
Landlord/Manager   Tenant

_____
Tenant

_____
Tenant

Move-In Letter

Date _____

Tenant _____

Street Address _____

City and State _____

Dear _____ ,
               Tenant

Welcome to _____

_____ (address of rental unit). We hope you will enjoy living here.

This letter is to explain what you can expect from the management and what we'll be looking for from you.

1. Rent: _____

_____

_____ .

2. New Roommates: _____

_____

_____

_____

_____ .

3. Notice to End Tenancy: _____

_____

_____

_____ .

4. Deposits: _____

_____

_____ .

5. Manager: _____

_____

_____

_____ .

6. Landlord-Tenant Checklist: _____

_____

_____

_____

_____

_____

_____

7. Maintenance/Repair Problems: _____

_____

_____

_____

_____

_____

_____

8. Semiannual Safety and Maintenance Update: _____

_____

_____

_____

_____

_____

_____

9. Annual Safety Inspection: _____

_____

_____

_____

_____

10. Insurance: _____

_____

_____

_____

_____

11. Moving Out: _____

_____

_____

_____

_____

12. Telephone Number Changes: _____

_____

_____

_____

Please let us know if you have any questions.

Sincerely,

_____   _____
Landlord/Manager   Date

I have read and received a copy of this statement.

_____   _____
Tenant   Date

Tenant's Notice of Intent to Move Out

Date _____

Landlord _____

Street Address _____

City and State _____

Dear _____ ,
            Landlord

This is to notify you that the undersigned tenants, _____

_____ , will be moving from

_____ ,

on _____ , _____ from today. This

provides at least _____ written notice as required in our rental

agreement.

Sincerely,

_____
Tenant

_____
Tenant

_____
Tenant

Move-Out Letter

Date _____

Tenant _____

Street Address _____

City and State _____

Dear _____ ,
                              Tenant

We hope you have enjoyed living here. In order that we may mutually end our relationship on a positive note, this move-out letter describes how we expect your unit to be left and what our procedures are for returning your security deposit.

Basically, we expect you to leave your rental unit in the same condition it was when you moved in, except for normal wear and tear. To refresh your memory on the condition of the unit when you moved in, I've attached a copy of the Landlord-Tenant Checklist you signed at the beginning of your tenancy. I'll be using this same form to inspect your unit when you leave.

Specifically, here's a list of items you should thoroughly clean before vacating:

- ☐ Floors
    - ☐ sweep wood floors
    - ☐ vacuum carpets and rugs (shampoo if necessary)
    - ☐ mop kitchen and bathroom floors
- ☐ Walls, baseboards, ceilings, and built-in shelves
- ☐ Kitchen cabinets, countertops and sink, stove and oven—inside and out
- ☐ Refrigerator—clean inside and out, empty it of food, and turn it off, with the door left open
- ☐ Bathtubs, showers, toilets, and plumbing fixtures
- ☐ Doors, windows, and window coverings
- ☐ Other _____

_____

_____

_____

_____

_____

If you have any questions as to the type of cleaning we expect, please let me know.

Please don't leave anything behind—that includes bags of garbage, clothes, food, newspapers, furniture, appliances, dishes, plants, cleaning supplies, or other items that belong to you.

Please be sure you have disconnected phone and utility services, canceled all newspaper subscriptions, and sent the post office a change of address form.

Once you have cleaned your unit and removed all your belongings, please call me at _____ to arrange for a walk-through inspection and to return all keys. Please be prepared to give me your forwarding address where we may mail your security deposit.

It's our policy to return all deposits either in person or at an address you provide within _____ _____ after you move out. If any deductions are made—for past-due rent or because the unit is damaged or not sufficiently clean—they will be explained in writing.

If you have any questions, please contact me at _____ .

Sincerely,

_____

Landlord/Manager

Index

 **NOLO** *Online Legal Forms*

Nolo offers a large library of legal solutions and forms, created by Nolo's in-house legal staff. These reliable documents can be prepared in minutes.

Create a Document

- **Incorporation.** Incorporate your business in any state.
- **LLC Formations.** Gain asset protection and pass-through tax status in any state.
- **Wills.** Nolo has helped people make over 2 million wills. Is it time to make or revise yours?
- **Living Trust (avoid probate).** Plan now to save your family the cost, delays, and hassle of probate.
- **Trademark.** Protect the name of your business or product.
- **Provisional Patent.** Preserve your rights under patent law and claim "patent pending" status.

Download a Legal Form

Nolo.com has hundreds of top quality legal forms available for download—bills of sale, promissory notes, nondisclosure agreements, LLC operating agreements, corporate minutes, commercial lease and sublease, motor vehicle bill of sale, consignment agreements and many, many more.

Review Your Documents

Many lawyers in Nolo's consumer-friendly lawyer directory will review Nolo documents for a very reasonable fee. Check their detailed profiles at **Nolo.com/lawyers.**

Nolo's Bestselling Books

 **Every Landlord's Legal Guide**
$44.99

 **Every Landlord's Tax Deduction Guide**
$39.99

 Every Landlord's Guide to Finding Great Tenants
$24.99

 **The California Landlord's Law Book: Evictions**
$44.99

 **The California Landlord's Law Book: Rights & Responsibilities**
$44.99

Every Nolo title is available in print and for download at Nolo.com.